Frances Newman

Frances Newman

SOUTHERN SATIRIST
AND LITERARY REBEL

BARBARA ANN WADE

THE UNIVERSITY OF
ALABAMA
PRESS

Tuscaloosa

Hardcover edition published 1998.
Paperback edition published 2012.
eBook edition published 2012.

Cover photograph: Francis Newman. Courtesy of the Atlanta
History Center

∞

The paper on which this book is printed meets the
minimum requirements of American National Standard
for Information Science–Permanence of Paper for
Printed Library Materials, ANSI Z39.48-1984.

Paperback ISBN: 978-0-8173-5739-9
eBook ISBN: 978-0-8173-8661-0

A previous edition of this book has been catalogued
by the Library of Congress as follows:

Library of Congress Cataloging-in-Publication Data
Wade, Barbara Ann, 1947–
Frances Newman : southern satirist and literary rebel / Barbara Ann
Wade.
p. cm.
Includes bibliographical references and index.
ISBN 0-8173-0902-0 (cloth : alk. paper)
1. Newman, Frances, d. 1928—Criticism and interpretation.
2. Feminism and literature—Southern States—History—20th century.
3. Women and literature—Southern States—History—20th century.
4. Satire, American—History and criticism. 5. Southern States—In
literature. 6. Patriarchy in literature. 7. Sex role in
literature. I. Title.
PS3527.E883Z95   1998   97-48396
813'.52—dc21   CIP

British Library Cataloguing-in-Publication Data available

CONTENTS

Preface

LIKE MANY OTHERS, I first became acquainted with Frances Newman's work through Anne Goodwyn Jones's book *Tomorrow Is Another Day*. Later, when trying to settle on a dissertation topic, I
kept returning to Newman's novels. Although her body of work
is small, her sparkling wit and dense, allusive style encouraged
rereadings that continued to unfold new meanings and pleasures. After the dissertation was completed, I was not content to
lay Newman's fiction aside, for it has still not garnered the critical
attention it merits, although that attention has increased, beginning with the republication of her two novels *Dead Lovers Are
Faithful Lovers* in 1977 and *The Hard-Boiled Virgin* in 1980. The
University of Georgia Press has recently published editions of
both novels with excellent forewords by Anne Firor Scott (*Hard-
Boiled Virgin*) and Anne Goodwyn Jones (*Dead Lovers*). In addition to the chapter on Newman in *Tomorrow Is Another Day*, Newman's fiction is the subject of a chapter in Kathryn Lee Seidel's
The Southern Belle in the American Novel, and Marjorie Smelstor
and E. Reginald Abbott have written articles on Newman for the
Southern Quarterly. Especially important in revealing Newman's
development as a writer are two dissertations: Margaret Manning
Duggan's critical edition of Newman's first (unpublished) novel,
The Gold-Fish Bowl, and Abbott's collection of Newman's critical

Preface

writings. In March 1996, I had the pleasure of exchanging ideas at the Twentieth-Century Literature Conference in Louisville, Kentucky, with two young scholars who were including Newman in their dissertations, and at the Southern Women Writers Conference at Berry College in April 1996, I was excited to be a part of a panel that focused on Newman and her work. Perhaps a Frances Newman revival has really begun.

Because no full-length biography of Newman has yet been published, this study begins with a chapter on Newman's life and writing career. Born in 1883 and raised to become a debutante in an upper-class family in Atlanta, Newman displayed courage in writing about women's private feelings and responses to their sexuality in an age and place that regarded such expressions as obscene. Considering marriage suicidal to a professional life, she never married but had numerous love affairs, usually with younger men. While supporting herself as a librarian, Newman wrote witty newspaper articles and book reviews that caught the attention of H. L. Mencken and James Branch Cabell. Although her first novel was never published, she found her unique voice with the second, and *The Hard-Boiled Virgin* became a sensational success and a best-seller banned in Boston. In 1928, shortly after the publication of *Dead Lovers Are Faithful Lovers* and while she was working on a translation of Jules Laforgue's short fiction, Newman died at the height of her literary powers.

The second chapter explores Newman's defiance of the genteel tradition and her satirizing rather than idealizing the restrictive role of the southern lady. Because Newman was writing within a tradition of southern women's fiction largely forgotten and often critically ignored, I have provided extensive comparisons with the fiction of Newman's contemporaries, southern women writers of the 1910s and 1920s whose novels are set primarily in the South. Thus I discuss Mary Johnston's *Hagar* (1913); Ellen Glasgow's *Virginia* (1913), *Life and Gabriella* (1916), *The Romantic Comedians* (1926), and *They Stooped to Folly* (1929); and Isa Glenn's *Southern Charm* (1928).[1] Mary Johnston and Ellen Glasgow were writing feminist novels that attacked and satirized the established social order of the South and the limited roles of women within it a decade before Newman began writing fiction. Isa Glenn, also a native of Atlanta, joined Newman in the twenties in revealing the injurious effects of the traditional image of the southern lady on the lives of women. One can appreciate Newman's work even more fully when comparing it with fiction by these contemporary women writers. Newman was not only avoiding the moonlight-and-magnolias tradition and instead exposing the difficulties of the southern patriarchy, but was also avoiding the often sentimental or doctrinaire writing of these women contemporaries. Her fiction is not just interesting historically as is Johnston's and Glenn's; rather, it is also the work of a superb stylist, whose writing is compelling as well. Nor is her irony heavy-handed or her sympathy cloying as Glasgow's sometimes tends to be. In satirizing the idealization and roles of the southern lady, Newman's wit is characteristically epigrammatic and often playfully humorous.

Chapter 3 compares Newman's ideas about the extent of social change occurring in her era, especially as it related to woman's "rightful" position in the southern culture, with historical accounts and with the fiction of her contemporaries Johnston, Glasgow, and Glenn. Although the 1910s and 1920s have been perceived as an era of widening roles and freedoms for women, women in the South were still denied any real power within marriage, an adequate education, and significant employment opportunities outside the home. Because Newman's fiction unveiled the pervasive sexism of the patriarchal southern society and thus violated the values and precepts of the Southern Agrarians, it was excluded from their canon of southern literature.

The subject of chapter 4 is Newman's revision and subversion of contemporary literary conventions to explode common stereotypes of women and their roles. *The Gold-Fish Bowl* (1921) loosely follows the two-suitors or marriage plot convention, a narrative convention with implicit assumptions about the nature and proper roles of women. Yet it subtly subverts that convention by questioning the role of the "right suitor" as the proper guide for his beloved and by questioning marriage as a happy ending for women. In *The Hard-Boiled Virgin*, Newman avoided marriage

Preface

as a resolution for the novel; instead, Katharine Faraday's decision to become a writer signifies her maturation, her affirmation of the right not to squeeze herself into the mold society has prepared. In this novel, Newman inverted aspects of the traditional male *bildungsroman* to portray the limitations of southern society for a young girl struggling to find her place in the world. In her last novel, *Dead Lovers Are Faithful Lovers,* Newman shattered the literary images of the angel in the house, the monstrous other woman, and the faithful widow to reveal the truth and commonality of women's experiences beneath culturally imposed facades and expectations.

In her writing Newman aspired to produce a "mutant," that is, according to this term that she used in *The Short Story's Mutations,* a work so strikingly different from its predecessors that it would influence the direction of subsequent fiction. Like other modernists, Newman abandoned the traditional structure of the novel; she experimented with narrative structure, point of view, and imagery to reveal the essence of southern aristocratic women's lives, their interior experiences, and the external constraints on their behavior and opportunities. Chapter 5 discusses Newman's stylistic experimentation and compares her writing with that of her British contemporaries Virginia Woolf and Katherine Mansfield. In *The Hard-Boiled Virgin,* Newman creates structure through her repetition of phrases and similar incidents and through a drama motif instead of through the traditional reliance on plot and action. Newman's complex, lengthy sentences mirror the complexity of the search for truth in a society of facades and "polite fictions," and her frequent negatives indicate the prohibitions of the restrictive southern society and the naiveté of young girls seeking to understand themselves and their place in that society. *Dead Lovers Are Faithful Lovers* resembles Virginia Woolf's *To the Lighthouse* and Katherine Mansfield's "Prelude" and "At the Bay" in its focus on women's thoughts and feelings as they are engaged in the repetitive, daily occurrences of their lives. Instead of narrating a series of causally connected events leading to a climax, the novel interweaves representative incidents and memories and discloses the climax only indirectly.

x

Preface

A powerful but neglected writer such as Frances Newman reminds us of the heritage of women's writing that is still obscured or buried. Our understanding of literature and our own culture has been impoverished by influential critics such as Louis Rubin and C. Hugh Holman, who in their book *Southern Literary Study: Problems and Possibilities* explicitly state that they will not discuss the role of southern women as revealed in southern literature (222), or Richard King, who explains that his exclusion of all but one woman writer from his book on the Southern Renaissance is because women writers "were not concerned primarily with the larger cultural, racial, and political themes."[2] Even Joseph Warren Beach, who speculates on Newman's influence on Faulkner's sentence structures, does not include a single woman writer in his anthology *American Fiction: 1920–1940.*[3] Fortunately feminist critics have begun to unearth the ideas and works of our literary foremothers and reveal an enriched heritage for us all. Frances Newman, who "has said discerning and devastating things about educational, moral, social, and artistic canons" (Hargrett), deserves a place of honor among them.

Acknowledgments

I WISH TO EXPRESS MY gratitude toward all the people who helped make this book possible. First, I wish to thank the Kentucky Foundation for Women for generously providing a grant at the inception of the project. My research led me to the archives of the Atlanta History Center, Emory University, the Georgia Institute of Technology, and the University of Georgia, and at each place I encountered expert, friendly assistance. Anne Salter of the Atlanta History Center was particularly helpful when I needed materials from a distance. Professors Sydney Janet Kaplan, Carolyn Allen, and Mark Patterson at the University of Washington encouraged me to revise my dissertation for publication and provided helpful initial suggestions. Subsequently, my colleagues at Berea College have read and commented on portions of the manuscript. I am indebted to Beth Harrison, Libby Jones, Mary Ann Murray, Jane Olmsted, Peggy Rivage-Seul, Richard Sears, Bill Schafer, and Mary Jo Thomas. Berea College reference librarians Steve Gowler and Susan Henthorn provided invaluable help. I would also like to thank my husband, Randall Roberts, for his continued encouragement and support.

Lengthy projects sometimes have disastrous moments. When my hard drive crashed and my backup disks were incompatible with any computers available to me, Tim Lamm provided the

Acknowledgments

expertise to switch to Apple Macintosh, and departmental secretary Phyllis Gabbard, who has provided computer assistance throughout the project, reformatted the jumbled manuscript. Her assistant, Leona Bowlin, edited the manuscript with a keen eye for details before I returned the final draft to the press. I feel fortunate to have worked with the fine editors at the University of Alabama Press. Editor-in-Chief Nicole Mitchell offered advice and encouragement during the publication process, and she secured excellent readers whose suggestions challenged me to make significant revisions. Kathy Swain provided clear recommendations for editing, and Kathy Cummins's copyediting was thorough and insightful. Any errors that remain are my own.

I wish to express my appreciation to the following archives for access to both published and unpublished works and to thank those who gave their permission to quote from the works:

Archives, Library and Information Center, Georgia Institute of Technology, Atlanta Georgia;

Atlanta History Center, Library/Archives, Atlanta, Georgia;

Hargrett Rare Book and Manuscript Library, University of Georgia Libraries, Athens, Georgia; and

Frances Newman Collection, Julian LaRose Harris Collection, and Frank Daniel Collection, Special Collections Department, Robert W. Woodruff Library, Emory University, Atlanta, Georgia.

I also wish to thank the following for their kind permission to quote extensively from works:

Selections from *"The Gold-Fish Bowl": Miss Newman's Five-Finger Exercise* by Margaret Manning Duggan, diss., University of South Carolina, 1985, used by permission;

Selections from *The Hard-Boiled Virgin* by Frances Newman, reprinted by permission of Liveright Publishing Corporation, copyright 1926 by Boni & Liveright, Inc.; copyright renewed 1954 by Louis Rucker;

Selections from *Dead Lovers Are Faithful Lovers* by Frances Newman, reprinted by permission of Liveright Publishing Corpora-

Acknowledgments

tion, copyright 1928 by Boni & Liveright, Inc.; copyright renewed 1955 by Louis Rucker; and

Selections from *Frances Newman's Letters,* edited by Hansell Baugh, reprinted by permission of Liveright Publishing Corporation, copyright 1929 by Hansell Baugh.

Frances Newman

1

Living as a Southern Lady and Literary Rebel

ARTICLES BY AND ABOUT Frances Newman, as well as her many letters, reveal a vibrant, independent woman who simultaneously defied and was influenced by the traditional southern society she satirized in her writing. It is difficult to measure the courage needed by this former debutante and member of Atlanta's high society to choose to be self-supporting, when that meant accepting a degree of economic hardship, and to write novels with allusions to such taboo topics as menstruation, sexual arousal, and syphilis, when that meant risking even her meager but respectable position as a librarian. Newman was known in Atlanta as a rather shy but polite and helpful librarian, and yet she sent that city "almost in convulsions" (*Frances Newman's Letters*, hereafter known as *Letters* 224) with her first published novel. Contemporary reviewers had difficulty reconciling Newman's feminine dress and fragile appearance with her sharp satirization of southern culture, yet her habit of dressing only in shades of lavender or purple during the last several years of her life was at the same time ultrafeminine and boldly eccentric. Newman explained the importance she attached to dress in her last interview with Winifred Rothermel: "It is not at all strange to me that persons who love the beautiful in art and music should love beautiful dress, for dress in itself is an art. One should wear colors and styles which reflect the personality of the wearer" (Rothermel). Newman's association of personal style and art suggests an affinity with aspects of the fin de siècle decadism of Oscar Wilde and Aubrey Beardsley.[1] Wearing only shades of purple and writing letters on lavender stationery, she can be seen as constructing an artistic persona. Newman also alludes to the culture of Oscar Wilde in her writing. In *The Hard-Boiled Virgin*, which has autobiographical elements, she attributes Katharine Faraday's appreciation for epigrams and her belief "that nothing is so immodest as modesty" to having "brought herself up on the literature of the Beardsley period" (94), and she almost immediately afterwards mentions *The Importance of Being Earnest*. Newman's own fiction is epigrammatic and self-consciously concerned with style, although she never mentioned Wilde's style as one she admired or emulated.[2]

Contemporary critics presented a portraiture of contrasts in describing Newman. One reviewer characterized her as "a strange mixture of a very modern woman, intellectually emancipated from conventionality and a Southern girl who has been carefully reared to remember all the proprieties" ("Frances Newman Shocked"), and another described her as having "a striking mind, brilliant and hard, and often a little alarming" as well as having "the excellent manners of a wellbred Southerner" (Brickell). Some considered her seemingly contradictory traits to be evidence of neurosis, unresolved conflicts, or an unfulfilled life as a single woman. However, rather than being consumed by conflicting and irreconcilable desires, Newman was fulfilling her own ideal of a complete person, a woman with intelligence and wit as well as charm and femininity. Her article entitled "The Rising Age of Heroines" applauded the demise of "the cheerless idea that aesthetic and intellectual charms could not be found in any one woman," and she once wrote to her friend Sylvia Bates, a writer whom she had met at Peterborough, New Hampshire, "I want people to be clever and to have the kind of manners I think of as good manners—somebody I can enjoy talking to in both ways" (*Letters* 324). Winifred Rothermel, the last person to interview Newman, found her a "mixture of Southern romantic, aristocratic ladyhood and modern sophistication," a woman and

2

writer who was "grossly misunderstood," especially in the South, but who nevertheless "retained her equilibrium" and displayed not even "the slightest signs of bitterness" over the attacks against her person and her work. The sense of good humor and perspective that Newman must have needed to achieve this balance of witty intelligence and charmingly polite manners, especially in the face of constant critical jabs, can be seen in Katharine Faraday's observation in *The Hard-Boiled Virgin* "that a southern lady's charms are estimated entirely by their agreement with tradition and . . . her intelligence is judged entirely by her ability to disagree with tradition" (244).

Frances Newman was born the fifth child and youngest daughter in a prominent Atlanta family on December 13, 1883 (E. Evans 253).[3] Newman's father, Judge William T. Newman, was a Confederate war hero who had lost his right arm in the Civil War and who became a highly respected lawyer and U.S. district judge after moving to Atlanta ("Judge"). Her mother, Fanny Percy Alexander Newman, was a direct descendent of the founder of Knoxville, Tennessee (Talmadge 622). In this upper-class conservative southern household, the person who provided Newman with her first skepticism concerning the southern tradition was Susan Long, a former slave who helped rear Newman and was known to the author and her family as "Mammy." Newman credited Long with being "mostly responsible for my lack of a southern lady's traditional illusions" (*Letters* 273): "When I was a little girl, she used to tell me about slavery times, and I thought Miss ———, her old mistress, was a woman and the devil was a man, and that was the only difference between them. If you grow up hearing of mistress's sons who set dogs on a little girl three years old to see her run, who beat the slaves, who didn't tell them they were free, you can't admire the ante-bellum south completely" (273–74).

Little else is known about Newman's childhood except that she was an avid and precocious reader in her father's library and that she began writing at an early age. In an article written for the *Atlanta Journal* the spring before she died, Newman tells of her first attempt at fiction when, "like nearly all other human

3

beings who learn to read and write at the age of six or seven," she wrote a novel at the age of ten ("Frances Newman Tells" 6). Soon afterwards, she overheard a suitor of her older sister reading a chapter from that youthful novel out loud and "without any trouble . . . gathered that . . . [they] found it very comical." Yet Newman did not attribute her early disappointment in literary endeavors to "a conviction of inadequacy" but rather to not having been "born into a literary environment." The "habit" of novel writing, she explained, was "very frequently caught in towns and in families and in colonies where a great many novels were written" (6), as opposed to Atlanta and her own nonliterary family. Writing novels was not Newman's only precocious activity; apparently she was reading Shakespeare's plays at that same age (Baugh 3).

Newman's early affection for her father's library and her early writing are often explained as a compensation for her lack of physical beauty. Isabel Paterson, for one, asserts that Newman "cultivated her fine intelligence as a substitute" for her "lack of beauty" ("Books"), and in his introduction to Newman's letters, Hansell Baugh includes a description written by her niece of Newman as a homely child: "She was an unattractive child, and she knew it. Only too often had she stood before her mother's mirror and compared the image of the pallid girl with stringy black hair and stringy black-stockinged legs with the visions of grace and beauty which were her three older sisters. And she realized that even in the remote distance when she would be grownup, she would never look as they did. So with remarkable intelligence, she decided that her only alternative was to cultivate her cleverness" (3).[4]

Even though Baugh insisted Newman later read "with satisfaction" this portrayal of herself, his and others' attributing her childhood proclivity for reading and writing to mere compensation is too facile. Newman's approval of this description of herself as an unattractive child who was thus attracted to intellectual pursuits parallels the taking on by nineteenth-century American women writers of ultrafeminine pen names such as "Fanny Fern" and "Grace Greenwood." Just as these earlier women writers dis-

4

guised "behind these nominal bouquets their boundless energy, powerful economic motives and keen professional skills" (Show-alter 35), Newman could avoid offending prevailing views of what was proper for women by agreeing to the explanation that her intellectual pursuits were compensation for not being beautiful. Newman's active social life and romantic attachments with younger men seem to indicate that far from feeling insecure about her physical appearance, Newman seemed rather to take her character Katharine Faraday's attitude that "she could not believe there was any really good reason why no one had ever told her that she was surprisingly pretty for a girl who was as clever as she was" (*Hard-Boiled Virgin* 41).

Despite her intellectual precocity, Newman's formal education was "extensive rather than thorough" (Talmadge 622); it was limited to that deemed appropriate for a southern female from a good family. Her early schooling began at the exclusive Calhoun Street School (F. M. Blake 305) and continued at Washington Seminary, "a fashionable girls' school" on Peachtree Street (Cole 19). After high school she was sent to two finishing schools—Miss McVeagh's School for Young Ladies in Washington, D.C., where she (like her character Katharine Faraday) made unchaperoned visits with other students to the Senate and House, and Mrs. Semple's School in New York City (Baugh 5), where according to her own recollections she "did nothing but attend West Point hops" (Essig). Newman also briefly attended Agnes Scott College in Decatur, Georgia, and then embarked on a three-month European tour in 1910 (F. M. Blake 305). After she returned from Europe, instead of seeking the proper marriage that her family and society expected, Newman continued her education, first taking courses in Italian and Greek at the Summer School of the South (the University of Tennessee's summer program) in 1911 and then completing a library science degree at the Atlanta Carnegie Library in 1912, in a program that later became the library school at Emory University (F. M. Blake 305–6).

After completing her library science degree, Newman worked for a year as a librarian at Florida State College for Women in Tallahassee. However, she so hated being apart from her family and Atlanta that she returned in 1914—after a Mediterranean tour with her sister Isabel—to a job at the Atlanta Carnegie Library. She once remarked that she had become a librarian because she liked books ("Frances Newman Tells"), and for a woman who chose to be independent when that meant to accept financial hardships, a library was an excellent place to continue her education. Newman later spoke of this period as one in which she had read "everything I could lay my hands on" and had "learned two-thirds all I know" (Essig). She displayed persistence in attaining her often-noted erudition; despite her lack of a university education, she became fluent in four languages and familiar with the literature of seven (Jones, *Tomorrow* 276).

During her early years at the Carnegie Library, Newman also began her writing career. As early as 1915 she was writing reviews for the *Atlanta Journal* ("Lady from Georgia"), in February 1920 her "Library Literary Notes" began to appear in the *Atlanta Constitution*'s Sunday editorial page, and she also began writing literary bulletins for the Carnegie Library. These early pieces revealed her broad reading, distinct tastes, and sense of humor. For example, in her essay "Exit Mr. Castle and Mr. Williamson" Newman first discussed a number of literary couples, some collaborators and others like Mary Shelley, who was "undoubtedly too clever a woman to make even the subtlest suggestion to her sensitive plant" (G-2). Newman then turned to unmarried novelists, observing that "with the notable exception of Mrs. Wharton, who would, of course, never have committed the social error of remaining unmarried, most of our other American writing ladies are stalwart spinsters." After an extensive list of American and English literary "spinsters" and "bachelors," including "Miss Ellen Glasgow and Miss Mary Johnston, of the unhappy endings," Newman commented: "Whether bachelors and spinsters take up novel writing as a solace or whether novel writing is a bar to matrimony seems difficult to settle beyond a reasonable doubt" (G-2). In her article "Freud and the Flapper," Newman playfully mocked Freud's "quite touching theory that the simplest way of curing a lady suffering from suppressed desires is to have her fall in love with the doctor—a noble idea but of a rather self-limiting nature, since even the most self-sacrificing doctor could hardly marry more than three or four of his patients." She also critiqued writers whose fiction depended too heavily on Freudian theory in "Literary Complexes," opining they were "obliged by a lack of imagination to fall back upon a set of complexes with frocks and boots and Christian names" (6). Evelyn Scott, whom she described as "very susceptible to the straws that the literary wind blows her way," peopled her *Narrow House* "with a family who suffer inferiority complexes, ego-complexes, compulsions—every conceivable complex except those that promote filial and fraternal affection" (4). In contrast, D. H. Lawrence "has read his Freud and his Jung, he has taken all that they have for him and then he has thrown the rest right away" (6), and Susan Glaspell's *Suppressed Desires* demonstrates "the moral that if one must write Freudian drama, it is far better to poke a sort of knowing fun at it" (4). Newman's bold, incisive articles attracted the attention of the Virginia novelist James Branch Cabell and the critic H. L. Mencken, who became her supporters and mentors. In his first letter to Newman, Cabell requested copies of all her literary introductions, saying he had "been wondering about this authentic voice from the wilderness for some while" (*Letters* 32). H. L. Mencken's first letter to Newman requested that she write an article for *The Smart Set* if she were a graduate "of any of the eminent women's colleges"; she ruefully responded that she would be unable to write the article since she did not have the "advantages of a college education" (64–65). Newman appreciated their encouragement and help, and she looked to Cabell for literary advice as well as intellectual friendship.

Cabell encouraged Newman to seek a publisher for her recently completed first novel, *The Gold-Fish Bowl,* in 1921, but she at first resisted, explaining she intended to keep it as a "skeleton in my own closet" (*Letters* 48) since it did not measure up to her own exacting literary standards. Later she decided to follow Cabell's suggestion, commenting to him: "I wish I could say that you had lured me into novel writing, as I need some such good excuse, but chronology would convict me. However, if Mr. Holt [Henry Holt of Henry Holt & Co.] should unthinkably find the

7

frivolous tale worthy, he will doubtless relate that you discovered me pining in the desert" (*Letters* 38). When the publisher Robert M. McBride rejected *The Gold-Fish Bowl* as a novel unlikely to be commercially successful (H[olt], unpublished letter), Cabell urged Newman to send it next to Knopf and if necessary to Harcourt, and he related his own difficulties in getting published (*Letters* 67). Newman, however, insisted her first novel "would never justify such fortitude"; she had already sent it to George Henry Doran and determined if he did not publish it not to send it out again. "Happily," she explained, "I care next to nothing about its fate" (69).

In August of the same year, "The Allegory of the Young Intellectuals" appeared in the *Reviewer* as the first in a series of Newman's articles published by this short-lived but important southern literary magazine newly founded by Emily Clark.[5] In several of these articles Newman satirized the propensity for gloom in the writing of young Americans, noting in "With One Year's Subscription" (1922) that whereas essayists "are still permitted a gentle cheerfulness," to be considered a worthy American novelist, one must "abandon all hope: having stumped his own toe on life, he must have decided that his own misfortune is nothing less than a law of nature" (375–76). In "Five Years of American Fiction," written in September 1922, Newman attacked "the complacent belief that the American short story is extremely clever technically" as "the fearful legacy of O. Henry and of the gentlemen and ladies who give prizes in his name and spread the legend that story writing is a merely mechanical art . . . easily learned over-night."[6] Instead, she asserted, the "inability to see the necessity of putting one's self to school in writing is the fundamental defect of American novelists" (6). She praised the experimental English writers Katherine Mansfield, Virginia Woolf, and D. H. Lawrence for their "delicately felt and beautifully fashioned stories" influenced by the "new psychology" ("Five Years" 5). In discussing the demise of the novel centered on external action and the ascent of that in "pursuit of the soul," Newman declared every novelist of the new school "a disciple of James Joyce and Dorothy Richardson" (" 'Quiet Interior' ").

Newman's own fiction was influenced by these modernist writers, as well as her acknowledged literary mentors Jane Austen and Henry James, although she developed a markedly individual style. She especially admired the fiction of Mansfield and Woolf and believed that American women writers similarly needed to focus their attention both on stylistic excellence and on the female experience, a focus that Newman's own fiction followed.[7] She insisted in a review of *To the Lighthouse* that "a woman must write the things a woman feels, and . . . she must avoid the things a man feels as carefully as a man who has never been east of Georgia must avoid describing the jungles of Africa." In her essay "The American Short Story," she praised Mansfield's rendition of the female experience: "No man knows the women of the twentieth century as Katherine Mansfield knew them, and the women who live in America in the twentieth century will not be painted until some American woman feels what Katherine Mansfield felt about English women, and feels it clearly enough to write stories as crystal as 'Bliss' and 'The Garden Party' " (193). However, Newman was aware of the danger of excessive literary influence even though she believed that "most women, apparently, must follow a master": "But the second woman who will have a place in the history of the short story will not be an American woman unless she follows a master as Katherine Mansfield followed Tcheckhov, instead of following him as Edith Wharton followed Henry James, and unless an American woman has already been born with the fineness of Mrs. Wharton, the sympathetic penetration of Ruth Suckow, and the gentle incredulity of Jane Austen, and the realization that, in spite of all those gifts, she must learn the difficult art of writing prose" (193).

A relentless reviser of her own prose, Newman had little patience for writers whose style was clumsy or for critics who praised such writers. In "Literary Independence," published in the first volume of the *Saturday Review of Literature* (1925), Newman deplored the lack of style in most American writing, including that of James Fenimore Cooper, William Dean Howells, Willa Cather, Sinclair Lewis, Theodore Dreiser, and Mark Twain, while she praised that of James Branch Cabell and Elinor Wylie. In

"Five Years of American Fiction," she commented that "though Nathaniel Hawthorne is a universally esteemed writer and no child has escaped a compulsory reading of *The House of Seven Gables*—which is not far from the most uninteresting novel ever written—his style is certainly not charming" (4). In contrast, she credited Henry James with being "the first American novelist who wrote distinguished and delightful prose," but lamented that "although he had quite enough style for a dozen writers, he had to go abroad to cultivate it" (4). An ongoing disagreement with Mencken and Cabell centered on their praise of Fitzgerald, whom Newman considered "an amateur of techniques" (Newman, "Herd" 431). She sought nothing less than perfection in her own writing and reported that her writing process involved "working over every sentence at least twenty-five times" before she was "satisfied with it" and "slaughtering whole essays and stories to make one good phrase" (Essig). According to her editor Emily Clark, Newman's "early manuscripts rivalled the Constitution of the United States in the number of their amendments, and corrections did not cease to arrive until second proofs were in the hands of the printer" (Clark 189).

Although Newman's extensive revisions arose primarily from her concern for artistry and exactness, her letters also reveal an insecurity about her writing. When she first started contributing articles to the *Reviewer,* she sent a revision to Clark with this note: "Little as the result discloses it, I am one of those people who must always be tinkering with their style, so probably I shall send you another tomorrow and then, I am afraid, you will give me up" (*Letters* 57). In a letter to Cabell concerning another article for the *Reviewer,* Newman urged him not to "be polite" if he did not like her "little paper," and she requested that he reject it for publication "if you find it unworthy of the Reviewer or even of me" (*Letters* 62). Similarly, she wrote to Mencken: "If you've settled against my review, just throw it away" (Undated, unpublished letter). Newman's insecurity about her writing was sincere rather than assumed; in an unpublished letter to her sister Margaret Patterson in July 1922, she confessed, "My things always make me sick when I see them in print." That same year she wrote to Clark

Living as a Southern Lady

about future contributions to the *Reviewer:* "You have so many of the great of the earth that I feel a little shy of offering myself to you" (Clark 195–96).[8]

In the fall of 1922 Newman began writing *The Hard-Boiled Virgin* after abandoning a conversational novel that she had dubbed "my Peacock" (Clark 199), probably referring to Thomas Love Peacock's conversational novel *Nightmare Abbey.* Making progress on this novel was complicated by her struggle to support herself and relatives. She was beginning to feel the stress of trying to write while working full-time as a librarian but needed the money her job and newspaper articles provided. She had been taking care of her mother since her father's death in 1920, and when her mother died in the spring of 1922, she continued to support Susan Long and her nephew Louis Rucker and could not afford to quit her job. Newman did consider applying for a job as a telephone operator in New York, where she could be in the center of literary activity, wryly commenting to her sister, "It would do no harm, I suppose, to see what they would offer—big corporations always deal more gently with their slaves than libraries and other high-minded institutions" (*Letters* 79). Nevertheless, she continued working at the Atlanta Carnegie Library until 1923, when she again went to Europe, this time to study at the Sorbonne. This trip offered a welcome respite from the library and an opportunity to concentrate her efforts on the collection of short stories that she was editing and translating, *The Short Story's Mutations.* Despite recurrent illnesses,[9] when Newman returned from Europe she was able to complete *The Short Story's Mutations* and three episodes of *The Hard-Boiled Virgin,* as well as write two short stories, "Rachel and Her Children" and "Atlanta Biltmore," before reluctantly accepting a position as librarian at the Georgia Institute of Technology in the fall of 1924.[10]

Much of Newman's ambivalence about accepting another library position came from the conflict between her writing and the demands of a full-time job. In a letter to Baugh about the offer of the librarianship, she had expressed doubts about accepting it, dubbing it the "age-old choice between literary indigence and dull respectability" and concluding, "I feel quite cra-

11

ven about taking the library, and as if I'd be silly not to take it—being fairly lucrative, seemly, and easy" (*Letters* 140). Part of her ambivalence is also embodied in her choice of the word *seemly*. As a southern lady, Newman was acutely aware that few careers were open to women of the upper class that would not be an embarrassment to them socially. When asked in an interview about "a woman's best chance to be self-supporting in the South," Newman responded, "Teachers and librarians are safe but few of them can save money and the professions are of course very hard for women to enter in the South" (J. C. Harris, "Interview"). Even to be a "literary woman" involved "horrid indignities"; "it's rather worse, I think, than running for office," she commented to Baugh, "and worse in very much the same way. . . . [h]umiliating" (*Letters* 140).

Newman also continued to feel insecure about her writing, especially as a career that might provide an income. She explained to Baugh that before the offer of the job she had been "feeling so off literature as an avocation": "Books and stories and reviews aren't *in* me. I have to create them with terrible agony and terrible work" (*Letters* 140). Juggling a job and her writing, she was assisted by her life-long companion and employee Susan Long, who served in some ways as the wife most male writers have to support them emotionally and to look after household details. Newman emphasized Long's importance to her work as well as her life; she wrote to Hudson Strode that they were "terribly attached to each other" (274) and spoke to Winifred Rothermel of Long's "carefulness to keep all distractions" from her when she was writing. That Long was more a surrogate wife/mother than simply a domestic servant can be seen in Newman's comment to a friend that Long "can play the faithful retainer perfectly with our friends" yet "keeps Louis [Newman's nephew] and me both in our places." This familial intimacy is also revealed in a letter to Long: "You must remember that Louis and I are your family, and that we both love you more than anybody in the world. . . . I never realize how much I love you until I am away like this" (*Letters* 275, 254).

Despite her misgivings about accepting the position at Georgia Tech and the continued conflict between a job and her writing, Newman was apparently happier there than she had been at the Carnegie Library. In January 1925 Newman wrote to her niece: "I am very much pleased with the library so far and I really think libraries are about the nicest spots in the world" (*Letters* 158). In contrast, she had written to her sister Margaret Patterson from Europe about Atlanta Carnegie Library: "I simply can't go back to the awful atmosphere of the library" (Unpublished letter, 19 Apr. 1923). Yet by February she was writing to Baugh, "Tech takes it out of me terribly—some people may be able to write at night after a day's work, but my mind and my body are both too feeble for that. I am sorry I took it" (*Letters* 159). She wrote to A. B. Bernd that same month: "This library is making writing of any kind impossible, and I don't think I should stay on after June—not unless I decide definitely to give up writing forever" (161–62).

Newman set June of 1925—the date of her nephew's graduation and, presumably, lowered expenses for herself—as a target date to resign from her position so she could finish writing *The Hard-Boiled Virgin.* Yet she continued to work full-time until August, when she again wrote to Baugh of plans for a part-time schedule: "I am to work just part of the day, send a weekly letter to the Journal, do some reviews for the Tribune and the Saturday Review and subsist on that and my small unearned increment until the Virgin makes my fortune—which won't be very soon" (176). As Newman's letter suggests, her newspaper writing was primarily motivated by finances; she wrote extensively for the *Atlanta Journal* and the *Atlanta Constitution,* and although she was critical of the sanctioned style and subject matter, she was practical about its rewards. "You would be horrified if you saw the things I am writing for the Journal here," she wrote to Clark. "But it's an extraordinarily easy way to pick up a little money. . . . I've learned to be extremely lucid and to write sentences about one line long" (*Letters* 116). Apparently Newman felt no danger that such writing would damage her style for her serious writing, although it robbed her of time, for she advised another friend: "I don't believe your newspaper work will hurt you except by taking

13

up your time. If you are like me, you can do it with some faculty that doesn't touch your real self at all" (157). Many of her newspaper articles concerned high society news, but she also wrote about her travels to Europe, New York, and Maine and about visits and interviews with writers such as Glasgow, Isa Glenn, Mencken, and Cabell.

In August of 1925 Newman applied for a year's leave of absence from Georgia Tech, and the next fall and winter she made several trips to New York City for stimulation for her writing, returning to Atlanta to recover from influenza. During this time she wrote a letter from New York to her friend Delia Johnston expressing ambivalence about her native city. "About every two days I get so homesick that I think I will come back to Atlanta as soon as I live up my month's rent," she confided. "Then I see a copy of the Atlanta paper and feel that I never can stand it again" (*Letters* 187). "Perhaps I'm hopelessly Georgian" (126), she had earlier written to Hansell Baugh from Maine, homesick for the sight of a peach tree, but when told by the New York publisher Benjamin Huebsch that nothing about her was southern except her voice, she responded: "Sometimes I think that he may be right—when I read a book like . . . Emily Clark's little Virginia sketches, I know that I will never write anything with a definitely southern quality like that" (133). Yet on another occasion she concluded: "I'm afraid that I at least have a tap-root and won't transplant" (Clark 205).

Newman's fall review of Sherwood Anderson's *Dark Laughter*, which praised its "beautifully simple prose" as "one with its idea and with its emotions" ("Dark Laughter"), brought a note of appreciation from its author, and in November she wrote to tell Anderson how "touched" she was by his note and to try to arrange a lunch or dinner with him and a young writer friend of hers (Unpublished letter, 6 Nov. [1925]). Newman appreciated Anderson's fiction because he chose to write about contemporary American life. She recognized him and Ring Lardner as "the only writers who have proved, in their best stories, that the current of American life can flow through an admirable and American form," and she credited Anderson's "I'm a Fool" with having

Living as a Southern Lady

"achieved a perfect blending of theme and form and style which has probably never been equaled in America" ("Short Stories of 1925"). Her alternating self-assurance and insecure deference in relating to prominent literary men can be seen in her requests to Mencken and Anderson to recommend her to the MacDowell Colony in Peterborough, New Hampshire. To Mencken she wrote, "Will you be an angel and . . . say that I am a woman of extraordinary creative gifts?" She then chided him for neglecting her: "You are making a great mistake not to call on me—I am bursting with ideas for Mercury articles, which I can't write until you approve. However, it is now too late, since I have had grippe [influenza] three times since January, and propose to go South next week" (*Letters* 187–88). In contrast, Newman deferentially asked Anderson if his "literary conscience" would allow him to recommend her, explaining, "I think perhaps I will never finish my novel unless I get into a more peaceable atmosphere than I have found either in Atlanta or New York, and Peterborough might just possibly be the right place" (Unpublished letter, 29 Mar. 1926).

Apparently Peterborough was the right place for Newman to concentrate fully on her novel. In two months during the summer of 1926, she was able to complete *The Hard-Boiled Virgin*, including extensive revisions and editing—a remarkable feat considering she had spent four years on the first seventy pages amidst the distractions of her other responsibilities. Newman's writing process for this novel, as for all her fiction, was meticulously analytical. She continuously searched for the exact word, metaphor, or scene to reveal the inner life and emotions of her character Katharine Faraday. One example is her puzzling out "a metaphorical way of saying what Katharine Faraday felt when she saw her tall young West Pointer again, and how she looked while she was feeling it." "I decided," she explained, "that some well-known and miraculous metamorphosis would be the way. And I brooded for an hour over various miracles before I thought of saying that 'she looked as calm as the wine which had been water one minute before' " ("Frances Newman Tells" 8). It was especially gratifying to Newman to be living among other writers who were similarly

Living as a Southern Lady

engaged in creative struggles; she found the MacDowell Colony a "charming and encouraging place to write" precisely because she was able to share her ideas and newly created lines with other writers such as Paul Green and Thornton Wilder (8). Newman spoke of "ideas and phrases which finally satisfy their writer" as the "only real reward for the terrifically hard work writing is," but added that few would persevere through the months of all-consuming labor "if their manuscripts were going to be laid tenderly away in an attic" (8). Thornton Wilder warned her of the "wicked publicity" her book would bring, but she responded that she was "not a magnolia blossom to turn brown at a cross word" (*Letters* 197).

When *The Hard-Boiled Virgin* appeared in 1926, Wilder's prediction proved correct, but Newman became reconciled to a notoriety that resulted in brisk sales of her book. "I haven't a particle of character left," she explained to a friend. "Lots of people think I've done everything in it, and although I point out that Hawthorne was never the mother of an illegitimate daughter and . . . that Kipling wasn't brought up by an elephant—it doesn't do any good. However, all of it sells the book" (*Letters* 229). At the end of December she wrote to Baugh: "The Virgin is in her fourth printing and in her second jacket. Apparently it has been damned and praised heartily enough to make it sell pretty well for a book with no conversation and only one seduction and our usual long sentences" (*Letters* 232). When she learned that it had been banned in Boston ("Boston Bans Sale") and kept off library shelves in Brooklyn public libraries (Stevenson), she responded, "Now that the Virgin has displeased an Irish Catholic policeman, I ought to become rich enough to buy a little house at once" (*Letters* 248). *The Hard-Boiled Virgin* was on the best-seller lists the same months as Hemingway's *The Sun Also Rises,* Sinclair Lewis's *Elmer Gantry,* and Glasgow's *The Romantic Comedians* ("Books of the Month"). Newman never bought a house, but she was now financially able to devote all her time to writing.

After another trip to Europe, this time with her nephew, Newman returned in the summer of 1927 to the MacDowell Colony in Peterborough, where she wrote the first half of *Dead Lovers Are*

16

Faithful Lovers. That fall she continued working on her novel while again struggling with illnesses. To Nelson Crawford, whom she had met at Peterborough, she wrote: "All the fall, I've been very poorly. . . . I have only about twenty-five more pages to write [of *Dead Lovers Are Faithful Lovers*], but I feel as if I'll never get them down, though I have them all somewhere in a mind which seems to be a rapidly sinking island" (*Letters* 303).[11] Newman's frequent illnesses, although they may be primarily the response of a delicate southern constitution to the harsh climate of New York, raise the question of possible psychological causes. In their book *Complaints and Disorders: The Sexual Politics of Illness,* Barbara Ehrenreich and Deirdre English discuss the "cult of female invalidism" prevalent in nineteenth-century England and America. The societal expectation for a lady to be frail and sickly continued to be an aspect of the southern culture, which retained many of the traditions of the nineteenth century, especially regarding roles for women. Were Newman's illnesses a means of punishing herself for exceeding the boundaries of acceptable behavior for a southern lady or a means of proving she still was a lady? Or were they, perhaps, a result of the stress of writing novels true to the experience of women that would also be acceptable to the largely male literary establishment?

Sandra Gilbert and Susan Gubar remind us that earlier women writers within a patriarchal system "were evidently infected or sickened by just the feelings of self-doubt, inadequacy, and inferiority that their education in 'femininity' almost seems to have been designed to induce" (*Madwoman* 60). Despite the success of *The Hard-Boiled Virgin* and her own sense of its artistic merit, Newman continued to express insecurity about her work when corresponding with male writers and publishers (*Letters* 272–73, 282). Newman's dependence upon male encouragement and approval for her writing conflicted with the feminist ideas present in her novels and many of her interviews. She once remarked in a letter that she believed "a woman can't write a book without a father for it any more than she could have a baby," adding that all three of hers "have had fathers as different as the fathers of Isadora Duncan's children" (*Letters* 310). Apparently she considered Lamar Trotti the emotional "father" of *The Hard-Boiled Virgin*. She sent episodes for him to read while she was in Peterborough and shortly after completing the novel claimed in a letter to him, "I never should have written the book if you hadn't goaded me. I certainly could never have gotten the same emotion into it if I hadn't known you" (*Letters* 214). In an unpublished letter to Trotti she assured him that he could not appreciate the book more if he were a woman "because of course you understand it in a way no other man can" and referred to her novel as his "handspring" (letter to Trotti, 26 Nov. 1926). Similarly, she wrote to Hansell Baugh from a ship on her way to France after finishing her third novel: "I wish you were here—when I have plenty of time. I never see you and when I see you, I don't often have plenty of time, though we did fairly well last May, didn't we? If we hadn't, I should probably never have gotten (yes, got*ten*) Dead Lovers begun. So you shouldn't be too hard on a book for which you are somewhat responsible" (*Letters* 339).

Regardless of the consequences to her health, Newman continued to travel to New York because she found it to be a stimulant for her writing, even though she was unable actually to write until she returned home. To Helen Stern she explained: "This time, I just went for a sort of pick-up to get me through the book [*Dead Lovers Are Faithful Lovers*], and it had a marvellous effect. . . . When I got back to work, I wrote a whole episode—three or four pages—every day, and before Christmas I'd been painfully screwing out half a page" (*Letters* 310). By the end of January 1928 the novel was completed, and Newman left before it was published for her last trip to Europe, explaining to Baugh: "I don't know what the publication date is, but I want to depart this town before much gossiping begins, as it is very irritating to me" (*Letters* 313).

In Europe, Newman began research for her translation of Jules Laforgue's short fiction, but her trip was shortened by a serious eye problem that was variously diagnosed but never successfully treated. In May she wrote to Baugh about a "congested right eye" that prevented reading (*Letters* 346–47), and in June she returned to the United States for medical attention. Although she had "a hellish time" with a number of doctors and was unable to attain relief from the incessant, throbbing pain or to see well enough to write herself, by September she managed not only to finish her translation of Laforgue's stories by dictation but also to begin making plans for researching her next book, all the while maintaining her sense of humor (353–61). Writing a business letter to her publisher about the delay of her translation, she joked, "I realize that it can't make any great difference to Horace Liveright, Inc., which will be prospering on the stories of the crucified and the electrocuted," and added, "having thought of that crack, you'll realize that I must use it" (357).[12] She asked her young friend Hansell Baugh to read over her proofs if she should die before they were ready to "be sure there are no inconsistencies and no howlers" (360). Although her problem had been diagnosed as related to her sinuses or perhaps her teeth, a visit to a specialist in Philadelphia raised the question of "intracranial pressure," and Newman was next referred to a neurologist in New York who suggested she enter a sanitarium (Baugh 351–52). A few days later, on October 19, 1928, she was found unconscious in her hotel room in New York City where she was waiting to consult yet another neurologist. Three days after that she was dead. Newman's death was first reported to have been caused by a cerebral hemorrhage complicated by pneumonia, but later reports blamed an overdose of a barbiturate with the trade name Veronal.

Newman's death occasioned a number of lurid newspaper articles that claimed suicide or poisoning and portrayed her as a neurotic spinster and "sensational sex writer" ("Authoress Dies of Poison," "Probers Seek," "Drug Killed"). Some were deliberately malicious. In his column "Books on Our Table," William Soskin extensively quoted H. E. Dounce, who claimed that those seeking the cause of Newman's possible suicide needed to search no further than her novel *The Hard-Boiled Virgin:* "The outer experiences of the heroine need not be the author's . . . but the inner story, the psychology, the revelation of an intensely neurotic life and temperament—that surely was done as with the aid of a mirror." He characterized Newman's heroine as "a miserable and pitiable creature, 'fixated,' mired in 'narcissism' to the most tormenting degree—one whose suicide, whenever a last illusion should shatter and leave her bankrupt, might be logical even without much immediate cause." Furthermore he saw Newman, unlike her heroine, as having "immediate cause" for suicide; in addition to being an object of "scathing criticism" and a "comic figure," she "had reached middle age, she was ill, [and] she was threatened with partial blindness, perhaps with disfigurement." An unsigned article concluded that in response to unfavorable reviews of her novels, Newman "had succumbed to futility, heightened with spinsterish complications" ("Says Newman Took"), and another argued that reasons for her "suicide" were "unimportant": "Like the types she wrote about—those deliberate sensualists, for example—she was above the vulgarity of a reason. She simply wanted to die" ("Frances Newman's End"). Newman's treatment by many newspaper journalists and critics at her death parallels the "rightful end" of romance novels discussed by Rachel DuPlessis; a woman achieved either "successful courtship, marriage" or "judgmental of her sexual and social failure—death" (1). Since Newman did not follow the traditional path for women—marriage and family—many critics assumed her life was a failure and tried to make the "plot" of her life fit the conventions of literature against which she wrote.

Far from being a frustrated spinster, Newman was an engaging woman who had excited the passions of a number of men but preferred brief love affairs and independence to marriage, fearing marriage would end her writing career. Her letters indicate several love affairs, often with younger men. For example, in the spring of 1925 she wrote to Emily Clark from Atlanta that she had fallen in love with "a youth twenty-five years old," whom she referred to as "my Gareth" after a character in Carl Van Vechten's novel *The Tattooed Countess*. In a June letter she disclosed "how charming it is to be loved in that fresh, garden-between-dawn-and-sunrise way, again" in contrast to attention from "all those fat, middle-aged lustful creatures" and claimed "when he doesn't love me any more I shall give up love forever" (*Letters* 172–74).[13] A year later she reported to Susan Long and her nephew Louis

Living as a Southern Lady

Rucker about "one man I was rather taken with, but he went away yesterday, so I got a good deal more work done today," and in a letter to Thornton Wilder that same month she referred to a visit from her "boy friend" (201–2). The publication of *The Hard-Boiled Virgin* in November 1926 brought a proposal from an "excited" young man, but she commented she had not begun "either a new love affair or a new book" (222). However, by May of the next year (1927), she wrote to three friends that she was "afraid" she was "falling in love again" and "such things are very disturbing to writing—for me anyway" (259–65). Newman's falling in love with younger men who admired her writing enabled her to retain her power in the relationship and, as they were unlikely candidates for marriage, to retain her independence. Thus Newman fits into the pattern of highly creative and talented women discussed by Carolyn Heilbrun in *Writing a Woman's Life* who " 'fall' into a condition where vocation is possible and out of the marriage plot that demands not only that a woman marry but that the marriage and its progeny be her life's absolute and only center" (51). Finding herself unable to write when involved with a man, Newman chose independence over marriage. She had once declared: "It would seem like suicide to be submerged in a lasting love affair . . . because I don't think it is possible to tie your emotions up in someone and still be free to do your very best work" ("Frances Newman Shocked").

Newspaper accounts also speculated on the coincidence of the appearance of a *Vanity Fair* parody of Newman's last novel entitled "Dead Novelists Are Good Novelists," which was published near the time of her death. In this parody, the writer Isabel Evelyn commits suicide by jumping out of the nineteenth floor of a building after realizing that her fears have been realized and she and her novel have been rejected by John Riddell (Riddell). Just as John Keats was believed to have been killed by a vicious review of *Endymion*, some newspaper articles implied that Newman took her own life after reading the parody. The article "Newman Parody Portended Death" (subtitled " 'Heroine' Was a Suicide") claimed that Newman heard excerpts from the parody shortly before her death and that she was "long known to be extremely sensitive to literary criticism" and recently "in a depressed frame of mind." These speculations also were unfounded. Newman had earlier responded lightheartedly to criticism of her writing, calling a review of her last novel by Donald Davidson "amusing" because he "said perhaps the South deserves me as the United States deserves Sinclair Lewis," and declaring she liked an intended insult that she wrote "like a child of Meredith by Ouida . . . as much as anything" that had been said about her (*Letters* 356). In an unpublished letter to Adrienne Battey (Saturday afternoon), Frank Daniel, Newman's friend and a journalist for the *Atlanta Journal,* commented that it was inconceivable that Newman would have taken the Riddell parody seriously, especially since she had looked forward to Christopher Ward's proposed caricature of *The Hard-Boiled Virgin.* Instead, Daniel suspected the publishers of the parody to be sensationalizing her death to advertise their work. Daniel's conclusion seems likely. Two newspaper articles that reported that T. R. Smith, editorial director of Boni and Liveright, had read the Riddell parody to Newman over the telephone gave a date for the conversation that was after Newman was already in a coma ("Parody on Novelist," "Newman Parody Portended"), and another newspaper article indicated the parody was not on sale until after she was unconscious ("Parody Newman Review").

In fact, the entire suicide issue is dubious. Although many newspaper articles assumed suicide once the presence of a barbiturate was suspected, for Newman to have deliberately taken her own life would have been entirely out of character. She had just finished the proofs for her book on Laforgue and would have wanted to see it published, and her brain was teeming with ideas for other books. Her letters discussed ideas for a book of criticism, "A History of Sophistication," and a volume of biographies, "Eminent Virgins," about the lives of Leonardo da Vinci, St. Francis of Assisi, Jane Austen, Cardinal Newman, and Henry James. Frank Daniel reported that Newman also had ideas for two novels, two short stories, and a play ("Miss Newman's Unwritten Books"). Apparently she had already begun research and writing on several, and she had estimated the spring before her death

Living as a Southern Lady

that she had a hundred pages "covered with phrases still out of employment" in a special notebook in which she jotted down "vagrant" phrases and ideas ("Frances Newman Tells" 8). She was undoubtedly discouraged and frustrated by her illness, but she had made an appointment with another neurologist in the hope he could help her. Even more significant was her planned outing with a friend. On the afternoon she was found unconscious, Newman had an engagement with Sylvia Bates to go to a concert and would not have wanted her friend to find her dead. Although it is possible that Newman took an accidental overdose of Veronal in order to get release from pain, her attending physician insisted there was no evidence of Veronal but only another sedative in an insufficient amount to cause death, and the chief medical examiner, Dr. Charles Norris, attributed her death to "natural causes" ("Finds Veronal in Body").[14] Furthermore, Bates, who stayed with Newman until her sister Margaret Patterson arrived, reported that Newman's left side was entirely paralyzed from what the doctors diagnosed as a brain hemorrhage (Battey, unpublished letter).

Seidel suggests Newman's reported suicide created an embarrassment among her "literary friends" that caused them to "disavow" her (*Southern Belle* 41), but apparently most of Newman's friends rallied to her defense. Cabell did write to Mencken that he was "horrified by Frances' death" and felt that she had "failed" him in not having lived to write "the planned History of Sophistication [that] would have made her future assured and enviable" (Wagenknecht 119), but despite his initial response, he dedicated his next book, *The White Robe*, to Newman, remarking he only regretted never having told her of his intention since he had planned the dedication as a surprise ("Cabell's New Book"). Mencken advised Julia Harris not to take the hints of Newman's suicide "too seriously" in an unpublished letter to her and indicated the reason for malicious attacks on Newman: "New York always concludes that a sudden death is a suicide. Frances had a good many bitter enemies and they are probably seizing the chance to dance around her coffin" (27 Oct. 1928). Similarly, Frank Daniel wrote to Adrienne Battey that Atlanta's headlines

23

were in retaliation for her portrayal of southern womanhood in *The Hard-Boiled Virgin* (Unpublished letter, Friday), and he suspected that the spiteful tone of one article was attributable to Harry Hansen's animosity over critical disagreements with Newman (Unpublished letter, Saturday). Daniel continued to write favorable articles about Newman in the Atlanta papers, including "Peachtree's Fame in Fiction: It Started with Frances Newman, Georgia's First Modern Novelist."

Several of Newman's friends were upset that her family took no steps to settle the allegation of suicide and to quiet attacks in the press. Daniel approached Newman's brother with his ideas for writing a rebuttal to a slanderous newspaper article but received the impression that Henry Newman was not interested (Unpublished letter to Battey, 30 Oct. 1928). Daniel had already begun to write an article in which he protested the idea that Newman's death had anything to do with comments from reviewers, and he challenged the implication that her problem with her eyes resulted from being unmarried. He also revealed that she had told relatives her pain had become unbearable (Draft). Adrienne Battey, who had taken dictation of Newman's last book, was disappointed Newman's family did not insist on an autopsy that included an examination of the brain to settle the question of suicide (Daniel, unpublished letter to Battey, 30 Oct. 1928), and she resented the family's treatment of Newman and her friends shortly after her death. In a ten-page typewritten letter, Battey described her own thwarted attempt to sit with her friend's body through the night and the hasty funeral service to which none of Newman's friends were invited (Unpublished letter).

Battey was, perhaps, somewhat unfair in her resentment of the family's behavior to her and in her conclusion that her dead friend was surrounded by unsympathetic relatives. When Battey learned of her friend's death and insisted upon talking with the family and seeing Newman's body, it was after midnight, and the quiet funeral service might have indicated a desire to escape publicity more than a disregard for Newman. However, several of Newman's New York friends would surely have wanted to attend

24

the funeral. Even Sylvia Bates, who had stayed with Newman while she was in a coma, was not notified in time to attend, and Hansell Baugh was also not invited (Battey, unpublished letter). Daniel, who was a friend of the family as well as of Newman herself, commented in a letter to Battey that the behavior of the Pattersons (Newman's sister Margaret and her husband John) reflected only on themselves and not on Frances. Perhaps they were embarrassed by their unorthodox relative and feared further scandal. Nevertheless, Daniel added, Newman's brother Henry and her nephew Louis Rucker were both genuinely grieving her death (Unpublished letter, Friday). In another unpublished letter he reassured Battey that her sister Margaret (with whom Newman had exchanged affectionate letters throughout her adult life) and her brother Henry both seemed anxious to carry out Frances's wishes, although all he mentioned was Henry's having provided the violet casket and orchids (30 Oct. 1928).

Newman was buried privately on Wednesday, October 24, in the West View Cemetery in Atlanta, her violet casket strewn with flowers in the shades of lavender and purple that she had worn for the last several years of her life ("Frances Newman Paid Last Honor"). For many years it seemed that the literary reputation of this controversial writer had died with her. Fortunately, after more than a half century of neglect, Frances Newman is finally receiving well-deserved and long-overdue critical attention.

2

Demythologizing the
Southern Lady

ONE OF THE DOMINANT SOCIAL and literary influences of the nineteenth century in the United States was the genteel tradition, which managed to coexist with more liberal ideologies. It was characterized by a prudish morality (with women as its exemplars and guardians) and valued cheerful optimism, high idealism, and decorous behavior. Reformers in the genteel tradition focused their efforts on keeping the home, and especially the women within it, untainted by the corruptions of society instead of battling against pervasive political and financial corruption and social injustice. The genteel tradition condemned literature with pessimistic or skeptical themes or with "anything derogatory, implicitly or explicitly, to religious ideals and moral standards," including discussions of the human body and sexuality (O'Connor 6–7). Malcolm Cowley compared the genteel tradition to British "Victorianism" but found it "even more stringent in its prohibitions" (*After the Genteel Tradition* 9). Books and magazines intended for the home were "supposed to express the highest ideals and aspirations" and be "as innocent as milk" (9–10): "If the young writer insisted on being pessimistic; if he portrayed women whose virtue was not laced in whalebone stays . . . then the doors of the institutions were closed to him" (15).¹ Newman, like her contemporaries Ellen Glasgow, Mary Johnston, and Isa Glenn, wrote against the grain of the genteel tradition, which

26

persisted into the twentieth century in the American South, and challenged the traditional images of the southern lady. Her satiric voice was startling amidst the moonlight-and-magnolias tradition of southern literature, and in her critique of the southern patriarchy, she was more audacious than other southern feminist novelists in revealing its sexism, classism, and racism.

A major facet of the genteel tradition, and one against which American women writers including Newman rebelled, was the "cult of true womanhood." Having abandoned, at least in practice, his religious and moral values in an increasingly materialistic society, nineteenth-century American man could assuage his conscience by making the American woman the protector and perpetuator of "all the values which he held so dear and treated so lightly" (Welter 151). According to Barbara Welter, keeping woman a "hostage in the home" provided the middle-class man with a sense of security and stability: "In a society where values changed frequently, where fortunes rose and fell with frightening rapidity, where social and economic mobility provided instability as well as hope, one thing at least remained the same—a true woman was a true woman, wherever she was found" (151–52). In surveying almost all women's magazines in the United States published for more than three years between 1820 and 1860, Welter found that the inherent virtues of "true womanhood" included "piety, purity, submissiveness and domesticity" (152). Any woman who deviated from any of these virtues was threatened with the dire consequences of total depravity, madness, poverty, or death (154–56).[2]

The image of the southern lady or belle was influenced by the cult of true womanhood, but as Elizabeth Fox-Genovese points out in her book *Within the Plantation Household*, the model of womanhood of the North "sought to deny the significance of class distinctions," which were pervasive in the South; its "specifically middle-class values" were portrayed as "universal" (41). Fox-Genovese also argues that while the rhetoric of domesticity in the slave-holding South was similar to that of the north, the meanings it implied differed. Domesticity in the urban and capitalistic northeast included the ideology of a separate sphere for women that was divorced from economic production. However, on the southern plantation, production was never separated from the household, which thus was never a woman's separate sphere but rather a shared world of males and females, owners and slaves. Also, the domestic labors exalted as the northern bourgeois woman's mission in life and symbol of her nurture and love were in the plantation household avoided by the southern lady and relegated to slaves. Even the kitchen, heart of the home in the separate sphere, was a separate building on the plantation, visited but not inhabited by the southern lady (79–81).

The southern version of true womanhood was thus modified by the South's aristocratic, racist culture; indeed, the image of the southern lady clearly developed from the need to rationalize and defend slavery. According to W. J. Cash in *The Mind of the South,* the planter class asserted its divinely ordained aristocracy to fortify its position as land and slave owners, with individuals securing aristocratic ancestors as soon as they became sufficiently prosperous.[3] From the immensely popular Sir Walter Scott novels, plantation owners acquired a chivalric vision of themselves and embraced the idea of *noblesse oblige* (59–81). Kathryn Lee Seidel similarly explains the element of aristocracy in the image of white southern womanhood as deriving from the southern planters' belief in their being descendants of the English aristocracy, who therefore ruled legitimately. In the era of Jeffersonian democracy, southern planters bolstered their position psychologically by comparing their undemocratic social order to that of the medieval age of chivalrous knights and fair ladies (*Southern Belle* 5).[4] Only privileged white women were considered ladies, and these upper-class women became "the objects of worship, the muses or guiding saints for those men who saw themselves as having established a chivalric and cultured world" (Westling 16).

Of course, this "chivalric and cultured world" had slavery as its economic base. Therefore, in addition to being a symbol of religious, moral, and social perfection like her northern sister, the white southern lady was a symbol of racial purity and a "perpetuator of white superiority in legitimate line" (Cash 84). As Diane Roberts notes in *The Myth of Aunt Jemima: Representations of*

Race and Region, white and black women were represented as "high and low, pure and polluted, bodies," and "this opposition became a part of the ideology of slavery itself: the sexual availability of slave women (who could not without danger refuse the Master), their ability to perform hard physical labour, their exposed bodies, their dark skin itself served to make the lady in the big house more ladylike: more untouchable, more angelic, more *white*" (4). Thus the white woman was considered the epitome of purity and innocence whereas the black woman was considered sexually promiscuous. Both Diane Roberts and Sara Evans explain the dualities of light/goodness/virginity versus dark/evil/sensuality as originating in Western European racial representations, myths, and metaphors that were easily translated into Caucasian/Negro (Roberts 4, 10; Evans).[5]

This idealization of the white woman and devaluing of the black woman intertwined with sexual behavior in a number of ways. In his study *Caste and Class in a Southern Town,* John Dollard discerned as the only absolute of the caste system its serving as a "categorical barrier" to sexual relations between white women and black men (63). Dollard also concluded that the idealization of the white woman caused sexual relations with her to be guilt-ridden for white men (136). In contrast to the symbolic figure of purity and sexual innocence projected onto the white woman, the black woman was seen as sexually promiscuous, and first slavery and later the caste system left her without an effective protector and therefore easily accessible. For example, Cash perpetuated the stereotyping by describing the black woman as "torn from her tribal restraints and taught an easy complaisance for commercial reasons" and explained her attractiveness to white men in that she was able to "give herself up to passion in a way impossible to wives inhibited by Puritanical training" (84). This idea of sexual promiscuity rationalized the rape of black women, who were seen as enticers and initiators of sexual relations rather than as victims (Hall 153; Hooks 52; Painter 58–59).

The sexual attraction the elite white male felt towards black women is explained by Lillian Smith as a result of the close relationship he had as a child with his black "mammy," who had

29

Demythologizing the Southern Lady

brought pleasure and comfort to his life but had no status and therefore became devalued as he grew older (123–29). Irving H. Bartlett and C. Glenn Cambor echo Smith's idea in Freudian terms; since the sons of white planters had both biological white mothers and surrogate black mothers who cared for them, they never had to reconcile their Oedipal complexes but could continue to be fascinated with black women, who had served as mother figures but were powerless to refuse sexual relationships (12–13).

Miscegenation also devalued white women, who represented "a racial purity which was required by her men for the maintenance of their caste but which many of them regularly transgressed in their own sexual behavior" (Westling 9). Supposedly compensation came in the form of being idealized, but Louise Westling remarks that "the white southern lady had been left in chilly isolation on her pedestal, for the facts of miscegenation spelled rejection and rendered chivalric tributes a painful lie" (23). Lillian Smith also laments "that lonely pedestal called Sacred Womanhood" upon which the white lady secretly mourned the painful and humiliating loss of her father, her husband, and finally her son to the arms of black women (133–35). Bartlett and Cambor discuss a more extensive devaluing of the southern white female, first through abandonment by a childish white mother to be cared for by a maternal but essentially powerless surrogate black mother, who both failed to serve as mature role models. Then in her adulthood, the southern white woman was "deprived . . . of her sexual identity and maternal identity" (20). The idealization of white women also arose from the guilty feelings of white men for being involved in sexual relations with women whom they had dehumanized (Cash 86; Tannenbaum 33). White men often projected their own sexual fantasies and practices onto the black man, whom they portrayed as sexual savages from whom white women needed protection.

This putative need for protection in turn served as an effective tool of social control for white women, who were expected to be obedient and submissive in return for protection. White southern womanhood involved an even greater expectation of submis-

30

siveness than the cult of true womanhood. Southern ladies were supposed to be so fragile and helpless that protecting them became a necessary role of the white male (Jones, *Tomorrow* 5). George Fitzhugh, a noted southern sociologist of the mid-nineteenth century, discussed the need for complete subordination of the southern woman: "In truth, woman, like children, has but one right and that is the right to protection." He added ominously: "The right to protection involves the obligation to obey," and he listed the appellation of "lord and master" with that of "husband" (A. F. Scott, *Southern Lady* 17). This submissiveness of women was especially important in the slave-owning South because, as Anne Firor Scott explains, "any tendency on the part of any of the members of the system to assert themselves against the master threatened the whole, and therefore slavery itself" (17). Without her submissiveness, the absolute authority of the planter was not assured (Clinton 111).

Since much of the justification for the white woman's need for protection and duty to submit was the black man's supposed unrestrained sexuality, even southern moderates approved the lynching of black men accused of raping white women. But lynching was more a means of controlling social caste than punishing crime. In *Killers of the Dream,* Lillian Smith explains: "We used those lynchings as a kind of symbolic rite to keep alive in men's minds the idea of white supremacy" (62). She views lynchings as opportunism; as men greedy for economic and political power taking advantage of "the terrifying complex of guilt, anxiety, sex jealousy" of other white men to keep the black population submissive. Lynching was a "symbolic killing of a black male" based on a "paranoid fantasy" and an "acting out of the white man's internal guilt and his hatred of colored man and white woman" (118). She notes the inherent irony in these lynchings: "In the name of *sacred womanhood,* of *purity,* of *preserving the home,* lecherous old men and young ones, reeking with impurities, who had violated the home since they were sixteen years old, whipped up lynchings, organized Klans, burned crosses, aroused the poor and ignorant to wild excitement by an obscene, perverse imagery describing the 'menace' of Negro men hiding behind every cy-

press waiting to rape 'our' women" (141). Statistics reinforce
Smith's charge that lynchings were motivated by a desire to control rather than concern for the safety and purity of white
women. Rapes of white women by black men, and even accusations, were rare, whereas rapes of black women by white men
were common both during and after slavery.[6] Of all the victims of
lynchings in the South between 1882 and 1946, only 23 percent
were even accused of rape or attempted rape, even though the
definition of attempted rape included "any act of a black man,
however innocent, that offended or frightened a white woman."
Twenty-six percent of the victims were accused of nothing more
than minor infractions of the racist code of behavior, which
could be nothing more than an insolent tone of voice (Hall 142–
51).[7]

Any violation of the caste system or step towards racial equality was deemed a threat to racial purity. Thomas Nelson Page,
essayist and novelist of the moonlight-and-magnolias tradition of
plantation novels, linked social equality with relationships between black men and white women in a 1907 article published
in *McClures* magazine: "Negroes understand by 'social equality,'
for the most part, one thing only: the right to stand with white
women on precisely the same ground as that on which white men
stand with them" (565). Reason was twisted to perceive a threat
to southern womanhood in simple offenses to white men. A
bishop of the Southern Methodist Church, Warren Candler,
warned that "possible danger to women is inherent in every offense against the white man" (Hall 147). The claims of a need to
protect white women justified segregation, and white politicians
used accusations of rape to regain control and functionally dis-
enfranchise black men (Painter 49–51; Ruoff 115–25).

The fear of rape and reprisals against blacks kept white women
as well as black men in their appointed places. As Jacquelyn Hall
observes in her history of the Women's Campaign Against Lynching, "it may be no accident that the vision of the Negro as threatening beast flourished during the first organizational phase of
the women's rights movement in the South" (at the turn of the
century), because "the fear of rape, like the threat of lynching,

Demythologizing the Southern Lady

served to keep a subordinate group in a state of anxiety and fear" (153).[8] Virginia Foster recounts an annual State Confederate Reunion in the early twentieth century in which she had listened as a girl to speeches about "the Lost Cause and Pure, White Southern Womanhood" and had "the feeling that the Civil War had been fought . . . entirely in my behalf," not recognizing until years later that "the cult of Pure, White Southern Womanhood also involved lynching—to protect it, of course" (51).

As Foster's recollection indicates, the image of the aristocratic, racially pure white southern lady persisted well into the twentieth century.[9] This image, together with the lingering genteel tradition, continued to influence white southern literature. In surveying the literature of the South as late as 1924, Addison Hibbard, professor of English at the University of North Carolina in Chapel Hill, lamented that just as in the previous hundred years, most southern literature remained "essentially romantic, still concerned largely with a time that has passed" (58). He hoped that the South would soon learn to laugh at itself and to look with keen eyes at actualities and thus engender satiric and realistic fiction. A year later, Paul Green, also of Chapel Hill and new editor of the *Reviewer,* wondered whether critics would continue to compile such collections as the sixteen-volume Library of Southern Literature with its works of "earth-departing spinsters . . . minute Alfred Tennysons, and nostalgic, whimpering Poes" (73) and called instead for "a truer and fresher interpretation of our environment and our relations to that environment" (75).

Despite Hibbard's and Green's assertions that literature in the South in the early twentieth century was almost entirely sentimental and steeped in the traditions of the past, when men were chivalrous and women were belles, fiction by white southern women was providing a realistic rather than sentimental portrayal of southern life, and the southern belle and lady had become objects of satire. Sarah Haardt painted a scathing portrait of the southern lady in her 1925 *Reviewer* article "The Southern Lady Says Grace." The southern lady, Haardt contended, "is still, and rather proudly, a slave of the conventions" since following conventions "saves her from thinking; and she has witnessed the

33

utter impossibility of thinking intently and looking pretty at the same time" (57). Haardt ridiculed the southern lady's "appealing demureness" in seeking minor changes in her role, believing rather that she should be straightforward in "taking her own stand": "Woman's sphere *is* the home, and she is not denying it, but surely there can be no harm in gently pushing the borders of that sphere. As long as there are women, there must be special laws protecting them, but, pray, let them be less binding and a little more decorative!" (57). Haardt claimed that the southern lady "pales at the thought" of "the new freedom"—"Freedom to do what? Work at a nagging, uninteresting job. . . . Be economically independent . . . ? No, indeed—not if she can help it! Her ambition is to marry and have her own home, with enough servants to run it" (58). The southern lady believes "a woman is most seductive when she is most reticent, trivial, demure," and "she has the feeling that it is somehow unbecoming for a woman to know too much about a subject" (61). "It is second nature for the Southern lady," Haardt continued, "to cling to what remains of extrinsic romance in the old regime": "She wants to preserve, even at a sacrifice, the divinely appointed role that the Southern gentleman has always held up to her: the painted halo, the remarkable virtues, the painful modesty, the piety, the irresistible tenderness, frailty, helplessness. It is the last, glamorous touch of chivalry in a harsh, unromantic age" (61).

Haardt was not the first southern writer to satirize the southern lady. Since before the turn of the century southern women writers had been questioning the role of the southern lady and criticizing a culture still bound by conventions of the genteel tradition. In addition, Frances Newman soon rose to the challenge implicit in H. L. Mencken's notorious essay "Sahara of the Bozart" to create a more dynamic, artistic literature. Mencken had characterized the South as "almost as sterile, artistically, intellectually, culturally, as the Sahara Desert" (136), claiming that with the exception of Cabell, the South did not have "a single southern prose writer who can actually write" (138). Newman's voice was satiric, like Mencken's, and shocked her contemporaries, but instead of lamenting the decline of the "old aristocracy"

Demythologizing the Southern Lady

of the South with its "great tradition," as did Mencken in his clas-
sist and racist invective (Mencken 139, 141), in her novels Newman revealed the injurious effects of the aristocratic southern
patriarchy with its traditional image of the southern lady.[10] In
doing so, she joined Mary Johnston, Ellen Glasgow, and Isa Glenn
in creating a women's tradition of southern white literature
counter to the male tradition that predominated at the turn of
the century. Carol S. Manning in her essay "The Real Beginnings
of the Southern Renaissance" names the "demythologizing of the
cult of Southern womanhood" as the central theme of female
writers of the emerging Southern Renaissance, and she mentions
Frances Newman as one of these "lone and isolated voices" (Manning 48–50). Instead of writing romantic plantation novels, these
southern women writers depicted the emptiness and frustration
of the life of the white southern female and exposed the racial
intolerance and class prejudices of the aristocratic southern society.

Newman was more audacious than most of her predecessors
and contemporaries in revealing women's actual position within
the southern patriarchy, and of these women writers, she was also
the most sophisticated and humorous satirist. Newman's satire is
usually urbane and playful; it is the Horatian satire of Voltaire,
whom she once called "my standard of perfection" (*Letters* 276).
In recognizing the similarity of her satire to Voltaire's, Evelyn
Hanna calls Newman "articulate and sophisticated, her weapon
a thin-edged rapier of wit such as a Frenchman would have used,"
and she notes that Newman's satire is directed towards "the de-
struction of the whited sepulchres that concealed smugness, intolerance and littleness of spirit." Newman's wit invites the laughter (or wry smile) of recognition not only at society's irrational
prejudices and dogmas but also at one's own foolish assumptions
and behavior. In her two published novels Newman manages to
maintain an ironic distance from her characters while still creating sympathy for them; she reserves her sharpest barbs for sexist institutions and ideas rather than her southern heroines. All
three of her novels have epigrammatic tendencies, funny lines
that startle and expose sexist assumptions. In an interview, New-

35

man discussed the role of humor in balancing "the cruel and uncomfortable side of life" (Rothermel), and she was irritated when Isabel Paterson wrote a review of *Dead Lovers Are Faithful Lovers* without "once suggest[ing] that it contained an amusing line" (*Letters* 349). Marjorie Smelstor says of this novel what might be said of all three: her humor adds "a dimension . . . which has often been missing in later so-called feminist pieces: the ability to laugh at and with characters." "Newman's theme is eminently serious," Smelstor continues, "but her authorial detachment gives her a vision that is both entertaining and provocative" (16).

Donald Davidson labeled Frances Newman's *The Hard-Boiled Virgin* "a scolding satire, almost vengeful in its exposure of what the author conceived to be the emptiness of southern traditions of gallantry and feminine behavior" ("Trend" 193). Similarly, William Curtis called the first part of the novel "one of the most bitter and vindictive analyses of social life and outlook in a small Southern city which has ever reached print," comparing it to Sinclair Lewis's *Main Street* but noting that Newman was "concerned with an older, a more finished, and a more deadly social code." Newman's satire of the southern code of true womanhood is devastating, but rather than being "vengeful," "bitter," and "vindictive," it is gently mocking and often playfully humorous, and she evokes an understanding sympathy for her characters. Instead of creating the one-dimensional, stereotyped characters typically found in satire (and in Mary Johnston's and Isa Glenn's fiction), Newman developed complex characters who internally rebel against society's dictates for proper southern women while externally striving to conform to them.

Newman particularly focuses on the code of proper behavior for the southern belle or lady through the rites of courtship, which foster competition between young women by making their success in attracting socially desirable males the measure of their worth and acceptability. Following her mother's advice, Katharine does not choose for intimate friends any "girls who are likely to be overlooked by men." Yet she also knows the danger of friends like Isabel Ambler who are more attractive to young men than she. Thus "her conscience did not hurt her when the

36

necessity of protecting her own masculine interests forced her to tell Isabel Ambler that she was prettier when her red hair was straight than when it was waved . . . [or that] although blue was not usually becoming to girls with red hair, forget-me-not blue was so becoming to Isabel Ambler that she must consent to borrow Katharine Faraday's embroidered chiffon tunic" (77–78). When Isabel accepts her opinions, Katharine is not chagrined but rather surprised at her friend's lack of "understanding of human nature" (78); the code that places male approval as the highest goal for a young woman is so pervasive Katharine associates it with human nature. She also realizes beauty to be a female's most important asset in this competition for male attention, and comparisons with her popular older sisters have made her doubt her own attractiveness. Invitations to dances inspire in Katharine a "terror of anticipation she would not have felt if her dentist had set his awful chair in the midst of Peachtree Street and invited her world to stop and see how Katharine Faraday supported his borings" (137). However, she knows she cannot simply refuse to attend because she fears being unpopular, and as a debutante she has officially entered the "uncomfortable years when she would be professionally engaged in looking out for a husband" (128). Therefore she must "go out and try to talk to men . . . whom she must please if she hoped to check off safely partnered dances as convicts may check off days without lashes" (137–38).

Katharine consults her older sister Eleanor as a "social dictionary" (153) of correct behavior for a southern lady, and from her she learns to "hide her more elaborate mental processes" (124) and her emotions. She writes her witty comments in a notebook rather than share them in the company of a male, and when she feels that her "reunion" with a young man is a "miracle," she nevertheless "look[s] as calm as the green laurel-tree which had been Daphne pursued by Apollo one minute before" (119). Even when she feels that she is in love, she remains aware of "the necessity of hiding it until a human being who could not have a baby asked affection from a human being who probably could have a baby" (151). Indicating affection even for a husband is "unbecoming a southern lady" according to her mother (50), and "elegance is the greatest of human virtues" (17). Katharine has learned from her mother that a girl or woman must never talk about her own interests but rather about what interests the particular man she is with. Accordingly, she endures a young suitor's sexist and racist religious pronouncements yet becomes increasingly annoyed by "the impossibility of contributing literary evidence against some of those faiths" (177).

As Katharine's impatience with her suitor's pronouncements and her repression of her own opinions indicate, Newman reserves her sharpest satire in this novel for the southern patriarchy. She exposes the "chivalry" of men like Katharine's suitor Neal Lumpkin and Katharine's own father who insist upon the innocence of their wives, daughters, or fiancées yet object to raising the "age of consent" on the grounds that "perfectly respectable young Georgians—who might even be sons and grandsons of the heroes who wore the grey—would be hanged for nothing more than the violation of fourteen year old virgins" (174). When she overhears her father and Neal Lumpkin discussing this issue, Katharine realizes that satisfactory conversation would be possible if southern women could only "admit that they understood the limited number of subjects men were interested in"; however, a southern lady is supposed to remain in a "state of innocence" (55). To admit knowledge of taboo topics would be to suggest a lack of good breeding. Young belles particularly are supposed to be ignorant of reproduction and sexuality; Katharine "knew that in Georgia no lady was supposed to know she was a virgin until she had ceased to be one" (174–75).

Newman further satirizes the doctrine of male supremacy by suggesting that male privileges are granted because of men's innate inability rather than ability. Even as a young girl, Katharine "knew that any boy is born to a more honourable social situation than any girl," but she "had observed that a boy's honourable situation seemed to be the result of his inability to produce a baby rather than to his ability to produce an idea" (30). Newman repeats this idea of male privilege throughout the book, as when Katharine fears she will not be asked up to West Point again and

Demythologizing the Southern Lady

wonders "why men can ask girls to dance with them and to marry them, and if it is because girls can have babies and men cannot" (93). Here Newman is satirizing the Darwinian biological justification for the subordination of women prevalent in the twenties. In perhaps her most humorously ironic single sentence, Newman undermines the idea of a southern lady's excessive frailty, which reinforces both chivalry and male supremacy. At lunch with her brother George, Katharine is not surprised when he does not offer her so much as one of the cherries from his cocktail, for "she did not suspect either the social or biological soundness of his demonstration that southern gentlemen consider alcoholic beverages unsuited to the fragile organisms which are capable of nothing more energetic than producing twelve babies" (110–11).

Although Newman credited Freud with influencing fiction through his studies in the subconscious realm ("American Short Story" 190), she pokes fun at the Freudian theory of penis envy, with its implicit belief in male superiority, in a scene reminiscent of Stern's metaphoric use of the nose as a phallic symbol in *Tristram Shandy.* Accidentally seeing her brother naked, young Katharine in *The Hard-Boiled Virgin* "felt almost sure that her oldest brother could not be made in God's image, and that he must be suffering from something like the disease Mildred Cobb said was responsible for her Aunt Ellen's increasingly enormous nose" (31). Katharine does "not become reconciled to her own sex," with its culturally prescribed limitations, but fearing that her brother might have the normal appearance of a man, she does discontinue trying "to kiss one of her sharp elbows," an accomplishment she believes would transform her into a male and thus avail her of the privileges that come with gender rather than ability (30–31). She is so far from envying a penis that she would rather suffer the restrictions of a southern female than acquire one.

The role of the southern male in reinforcing the image of the southern lady is also a theme in *Dead Lovers Are Faithful Lovers.* Evelyn's father considers her the "last of the Virginia belles" (29), and although he is generally critical of the pretensions of the southern aristocracy, he has advised his daughter to defer to the

39

male ego by never introducing topics she knows more about than her current companion. As she casts about in her mind for a topic suitable for conversation with the president of Southeastern Railway, Evelyn rejects several as not polite or deferential enough and remembers her father telling her that "frivolous femininity is always a charming refuge" (101). Like Katharine Faraday, she feels compelled to keep her witty observations to herself (or occasionally to write about them to her father) rather than tell them even to her husband, who considers her the frivolous female her father has told her men appreciate. Evelyn has so successfully hidden her potentially threatening mental processes and clever ideas that her husband Charlton Cunningham is unaware she has any. Charlton makes an oblique reference to Evelyn in telling Isabel, the young woman he has fallen in love with, that he wishes southern aristocrats "would bind their women's feet instead of their brains" but that in Richmond (where Evelyn was born and reared) he doubts "binding the women's brains has often been really necessary" (274).

Yet despite his protestation that he wishes southern women were more intellectual, Charlton too is a traditional southern gentleman who expects his women to be pure, innocent southern ladies. Isabel recognizes the irony of Charlton's "saving her from himself for himself"—even though he is seeing her surreptitiously while still married to Evelyn—because her sexual involvement with him would sully her in his eyes and thus make her an inappropriate choice for his affections. Thus "she could not come to him until she could come to him in the legal and immaculate state in which a southern gentleman thinks he should receive his bride" (271). This standard of purity is imposed by the male as seen in Isabel's rueful reflection that "if Charlton Cunningham went on saving her from himself for himself, she would be like the letter which she had once dropped down on that hearth, and which had become ashes without ever becoming fire" (266).

Evelyn Page Cunningham has been more thoroughly indoctrinated in the proper behavior and attributes of the southern lady than Isabel, and she wishes at least to project the image of a "completely virtuous" lady (62). In fact, she aspires to become "one of

those impregnable great ladies who can revive the dying reputation of a pregnable acquaintance merely by ringing the bell at
her door and leaving a small white card on a small silver tray"
(29). In seeking this goal, she realizes her need for chastity, deference, and beauty, and although she may not agree with all of
her society's verdicts, she keeps dissenting opinions to herself.
Evelyn recognizes that in Virginia a lady never allows herself to
be kissed by another man after "her husband's first kiss" (132),
and although she wonders what women do after the excitement
of their love relationship with their husbands dulls, she only decides to renew her own efforts to make herself more alluring to
her husband. Her faith in the power of beauty is so absolute that
she suspects "beautifully disarranged hair and a flattering deference" are as pleasing to God as to "all the men he had created
in his own flexible image" (110). Newman pokes fun at the social
edicts that seem so powerful to Evelyn that she thinks even God
powerless to change them: "She knew that her god could interfere with the laws of nature to stop a sun which was already fixed,
and to raise men and women from the dead, but that he could
not interfere with the social dogmas of Virginia" (132).

Newman further attacks the cultural conditioning of white females and the idealized image of the southern lady by revealing
the racism, class prejudice, and false piety that reinforce the image. In *Dead Lovers Are Faithful Lovers*, Evelyn Cunningham decides
to become a "great lady" without a recognition that southern ladies do so "by admiring their world enough to accept its verdict
on love and on religion, and on the status of women and of negroes" (29–30). Similarly in *The Hard-Boiled Virgin*, Katharine is
forced to listen politely to a suitor's championing of "all the faiths
of his fathers which concerned God and women and negroes"
(177). In both passages, Newman draws a parallel between stereotypes of women and blacks and also implies an ironic relationship between these attitudes and Christian values.

In *The Gold-Fish Bowl*, protagonist Anne Delaney sees no solu-
tion for racial problems but feels responsible as a white southerner for their existence. She compares her guilt to that of the
English over the plight of the Irish: "I suspect that all decent

Englishmen are rather miserable about Ireland," she says to Stephen, "just as all decent Southerners firmly expect to go to hell on account of the negroes. And neither of us can do much to help out a painful situation" (208). Earlier when Stephen admired the British look of her "celebrated house" while adding that he read it was built by her grandfather's slaves, she quipped, "Like the noble character of Mrs. Stowe's Uncle Tom, Clarendon is a monument to the virtues of slavery" (6). Like Anne, Isabel in *Dead Lovers Are Faithful Lovers* is distressed by injustice towards black people, but in this novel Newman avoids the flippant tone of her earlier heroine's protestations. Isabel Ramsay silently opposes the Jim Crow laws. She is especially annoyed when white bus passengers ignore signs asking them to seat themselves from the front to leave sufficient room for black seating and when the bus drivers delight in reminding black people to seat themselves from the rear. But her protest is ineffectual and personal. She decides to stop riding the bus after hearing a young "primrose-coloured" woman declare her intention to leave a town where she "could not sit down beside a man whose body was legally entitled to the adjective white, even though the man had been sleeping beside her two hours before" (228). While pointing out the irony of a code that would permit a white man and a black woman to sleep together but not sit on a bus together, Newman also touches on the arbitrary nature of legal definitions of "white" and "colored" and raises questions about the doctrine of white supremacy and racial purity symbolized by the white southern lady.

Newman was troubled by the status of black people in the South, as seen through her correspondence. When A. B. Bernd requested information for Harlem Renaissance novelist Walter White about the exclusion of blacks from prominent Atlanta churches, Newman sent details and then revealed she had not read White's novel *The Fire in the Flint*, "because I already suffer agonies about the negroes" (*Letters* 171–72). In a letter to Scott Cunningham in 1927, she again expressed concern about black people, but revealed she was not in circles that socialized with them: "I've never been asked to a Van Vechten mixed party. Of course, I don't know any new negroes, but I'm far from disliking negroes—in fact, I suffer tortures over their sorrows, because I don't see what can be done about them" (*Letters* 240).[11] Newman's protests against racism primarily came indirectly through her fiction, but she at least intended to write an article about race relations. In a 1924 letter to A. B. Bernd, who had requested an article from her on "The Revolt in Georgia, Literary Phase," she replied: "So far as I know myself, I should say that my interests are too literary, too much concerned with style and form, to make a very good rebel. But when I think of the article I mean to write concerning the effect of the negro on the southern mind, I rather think I must be one" (*Letters* 134). Newman may or may not have written this article,[12] but she was certainly aware of the strictures in writing for a southern newspaper. In a later letter, she advised Bernd not to give up his revolt but to write of it in "an allusive, insinuating fashion" and mentioned her own use of that technique in "circumventing the Atlanta papers" (144). At a time in Atlanta when the American Fascist Association and Order of Blackshirts was increasing in strength because of the absence of newspaper protests against it and its white supremacist goals (Dabney 261), Newman's attacks on racial hatred through her fiction are impressive although tangential.

A passage from *Dead Lovers Are Faithful Lovers* indicates both the difficulty of getting criticism of the South published in southern newspapers and Newman's outrage at the violence perpetuated against black people. Isabel Ramsay remembers her journalist father's having "discovered early in life that he could not afford to have opinions" because he had two daughters to raise. She especially remembers the morning when he experienced anguish because he knew the papers would not print what he would like to say about a lynching:

> She always remembered her father's sufferings on the day when he had wanted his words to scream out his horror of a state in which hundreds of young gentlemen from America's oldest state university could stand still and hear another human being scream out of the agony of a body which was burning a slow exit

43

from a world that dozens of virgins' sons had lived and died to save. And she always remembered her father's sufferings when he had written only the words he had known his paper would print—when he had written nothing more than one editorial column . . . on the opening of a new hotel . . . and the half column about the official appearance of the spring's straw hats. (219–20)

During the twenties in the South, the torture, mutilation, and burning at the stake of black men were common aspects of lynchings (Dabney 249–50). Newman draws an ironic contrast between the South's attitude towards its Confederate soldiers as Christ-like sons of virgins and their actual position of having fought a war to perpetuate a slave-based society that even generations later condoned the savage racism epitomized in lynching.

In addition to attacking the South's racist attitudes in her fiction, Newman also reveals its aristocratic pretensions. In *The Hard-Boiled Virgin*, little Sarah Rutledge has just moved to Atlanta from Charleston, where family name and class distinctions reign. She has difficulty believing in this new town "where personal charms, including frocks and houses and even brains, were more useful than ancestors who had signed their names to a document called The Declaration of Independence." She can scarcely endure being snubbed by little girls "who would never be allowed to dance, or to eat terrapin, or to drink champagne at a Saint Cecilia Ball," much less marry "a Middleton or a Pringle or a Pinckney" (21). Family names were important, and having an ancestor who had fought as an officer in the Civil War identified one as a member of the upper class, regardless of current economic status. Newman again expresses a skeptical attitude towards the veneration of Confederate soldiers and their offspring in *Dead Lovers Are Faithful Lovers*. When Evelyn's aunt and uncle are upset because she has decided to marry Charlton instead of George, who is "the only living grandson of two Confederate generals," Evelyn's father defends her choice: "She may feel as I do about George. Every time I see his chin rushing away from his profile into his collar, I remember that Confederate armies were led into unusually bloody battles by the men who begot his father and mother. And I am afraid of understanding why the Confederacy is a lost cause" (25–26). Nevertheless, Evelyn's uncle continues to express his disappointment that she will be marrying a young businessman instead of a member of the Richmond aristocracy and will move to Atlanta "where people have no ancestors and no manners of their own" but invite others to dinner for pleasure or business and not "because the position of their guests makes an invitation unavoidable" (26). He is concerned that when his niece leaves Virginia, no one will know "her father belongs to the elder line of Virginia Pages" or "her mother is as nearly related to Evelyn Byrd." Evelyn's aunt commiserates that people will ask her if she is a North Carolina Page "and have no idea they are being rude" (24). Evelyn's uncle and aunt embody the southern psychic link to European aristocracy that rationalized the hierarchical southern social structure, especially during slavery but even afterwards. After they leave, Evelyn's father remarks of his brother's pretentious attitude that with another drink, "I'd have asked him if he would like to have Evelyn formally renounce the possible inheritance of Shadwell for herself and all the heirs of her body—as if she were a Hapsburg archduchess renouncing the possible inheritance of the Austrian crown" (27).

Organized religion reflected the secular social strata, and this social hierarchy did not escape Newman's ironic voice. Katharine Faraday never suspects "that people ask the names of each other's religions for any other purpose than the establishment of their probable social importance," and when she sees the musical director of her Sunday school repairing a furnace, she begins to suspect "that membership in the First Presbyterian Church was not a complete social reference" (48–50). The Church of England is a better social reference, and when Katharine's friend Mildred Cobb joins, she speaks of Good Friday "as if it celebrated the heroism of one of her own eminent ancestors" (91). In Newman's short story "Atlanta Biltmore," Atlantans whose wealth came from prohibition display their common origins by "betraying the evangelical piety of their upbringing by the absence or

Demythologizing the Southern Lady

the elementariness of their dancing" (641). The library's first director in *Dead Lovers* carefully hides her own common Methodist Episcopal origins but betrays them in choosing her successor, Miss Currier, and thus ruins "the Carnegie Library's usefulness as a social reference" (175). Isabel Ramsay realizes that this new library director "would be happy if she could walk beside a man or a woman whom she considered an aristocrat, even if she were walking up the steps of a crimson scaffold," but she instead "could only walk beside another hereditary follower of John Wesley" (216) in a society that makes distinctions between the Virginia Pages and the North Carolina Pages but not between "overseers and sheriffs and hereditary followers of John Wesley" (136).

Although Newman deflated the pretentiousness of the upper class in making caste distinctions based upon religious affiliation, she also satirized the religious intolerance of lower-class fundamentalists. In *The Gold-Fish Bowl*, Newman's satire of religious fundamentalists is lightly humorous. After Anne Delane is approached in the library by a preacher who gives her a religious tract and asks her if she is a Christian, she relates her experience to Stephen and then adds, "I wish I had asked him to pray that I might learn to suffer fools gladly or that someone would leave me a hundred thousand dollars so I shouldn't need to" (45). In *Dead Lovers* Newman portrays religious fanatics such as "the bald old man who would spend his day interpreting the Book of Revelations unfavourably to every person and every object he disliked" and the woman "who had often told her that a book called Science and Health with Key to the Scriptures was placed in libraries as a pail of water would be placed in a desert" (167–68).[13]

Newman's ironic voice is especially evident in her treatment of southern prejudice against Catholics. In *Dead Lovers,* the young librarian Isabel interacts with patrons who consider "Romanism" a "menace" to the country (168). She reflects that "her face and her mind must be almost as different as Abraham Lincoln and the Lincoln Memorial" as she returns greetings from the narrow-mindedly pious library patron who reads Erasmus to support ideas in an anti-Catholic pamphlet she is writing. Later Isabel

46

thinks her own smile must be as artificial "as the smile of the white-haired Christian Scientist who had apparently forgotten her church's prejudices long enough to copy a smile from a photograph of Pope Leo the thirteenth" (173–74). Her most scathing reference to anti-Catholic bias comes when Evelyn, although "an extremely Protestant Episcopalian," does not join those at an opera "applauding themselves" for noting that "the Holy Father . . . was Baron Scarpia's master . . . in whose service his villainies were presumably planned" (99).[14]

Prejudice against Catholics was largely based upon a bias against immigrants and thus was linked to racist attitudes. In a 1926 article entitled "The Klan's Fight for Americanism," the Klan's Imperial Wizard, Hiram Wesley Evans, described the Catholic Church as "actually and actively alien, un-American and usually anti-American" and the Pope as "the most dangerous alien power with a foothold inside our boundaries" (143). Evans characterized immigrants as "low living and fast breeding" and incapable of becoming true Americans regardless of education, oaths, or attitudes (139–44). This xenophobia is ironically treated in *Dead Lovers*. When Mrs. Abbott praises a school for young Anglo-Saxon girls in the Georgia mountains that is "preserving them to save their country" from the influence of immigrants, Evelyn reflects that Mrs. Abbott did not say the country was being saved from the influence of "the mere compatriots of Plato and Leonardo da Vinci and Jesus Christ" (42).

In exposing the sexism, racism, and class distinctions involved in the idealization of white women, Newman was writing within a tradition of satire by white southern women. As early as 1913, Mary Johnston and Ellen Glasgow began questioning established roles for the white southern lady and providing alternative visions for women in their respective novels *Hagar* and *Virginia*. Glasgow continued with her portrayal of the southern lady as an old-fashioned ideal in *Life and Gabriella* (1916) and in *The Romantic Comedians* (1926), published the same year as *The Hard-Boiled Virgin*. Isa Glenn echoed this theme in her 1928 novel *Southern Charm*, published the same year as Newman's *Dead Lovers Are Faithful Lovers*. Johnston and Glenn, unfortunately, subordinate realistic character development to the feminist ideas that they wish to present. Although both tend to be biting in their satire, Glenn's satire especially is more Juvenalian than Horatian; it is often harsh and unsympathetic in its critique of the southern lady and southern institutions. Johnston has idealistic hopes for a near-utopian future, even as she exposes the continuing sexism of the southern culture. Ellen Glasgow's hopes for women are far less than utopian, but her Gabriella, like Johnston's Hagar, escapes from the confining roles of southern females only when she travels north. Glasgow's southern ladies, like Newman's, are more fully realized and more sympathetically treated than Johnston's and Glenn's, but her ironic voice is usually more ponderous than Newman's.

Newman was familiar with the works of these women writers, and although she praised Glasgow for much of her fiction, she found her sometimes too didactic and had serious reservations about the fiction of Johnston and Glenn. In her column "Library Notes" in the *Atlanta Constitution,* she charged Glasgow and Johnston with having "written some of the dullest books that they or anybody else ever wrote" on suffrage and women's rights, "in which the propaganda is so vigorous that the story is lost to view" (2 Aug. 1920). Similarly, in an unpublished letter to Mrs. Harris, Newman confided that "Isa's book [*Southern Charm*] bored me so much that I could have cried with the effort of getting through it." She characterized Glenn's novels as "very thin and unimportant—like long slick magazine stories," noting Glenn knew little about the contemporary South since she had left thirty years earlier (1 Mar. [1928]). Nevertheless, these southern women writers were literary precursors of Newman who provided a tradition to build upon and, perhaps, a determination not to sacrifice artistry in expressing her perceptions of woman's place in the southern patriarchy.

Mary Johnston's 1913 novel *Hagar* presents a sharp criticism of the southern patriarchy and an idealized version of the eman cipated woman. Whereas Newman cleverly and implicitly portrays religion as reinforcing societal attitudes towards women (as in Evelyn Cunningham's belief in God's preference for beautiful and deferential women), Johnston depends upon more explicit statements. For example, Mrs. Ashendyne lectures her daughter-in-law Maria: "The Lord, for his own good purposes,— and it is *sinful* to question his purposes,—regulated society as it is regulated, and placed women where they are placed" (16). Long after her death, Maria is accused of corrupting her daughter Hagar by failing to set an example as a properly submissive woman. When Hagar refuses to obey her grandfather and disavow an early love, Hagar's grandmother again links women's struggle for independence with godlessness, expressing her outrage and scorn at "women deserting their natural sphere, atheists denying hell and . . . young girls talking about independence and their own lives—their own lives! Ha!" Hagar should bow to her grandfather's wishes: "Fitness, propriety, meekness, and modesty, consultation with those to whom she owes duty, and bowing to what they say"—the characteristics of a true woman— demand obedience (118). Ironically, the strong-willed, domineering Mrs. Ashendyne is considered a proper southern lady because she affirms her proper sphere and serves the patriarchy, yet her fragile daughter-in-law Maria is seen as a threat to the entire social structure because of her ineffectual protests against women's roles and restrictions, which she escapes only through death.

Johnston's satiric treatment of southern womanhood is more clumsily handled than Newman's; her style is preachy and her characters are more mouthpieces for particular positions or ideas than fully realized characters. Many of them deliver long, improbable speeches to one another about social issues in addition to the speeches they deliver on public platforms, and her typical southern ladies, as Anne Firor Scott asserts, are simply "foils for Hagar" (*Southern Lady* 224). Instead of treating them with the warmth and sympathy that Newman displays towards her southern ladies, to a large extent Johnston caricatures them. Miss Serena, for example, is an ill-tempered spinster who upholds the doctrines of masculine supremacy and zealously attacks any minor infractions of the southern code of behavior, especially in Hagar or Maria. Her name seems an ironic comment on her irritability and underlying dissatisfaction with her life, which erupt in sharp comments to others despite her pronouncement that being "discontent with your lot in life" is "a heinous sin" (302). Although Johnston, as Jones observes, "clearly links the perpetuation of . . . destructive definitions of women . . . to the perpetuation of the culture of the South" (*Tomorrow* 194), she also blames women for not escaping the destructive roles assigned to them and even for perpetuating the ills of society in their dependency. Her character Rose Darragh, the social reformer whom Hagar admires, attacks dependent women in general, whom she compares to leeches, "with their mouths glued" to their husband's or father's pockets (336–37), causing the wealthy male to exploit working-class men and women "because he's got to 'provide' for . . . perfectly strong and healthy persons in jewelry and orchids . . . to keep filling and filling the pocket because they suck so fast" (337).

Even Hagar, who is much more fully developed than any of the southern ladies or minor reform-movement characters, sometimes acts in ways that are implausible. Her blithe disregard of her family's response to her violations of the proper behavior of a southern lady, for example, seems psychologically unrealistic. Instead of feeling anguished or angry over the conflict between her family's mores and her own ambitions and beliefs, she remains serene. She feels trapped like her mother for only an instant. Then she envisions a "Fourth Dimension" of "inner freedom, ability to work, personal independence, courage and sense of humour and a sanguine mind, breadth and height of vision . . . her work, the story now hovering in her brain, what other and different work might rise above the horizon." Readily she concludes, "there was her land of escape. . . . She crossed the border with ease" (318). Hagar's idealistic, grandiose visions are not treated with humor or irony as Katharine Faraday's illusions are in *The Hard-Boiled Virgin;* instead, they appear to be the visions of Johnston herself. In her article "The Woman's War," Johnston called the "Woman Movement" the "most significant, most vital, most important" movement of the age, which must progress, "for behind it is the life-force, the stream of tendencies, the evolutionary will" (561). Her imagery is that of powerful, moving water, a "cosmic tide," which cannot be resisted. In both her novel and her essay, Johnston discounts the weight of social conditioning and social censure in controlling behavior and in inhibiting change, and thus she caricatures and condemns rather than sympathizes with most of her southern female characters.

Isa Glenn's indictment of the southern lady in *Southern Charm* (1928) is similar to Johnston's in its harsh, bitter satire and unsympathetic portrayal of the southern lady as represented by Mrs. Habersham and her spoiled daughter Alice May. Mrs. Habersham's name is a thinly veiled allusion to her life of pretense and her willingness to sacrifice even her own daughter to retain her good name. The innocence or high-minded morality associated with the traditional southern lady has degenerated into smallminded respectability.

Out of concern for society's approbation, Mrs. Habersham had abandoned her pregnant adolescent daughter Laura in Europe years before, leaving her in the care of strangers with a small inheritance for her support and creating the fiction of her death by fever in Rome to avoid scandal. Mrs. Habersham's entire concept of good breeding consists of maintaining appearances and following all the trivial rules dictated by society as proper and becoming for a lady, rules that she tirelessly repeats to her "respectable" daughter, Alice May, or uses as standards in judging others. "It's unladylike to rush" (15); "it isn't well-bred to show your feelings" (194); "it was not good breeding to emphasize what one said" (156); "southern ladies were brought up to be helpless" (171)—these are the rules for the southern lady perpetuated by Mrs. Habersham. Seidel comments that novels written during the Southern Renaissance "show that the virtues southern tradition has reserved for the belle are actually destructive to her and to others" (*Southern Belle* 31). This observation is particularly pertinent to Alice May, a caricature of the spiteful, vain belle who manipulates men with her pretense of helplessness and frailty. She is certain her husband admires her "because he thinks I'm so helpless he has got to wait on me" (16). When he comes home, she becomes "languid" and "plaintive," playing the part of a semi-invalid while telling him she wishes she were stronger for his sake (36–37). Having learned the importance of being pretty from a southern father who joked that "a plain girl baby should be strangled at birth" (20), she complains each time her husband caresses or embraces her that he is messing up her hair or clothing, and the very shape of her features suggests a "cold chastity" (46).

Glenn's characters are not convincing, nor are they consistent in their behavior and beliefs; rather, they seem mere vehicles for Glenn's ideas. For example, although Mrs. Habersham continuously harps on the minutiae of correct behavior for a lady and deplores even the slightest changes in that traditional behavior, she also inconsistently criticizes that tradition for making women incapable of being friends instead of competitors for male attention. The inconsistency of Mrs. Habersham's ideas is apparent when Alice May and Minnie Lou inch their skirts higher and higher in vying for the attention of each others' husbands as well as their own, causing the outraged Mrs. Habersham to comment bitterly that she tried to bring her daughter up correctly but "the present generation has no conception of what it is to be a lady" (63). However, their competitive behavior for male attention is a direct outgrowth of the vanity and superficiality that Mrs. Habersham has always encouraged in her daughter. The self-reliant "fallen" daughter Laura, who has escaped her mother's influence and the dicta of behavior for the southern lady, is Glenn's clear model for genuine good manners and social behavior. When Mrs. Habersham begins to admire Laura and question her own beliefs about the proper role of women, her switch in perspective is too sudden to be plausible. Although Glenn's characters never breathe life as do Newman's, and although they change their beliefs and behavior without sufficient motivation, Glenn does present a sharply satiric critique of the idealized southern lady.

Ellen Glasgow's novels more realistically portray women trapped by social restrictions or struggling to surmount them. The southern lady and young belle do not escape her ironic treatment, although she, like Newman, develops more sympathy for these characters than do Johnston and Glenn. Yet, like Johnston

Demythologizing the Southern Lady

and Glenn, Glasgow is more straightforward and explicit in her use of satire than Newman. Her characters often articulate specific positions that are handled satirically, and frequently they find themselves in ironic situations. Glasgow's tone can be gentle and sympathetic as in *Virginia*, or it can be sharp and more distanced as in *The Romantic Comedians* and *They Stooped to Folly*.[15]

In *A Certain Measure*, Glasgow explained that she tried to portray the vanishing southern lady "with sympathy, though not entirely without that cutting edge of truth which we call irony." She revealed that in writing *Virginia*, "I had intended to deal ironically with both the southern lady and Victorian tradition, [but] I discovered, as I went on, that my irony grew fainter, while it yielded at last to sympathetic compassion" (78–79). As the novel opens, Virginia is a perfect young belle. Oliver falls in love with her because of her beauty, her passivity, and her "look of angelic goodness" and places her on a pedestal: "To have her always gentle, always passive, never reaching out her hand, never descending to his level, but sitting forever aloof and colourless, waiting eternally, patient, beautiful and unwearied, to crown the victory—this was what the conquering male in him demanded" (158). He also eulogizes her as "perfect in unselfishness as all womanly women are" (160). Ironically, Virginia has just been chafing under the enforced passivity of her role: "Was that a woman's life, after all? Never to be able to go out and fight for what one wanted! Always to sit at home and wait, without moving a foot or lifting a hand toward happiness! Never to dare gallantly!" (152). Yet Virginia becomes the embodiment of Oliver's vision just as she becomes his wife.

Edgar MacDonald calls *Virginia* "the first classic study of the evasive idealism that stifled thought in the South" (267), and this idealism of the genteel tradition was instilled in Virginia by her parents. Just as Newman's Katharine Faraday learns as a child "that southern ladies and gentlemen respect the polite fictions of society" (51), Virginia's parents "both clung fervently to the belief that a pretty sham has a more intimate relation to morality than has an ugly truth." To them, "to 'take a true view' was to believe what was pleasant against what was painful in spite of evi-

53

dence" (35), and they carefully educate their daughter to take this view. Years later when Virginia decides to confront her husband's lover Miss Oldcastle, her idealism, with its "obligation to keep the surface of life sweet," prevails: "It was impossible to say the things she had come to say, because even in the supreme crises of life she could not lay down the manner of a lady" (486–87).

This idealism and clinging to the "manner of a lady" is also seen in Mrs. Carr of Glasgow's *Life and Gabriella* (1916), who focuses her entire life on maintaining her position as a lady, despite her reduced circumstances. A widow, she has raised her two daughters in "genteel poverty which must keep up an appearance at any cost" (37). Glasgow's description of Carr's older daughter Jane is an ironic comment on the traditional image of the southern lady, which is worshipped only in the abstract. Jane "had started with a natural tendency to clinging sweetness," but as she grew older, "the sweetness, instead of growing fainter had become almost cloying, while the clinging had hysterically tightened into a clutch." At thirty, she is "one of the women whom men admire in theory and despise in reality" (5). Glasgow also suggests that the image of the southern lady persists even when reality contradicts this image. Arthur Peyton thinks of his fiancée Gabriella in similar terms of fragility despite his awareness of her "character and determination," for "by the simple act of falling in love with her he had endowed her with every virtue except the ones that she actually possessed." Instead of valuing her for her strength and positive energy, he sees in her his "ideal woman," who is "essentially starlike and remote," "gentle, clinging, so perfectly a 'lady' that she would have perished had she been put into a shop" (37). Just as traditional southern lady characters serve as foils for Hagar, so do they also for Gabriella, who escapes to a certain extent from the prescribed boundaries of behavior by her determination not to be helpless like her sister and mother. Also like Hagar, she must leave the South to escape the confining roles of the southern lady.

The southern lady is seen as an old-fashioned ideal in both *Virginia* and in *Life and Gabriella*, but she appears even more old-fashioned and ineffectual in Glasgow's later novel *The Romantic Comedians* (1926). Amanda Lightfoot was her generation's and Gamaliel Honeywell's "ideal" (100) with her hourglass figure, beautiful face, and sweet disposition. She has been faithful to the memory of her youthful lover Gamaliel, wearing his favorite color and dressing her hair in the style popular when they were engaged, even though he married another woman nearly forty years before the novel opens. Polite and gracious, she maintains a facade of cheerfulness, hiding her feelings even when her old lover remarries a young woman after the death of his wife. Instead of being portrayed as an admirable figure who maintains the traditional values, she is seen as pathetically clinging to illusions of the past. Even in the past, Gamaliel's sister Edmonia insists, the stereotype of the perfect southern lady was less a gracious ideal than a cruel standard used to limit possibilities of behavior for women: "So long as you were different from the wasp-waisted morality of the period," she declares, "it scarcely mattered whether you were a saint or a sinner, for both got the same punishment, though, if anything, the saint got the worst of it." Alluding to her own fall from honor because of a youthful seduction, she continues, "The venom with which they pursued me was nothing compared to the ribald mirth they showered upon poor Johanna Goodwin, who was as sexless as an amoeba but had a mind of her own" (216–17).

Although Johnston championed social equality in general, Glasgow was the only one of these women writers besides Newman to question seriously her culture's racism, which she related to the idealism and selfish materialism of the genteel tradition. Glasgow is more direct than Newman in her criticism of racism, even though her depictions of blacks in *Virginia* are fairly stereotypical. Mrs. Pendleton, like her husband and daughter, never questions any aspect of her society, and she is "incapable of looking an unpleasant fact in the face" (65). Thus she avoided recognizing the cruelty of slavery even while she was in the midst of it: "In the old days, she had known where the slave market stood, without realizing in the least that men and women were sold there. 'Poor things, it does seem dreadful, but I suppose it is better for them to have a change sometimes,' she would doubtless have reasoned had the horror of the custom ever occurred to her" (67). Glasgow also satirizes the assumption that blacks were happy and contented with their lot. Viewing the house of his family's former slave, Gabriel Pendleton thinks, "there never were happier or more contented creatures than the darkeys" (374). Ironically, the "decrepit negress" inside the hut speaks to him of "no end er trouble" (375), and it is her grandson whom the preacher finds a few minutes later about to be tortured and killed by three white drunks for accidentally bumping against a white woman.

Glasgow's satire is even sharper concerning Cyrus Treadwell's attitudes towards black people and slavery. He fathered a son by a black servant girl, who was turned out of the house by his wife when her pregnancy became obvious. He assumes no responsibility for the child or its mother and is outraged when Mandy mentions their son years later. Cyrus decides at that moment to help his errant nephew with whom he has had a violent argument: "Even if the boy's a fool, I'm not one to let those of my own blood come to want," he self-righteously thinks after denying any responsibility to his own mulatto son (173–75). Later when Mandy comes to him to beg for his help to keep their son from being lynched after shooting a white policeman, he replies unsympathetically, "Your race has got to learn that when you break the law, you must pay for it" (366). The southern attitude towards miscegenation, which allowed a white man to feel no sense of responsibility for his own son and only contempt for his former black lover, is also handled ironically in *They Stooped to Folly*. Mr. Littlepage's statement that a woman has a claim on her seducer, especially if a child results, surprises his wife, who reminds him that he had said the opposite recently about his Uncle Mark. "Startled but undefeated," he explains: "That . . . was the case of a mulatto child" (259). Glasgow's fully realized characters and realistic assessment of the social force of sexism and racism make her writing most like Newman's among these three writers, despite the differences in their style.

Most contemporary critics tended to blame women for the perpetuation of the genteel tradition rather than to explore the writing of women who questioned or satirized it. In her article "The Flapper's Wild Oats," Elizabeth Brewer characterized the young woman writer in the twenties as dressing her ideas "in the hoops and bustles of a Victorian day" while only "rumors reach her of a world which has long since dispensed with such plumage" (2–3).[16] In his 1921 article "The Feminine Nuisance in American Literature," Joseph Hergesheimer expressed his "conviction that literature in the United States is being strangled with a petticoat" (718) and accused women of establishing the standard and tone of the mediocre, moralistic American novel since they were the primary readers (718).[17] The novelist Robert Herrick scorned the "feline world" of women's fiction as "not a world of idealisms or social experiments" or "of ideas or theories," but rather a "comfortable and convenient place" with "a lot of demure, softly-spoken and prettily dressed little pussies running about it" (5). The *Double-Dealer,* then a new literary magazine in New Orleans, also blamed women writers for the perpetuation of standards of the genteel tradition. "We are sick to death of the treacly sentimentalities with which our well-intentioned lady fictioneers regale us," it declared in its first issue in 1925 (Bradbury 8). All of these attacks on women's fiction ignored the existence of the many male writers of sentimental fiction such as Thomas Nelson Page as well as women writers like Frances Newman who boldly challenged the genteel literature and satirized rather than sentimentalized the traditional image of the southern lady.[18]

Newman's own satire and humor are clearly feminist. As Judy Little notes in her book *Comedy and the Woman Writer: Woolf, Spark, and Feminism,* satire has traditionally attacked deviations from the norm or accepted standards of behavior (8–11).[19] In contrast, like Virginia Woolf and Muriel Spark, Newman mocked the norm and accepted values. Traditional humor is directed downwards, towards the more vulnerable, and women in this tradition are expected to create and identify with humor that insults women. In feminist humor, however, "the context and the characters interact in such a way as to stir our empathy as much as our amusement. It is the situation which is ridiculed, rather than the characters struggling to negotiate their circumstances" (Merrill 273, 279). Newman's humor destabilizes the southern hierarchy with its sexist and racist ideology instead of targeting the southern belle and southern lady as objects of ridicule and scorn. By focusing on the institutions and customs that enforce irrational behavior, Newman's fiction avoids the stereotyping common in traditional male satire. Her satire is essentially optimistic and empowering because it does not accept injustice and inequality as inevitable but rather as ludicrous and in need of change.

3

Questioning Social Change

THE 1910s AND 1920s are widely regarded as times of sweeping social change in the United States, especially in regards to morality and women's roles.[1] Although materials on southern women in the post–World War I era are limited (Ruoff 6; A. F. Scott, *Southern Lady* 13), a number of writers have discussed social changes in the South during this time. For example, in an article written in 1930, "Women in the New South," George Britt asserted that after World War I, "old ideas were questioned in the South no less than elsewhere" and that "Southern girls and Southern women . . . have gone about as far as elsewhere in casting off restrictions to their conduct" (416–17). He credited the war with "supplanting the belle by the flapper" (416) and concluded that the "emancipated new woman of the South" faced "no obstacles worth considering as to what she may do morally, socially, economically, and politically" (419). Others made less sweeping statements about changes in moral codes and women's roles in the South during the early twentieth century. In her article "The Emancipation of Pure, White, Southern Womanhood," Virginia Foster described her adolescence in Alabama during World War I, when "girls began to take off their corsets and girdles and roll their stockings," and commented that "while this was at first considered to be fast, it soon became the usual thing" (52). Similarly, a 1920 article in the *Atlanta Constitution* described contemporary dress as "daring to excess, unruly, even

59

a little savage in appearance" and reflected the ambivalent feelings towards it common throughout the country: "It is not concerned with any of the old-fashioned virtues, yet, undoubtedly it
has . . . certain qualities . . . which speak for common sense. The
freedom from bones is always something in its favor" ("Latest
Fashions").

Nevertheless, Anne Goodwyn Jones indicates the superficiality
of the changes in dress and moral behavior, asserting that "although some of the most famous flappers came from the South
. . . their sexual emancipation stopped short of challenging the
patriarchal image of the lady" (*Tomorrow* 16).[2] In the early twenties Jane Addams even suggested that the "breaking down of sex
taboos" epitomized by the flapper led not to liberation but to a
de-emphasis on women's rights and contributed to the disinte-
gration of the women's movement as young women focused on
fulfillment through sexuality and marriage (Ryan 219). Similarly,
Lois Banner observes that although young people were rebelling
against the morality of the Victorian culture, they were taking
"new liberties" but retaining "old attitudes," failing to "overcome
woman's greatest difficulty: the sex-role conditioning that was an
integral part of their upbringing" (153, 160). Even Britt, after his
extravagant claim about the emancipation of southern women,
painted an extremely traditional portrait of the young southern
woman: "The Southern girl may like to earn a little money and
have her fling, but the ideal in the back of her head is a nice
house in the home town and a decorative position in society"
(419).

Just as Newman and other southern women novelists satirized
rather than idealized the role of the southern belle and southern
lady, they also questioned the extent of changes in social mores
and women's roles during the early twentieth century and the
liberalizing effect of these changes. Newman, especially, implies
that these changes are superficial rather than substantial, and
her characters are often uncomfortably caught between two
standards of behavior. Newman, Johnston, Glasgow, and Glenn
also reveal the lack of significant social change for women by
specifically exploring ways in which southern expectations con-

cerning marriage, education, and activities outside the home narrow their horizons. Newman goes further than her contemporaries, though, in satirizing the institutions that perpetuate women's constricted lives.

Anne Firor Scott describes *The Hard-Boiled Virgin* "as a kind of minor Don Quixote, a satire designed to provide the coup de grace to an outworn tradition": "The whole book is an ironical treatment of the attempt . . . to impose the southern lady image on a bright girl who, as she grew up, was exposed to one experience after another which her southern lady upbringing had not prepared her to handle" (*Southern Lady* 224). Katharine Faraday has been brought up with the moral standards of one age and has difficulty adjusting to the standards of the new age. In explaining her intentions for the novel, Newman discussed the predicament of her heroine in believing all that she has been taught or at least compulsively continuing to act as if she does: "I discovered that I was going to write a novel about a girl who began by believing everything that her family and her teachers said to her, and who ended by disbelieving most of those things, but by finding that she couldn't keep herself from behaving as if she still believed them—about a girl who was born and bred to be a southern lady, and whose mind never could triumph over the ideas she was presumably born with, and the ideas she was undoubtedly taught" ("Frances Newman Tells" 6).

Even though society may have changed enough so that Katharine Faraday has the freedom to travel without a chaperone, her ingrained inhibitions and sense of propriety serve effectively as interior chaperones. Mrs. Randolph allows the young ladies in her school in Washington, D.C., to travel to the House and Senate alone or with only another student, but Katharine does not exult in this freedom. On the contrary, she feels guilty when she and a friend have tea with two young southern gentlemen to whom they have not been properly introduced. She fears attracting the wrong kind of man who will not be able to take her to St. Cecilia's Ball or even to the Piedmont Driving Club. During a trip to New Orleans to attend St. Cecilia's Ball with Edward Cabot, Katharine is disconcerted by changes in social mores rather than feeling liberated by them because they catch her by surprise and shatter her illusions. Having learned how to behave with a man and what to expect during a proposal from nineteenth-century novels and advice columns to young girls, Katharine is dismayed when Edward Cabot presents her with "an unbetrothed kiss," for she believes it can only mean that he does not respect or care about her, and she leaves abruptly. Her older sister, who is a custodian of the old values, agrees with Katharine's assessment and upbraids her for "the damaging effects" of her "entirely unconcealed affection" (153–54). Ironically, whereas Katharine's culture considers marriage the only appropriate role for a woman, the overemphasis on purity and innocence leaves young Katharine unready to face the slightly more liberal ideas about morality developing in the 1910s. She is shocked and offended by any signs of physical attraction from men she is interested in and mistakes her own sexual arousal for "an emotion she did not doubt was love" (151).

Although Clement Hoyt commented that *The Hard-Boiled Virgin* was "more applicable to the girl of a decade and a half ago than it is to the girl of this modern generation of gin and jazz and fictitious intellectual renaissance," tradition rather than change is also triumphant in *Dead Lovers Are Faithful Lovers,* which takes place largely in the twenties. Isabel Ramsay, a self-supporting librarian in love with a married man, does not ultimately win that man away from his traditional wife. Rather, he continues to make excuses about needing to have his financial affairs in order before divorcing his wife, and he does not even consider consummating their affair until he is free to marry Isabel. When he becomes fatally ill, it is the wife and not Isabel who is by his side. Despite superficial changes in social mores, Newman suggests, a woman's position in the South remains essentially the same and is reinforced not only by society but also by the continuing psychological restraints learned from the past.

Like Katharine Faraday, Ellen Glasgow's title heroine Virginia has difficulty adjusting to the new mores and roles for women, and her husband, like Evelyn Cunningham's, is attracted to a younger, more modern woman. Even before she learns of

Oliver's interest in another woman, Virginia feels that her world has changed and she has been left behind: "She felt . . . that she was left behind like a bit of the sentiment or the law of the last century. . . . Her ideals were the ideals of another period" (443–44). In a chapter significantly entitled "The Changing Order," Virginia reflects on the difference between her life and her daughters'; although Lucy enjoys masculine attention, "it isn't her life," and Jenny talks only about going to college (406–7). The changes widen opportunities for her daughters, but they leave Virginia, who cannot change with the times, feeling utterly old-fashioned and useless.

Glasgow deals with the idea of changes in social mores and the effects on women more fully in *The Romantic Comedians* and *They Stooped to Folly*. Like Virginia, Amanda in *The Romantic Comedians* continues to fulfill the role of the ever-sweet and fragile traditional southern lady, but even the elderly Judge Honeywell sees her as a remnant of a past world, and although she has remained faithful to him for forty years since their broken engagement, when his wife dies, he marries a thoroughly modern young woman. After his new wife Annabel leaves him for a young man, the judge ponders the "revaluation of morals" (201), and Annabel's mother wonders "if ruined women, like fragments of Colonial architecture, 'dated' . . . a period in history? Or were all moral laws engulfed in some recent volcanic eruption?" (187). Society's change in its treatment of "ruined women" was a significant one; Edmonia had virtually been driven out of town because of an early fling, and she was never forgiven by her brother because she "wasn't satisfied simply to stay ruined and to stew in the consciousness of sin" but rather made a new life for herself (159). Back now for a visit, she is "eagerly sought after by the inquisitive youth of the period," who regard "her scarlet letter less as the badge of shame," her brother reflects, "than as some foreign decoration for distinguished service" (60). Yet despite the change in moral standards, Glasgow suggests that little has changed essentially as long as women cling to the same ideas about love and the same roles in love relationships. Mrs. Upchurch thinks that "the modern point of view had scarcely dam-

aged the popular superstition that love and happiness are interchangeable terms. . . . She beheld the world enslaved by this im-
memorial illusion" (187).

They Stooped to Folly (1929) deals even more centrally with the
idea of the changing morality, especially regarding the "ruined"
woman. This novel compares the treatment of three women from
different generations who are involved with a man sexually outside of marriage. Agatha Littlepage was involved with a married
man forty years earlier and was sequestered in a back bedroom
by her family as an object of shame. Two decades after Miss
Agatha's "fall," Mrs. Dalrymple was implicated in a scandal with
another man and was divorced by her husband, while her lover
married a young bride with an unblemished reputation. Mrs.
Dalrymple survived and made a new life for herself, eventually
leaving town and even remarrying, but she still accepted the
code that she had fallen. In contrast, the young Millie Burden,
an unmarried mother abandoned by her lover, sees herself as having done no wrong by getting sexually involved with the man
she loves. However, the present also retains much of the double
standard. Millie Burden is not condemned to a back bedroom,
but she is condemned by her mother for her sexual affair and
considered a wicked woman by Mary Victoria, who considers Millie's lover blameless and persuades him to marry her.

As Newman and Glasgow suggest, changes in moral codes were
not as substantive or liberating for women as popularly believed.
Also, women's social roles remained virtually the same. Barbara
Harris points out that the growing sexual liberalization of the
1920s occurred hand-in-hand with belief in the Darwinian idea
that the roles of women and men were biologically determined
and thus women were best suited to maternity and the house
(132–36). Susan LaFollette, one of the most outspoken feminists
of the twenties in her ideas about women's relationship to marriage, described marriage as the "most pronounced distinction"
between men and women: "For man, it is a means of ordering
his life and perpetuating his name, for woman it is considered a
proper and fitting aim of existence." She compared the prevalent
argument for the extension of women's rights so that they could

be better wives and mothers—an argument that operated within the cult of domesticity and true womanhood—to the writers of the Declaration of Independence "arguing with King George that a little more freedom would make them better husbands and fathers" (553). Despite some shifts in attitudes about marriage, which in the 1920s included proposals for serial monogamy, trial marriages, and divorce and remarriage, trends towards liberalization were soon replaced by pressure for conventional roles and marriage relations (Ryan 231–33). In a 1924 article, Florence Seabury reasoned that as long as women were stereotyped into roles rather than treated as individuals, nothing had essentially changed: "As long as women are pictured chiefly as wife, mother, courtesan . . . nothing new or strange or interesting is likely to happen. The old order is safe" (231).

Frances Newman and her contemporaries portray the "old order" in the South as alarmingly safe and traditional marriages as fraught with dangers for women. In Newman's *Dead Lovers Are Faithful Lovers* and Glenn's *Southern Charm,* marriage is a diminishment for women, within which they feel compelled to play false roles. Johnston and Glasgow, while portraying most marriages as an entrapment for women, also optimistically envision marriages of equality for some of their characters. The inadequacy or misery of traditional marriages for women is a common theme among these women writers, but Newman deals with marriage itself most satirically, comparing it to prostitution in both *The Hard-Boiled Virgin* and *Dead Lovers Are Faithful Lovers.*[3]

In *The Hard-Boiled Virgin,* Newman directly compares marriage to prostitution. When Katharine Faraday declines Neal Lumpkin's proposal, "she would also have liked to tell him that if she should ever be reduced to making her own living, she would rather make it by day than by night," but she is unable to write or even tell her closest friends "anything so unbecoming a southern lady" (193). Although "a satisfactory husband between eight and twelve is necessary to a woman's dignity," Katharine plans to "postpone . . . a husband" by going to Europe (191–92), and eventually she decides that she can live very well without one. The allusion to prostitution is subtler and more diffused in *Dead*

Lovers Are Faithful Lovers. Aware that her beautiful, carefully tended body is her primary means of retaining Charlton's interest in her, Evelyn continuously buys new negligees and considers which to be the most alluring. She even attempts to match the decor whenever they travel and prays to her god to remember that "even in early maple beds, men drop helplessly to the bottom of their emotions as soon as they lie down in a horizontal position" (136). Although her mother had recommended "nainsook and linen lawn as more enduring and less revealing fabrics than crepe de chine" (32), Evelyn chooses crepes and fragile laces for her negligees. Isabel Paterson criticized Newman for her "extreme and pathetic preoccupation with details of the feminine wardrobe as a means of evoking the atmosphere of intimacy," arguing that Newman "succumbs to the sentimental nonsense of women about women" (6). However, Evelyn's fixation on dress and her appearance goes beyond female vanity. Newman implies that Evelyn's livelihood—her marriage—depends on her sexual attractiveness and thus is similar to prostitution. Evelyn's entire life centers on retaining her husband's love, and other women threaten Evelyn's hold on Charlton. She speculates that married life would be "less difficult" if all women were safely shut up in monogamous harems "guarded by fat eunuchs with curved swords" instead of harems "guarded only by elderly ladies with invitations to dinner," especially when she thinks of "her own red-haired cousin" with whom her husband of one month has been flirting (77–78). When married less than a month and still a bride "according to the [social] law which allows a bride her dignity for one month" (75), she "began to wonder what her mother had been thinking about . . . when she had commended marriage as a state for women" (31).

A woman's powerless and diminished position within marriage is perhaps best expressed when Evelyn receives a calling card from Mrs. Perryman that substitutes her husband's first name for her own: "When she read Mrs. Andrew Harvey Perryman's name, she knew that her second caller's name added only a small letter s to the names birth and baptism had given the Southeastern Railway's most important vice-president" (34).

Newman was exasperated by the critic Isabel Paterson's obtuse-
ness in seeing this passage only as having "elaborated . . . unnecessarily" the statement that "in brief, Mrs. Perryman was the wife
of the vice-president of the Southeastern Railway" (Paterson 3).
In a letter to Hansell Baugh from Paris, Newman suggested that
he write to Paterson using a pseudonym to tell her that "she
didn't see the point about the small letter s—that an important
man's wife had no existence of her own, usually, and that Mrs.
Perryman had less than most of them" (349). Fortunately other
readers were not as obtuse as this critic. In a letter to the editor
of the *New York Herald Tribune Books*, one woman responded to
Paterson's review much as Newman had: "Mrs. Paterson apparently did not realize all the overtones supplied by 'added only a
small letter "s" to the names of the Southeastern Railway's most
important vice-president.' That was a very obvious commentary
on the unimportance of women whose whole distinction comes
from 'making unimportant marriages that have become important marriages,' and in general on the status of married women"
(Mitchell).

   Like Newman, Glenn suggests a parallel between marriage
and prostitution. Alice May keeps remembering her unmarried
sister's pride in not being a "kept woman" but a "free woman"
because she supports herself (99, 180), and Alice May grows im-
patient with her own dependent role as a wife. Yet most of
Glenn's satire is directed towards the selfish child/wife who has
learned from her mother that men will not "stick to women unless those women are full of wiles" (100). Glenn depicts the narcissism engendered by the attention placed on a southern girl's
physical beauty and her ability to attract males and the childlike dependency and helplessness encouraged as a means to elicit
male chivalry and protection. Seidel discusses the "vain narcis-
sist," whose self-esteem is based upon the attention of others, as
logically developing into the self-abnegating matron who devotes
herself to others out of her own lack of a sense of worth and need
for approval (*Southern Belle* 36). However, in the instance of Alice
May, the belle has not transformed into the sacrificial wife and
mother but instead manipulates others and imposes her own will

through a combination of flirtatiousness and a pretense of help-less frailty, keeping her husband "in a state of willing subjection" (13). Her mother has encouraged this childlike dependency and flirtatiousness; she has trained her daughter to be "the delightful parasite" (72). Glenn's satire is obvious here, but it is also out of control, since it is Mrs. Habersham who thinks of her daughter as a "parasite" and yet is pleased with her own efforts in having made her one.

Mary Johnston is the most idealistic of these writers about the possibilities of married life for women, yet even she sees tradi-tional marriage as potentially disastrous for women. Hagar de-cides to marry the gentle bridge builder and women's rights advocate John Fay only after a storm off the coast of Brittany, during which they fear for their lives and Hagar recognizes the depth of her love. It may be psychologically realistic for Hagar to need a crisis to make her consider relinquishing her inde-pendence, but the fierce storm is a rather melodramatic device. In their talk after the storm, Hagar makes it clear that she intends to continue writing and working for the women's movement, and John Fay affirms that he intends to help her, but she also desires a child, and the book ends before she has to confront the con-flicts of multiple roles and even without a sense that there will be any conflicts for her to reconcile. Jones's judgment of the novel as an artistic failure because of the "failure of realism to hold its ground against the force of authorial hope" (*Tomorrow* 222) is sound. Just as Johnston unrealistically portrays Hagar as immune to her family's and society's disapproval of her advocacy of women's rights and the women's movement, she also paints an idealistic, even idyllic, picture of the union of the "new woman" with the "new man." In contrast Johnston offers the story of the young marriage of Hagar's friend Rachel, whose husband is un-faithful to her even on their honeymoon and whose second child is born blind from syphilis. Rachel's husband squanders his in-herited fortune, leaving his family penniless for weeks at a time, yet her parents insist that she should stay with her husband. Ra-chel is determined that her daughter will grow up able to support herself and without the romantic lie of "happily ever after" that ruined her own life (216).

Like Rachel, Glasgow's Gabriella marries a handsome young man who soon proves to be dissolute and philandering, but like Hagar she ends up with a marriage portrayed as potentially fulfilling. As in many of Glasgow's novels, in *Life and Gabriella* love can be a great deceiver. In loving George, "so complete was the subjugation of Gabriella that she exacted nothing, not even a return of her love" (96). Like the traditional self-sacrificing true woman endorsed by southern ideology, she "passionately" agrees with him "that the aim and end of their marriage was to make George perfectly happy" (96–97). Soon after their marriage Gabriella learns—as Rachel had of her husband—that George's parents hoped marriage to a nice girl from a good family would cause their errant son to reform, but instead he rarely goes to work, stays out late, treats Gabriella with "casual indifference" and "explosive violence," and after only four months of marriage begins seeing other women (170–79). Gabriella determines not to be a victim and accept endless abuse as her sister had in the name of the "sacred duty of marriage" (57). Nevertheless, she tries to make the best of her situation, especially since one child is already on the way. When George finally leaves her for another woman, she sheds no tears but is determined to support herself and her children. After a decade of putting all her energy into her children and her work, she rejects a proposal from her childhood sweetheart Arthur Peyton, realizing that to marry this perfect southern gentleman whom she has idealized throughout the years would make her "an old, patient, resigned woman" (520). Her decision to accept an energetic Irishman's earlier proposal is portrayed as a victory: "The will to live, to strive, and to conquer—this had risen superior to the empty rules of the past" (527). Choosing O'Hara instead of Peyton constitutes her relinquishing the idealism of southern gentility and its self-sacrificial roles for married women. Seidel's assertion that "for a Glasgow heroine, the only way to avoid suffering . . . is to reject sexuality altogether" (83), although true of many of Glasgow's novels, is not true in this instance. Gabriella has clearly been physically attracted to O'Hara, yet Gabriella's lack of idealization of O'Hara and their frank conversations and genuine respect for one another, as well as her own strength and maturity, indicate that this time she will not be a subservient victim but an equal partner. Glasgow is not so optimistic about marriages for her other southern women in novels of this period. Virginia devotes herself to her husband and children, following the self-sacrificial pattern of a true woman she learned from her mother, but finds herself at age forty—the age when Gabriella was beginning a new life with O'Hara—having "outlived her usefulness" (443). Her children are grown and no longer need her, and her husband announces his decision to divorce her to marry an actress. Virginia feels that "her life was over" and wishes she could die since "her universe lay in ruins" (501). For the first time since her marriage, she thinks of herself: "She, who had effaced herself for a lifetime, found suddenly that she could not see beyond the immediate presence of her own suffering" (501).

In *They Stooped to Folly* (1929), Glasgow is more satiric than sympathetic in her treatment of this theme of a wife's self-sacrificial, dutiful behavior driving a husband away instead of eliciting a grateful loyalty. Mrs. Burden, appropriately named for her pious attitude towards life as a burdensome vale of tears, was from her own perspective "respected" by her husband but "deserted for a loose woman" (217). Mrs. Burden never questions her role in her marriage but sees it as divinely ordained; she is proud of having never flinched in her duty, although one suspects from Glasgow's tone that a little less duty and a little more warmth and love might have kept her husband at her side. Their daughter Milly later reveals that her father sent them money as long as he lived, but "he couldn't live with Mother's duty. Nobody could" (292).

Mary Victoria is also obsessed with the idea of a woman's duty in marriage, but she is less self-sacrificial than self-deceiving in her sense of duty. She justifies her marriage to Milly's former lover Martin as motivated by her desire to "save" him not only from his suicidal tendencies but especially from a "bad woman,"

70

Milly, whom he abandoned when she was pregnant. Mary Victoria's own father pities Martin for becoming the object of her reforming energy, reflecting that "intemperate virtue is almost as disastrous in marriage as temperate vice" (268). Like Glenn's *Southern Charm,* Glasgow's later novels suggest not only that women are miserable within traditional marriages but also that they sometimes bring this misery upon themselves and others by embracing the destructive aspects of true womanhood.

Because young white women in the South were expected to devote their energies to marrying well rather than seeking careers, their education was primarily aimed towards making them charming and decorative members of society. In writing of the "Old South," Edwin Mims discussed the inadequacy of women's education, a "finishing school" education that southern women novelists indicate was still prevalent in the early twentieth century: "As domestic and social accomplishments were considered of first importance, any education aimed at any other object was considered unnecessary and undesirable. Education was left to governesses or to poorly equipped colleges that taught the conventional subjects of music, china-painting, elocution, and *belles-lettres*" (240). In 1910, only one out of twenty-eight of the nation's female college students was from the South Atlantic states (Hall 170), and even in the early 1920s, Mims found "less than a half dozen" women's colleges in the South that had standards equal to those of the best men's colleges, and they were woefully inadequate in their equipment and inferior in their financial resources (234).[4] Virginia had private colleges for women, but the state itself was the last one, in 1918, to provide collegiate education for women (Dabney 377). Although some southern women went to the north and west for adequate college educations, many could not afford to do so, and efforts to open men's colleges to women or to establish sister colleges that would share resources met with strong resistance (Mims 233–35). For example, Beverly Munford's efforts to establish a coordinate college for women at the University of Virginia were met with outraged protestations in the student newspaper that the presence of women— even though they would have a separate campus and separate classes, sharing only classroom facilities and lecturers—" 'would destroy all of the traditions and high ideals for which the University of Virginia has always stood.' " Students evoked the image of the southern lady in claiming that simply having women on campus would have " 'a demoralizing influence' " since only " 'female riff-raff' " would have " 'such a lack of modesty as to put herself on an equal footing with men, free from all restriction, unsexed into a depreciation of womanhood by the allurement of women's rights' " (Mims 233–34). Although the pervasiveness of this attitude may be impossible to measure, the coordinate college did not receive the needed support from the state legislature.

Frances Newman, as well as Mary Johnston, Ellen Glasgow, and Isa Glenn, realistically describes education for upper-class southern girls and women in the early twentieth century as more a means of perpetuating the social dogmas and the *status quo* than of providing any significant opportunities. These writers satirized the "finishing school" education available to southern girls as preparing them for nothing more than attracting a man and later bringing grace and beauty into the home. Many of the girls in their novels are literally schooled in how to become ladies, and when their schools are coeducational, they meet institutionalized sexism.

Julian Symons observes that *The Hard-Boiled Virgin* "might have been sub-titled 'The Education of a Southern Lady' " ("About Frances Newman" 41); although Katharine Faraday is sent at first to a coeducational public school instead of a private girls school, she nevertheless is schooled in the proper position and roles for females. As a young schoolgirl, Katharine quickly discovers that females are relegated to an inferior, subordinate position. When Katharine's name is at the top of the honor roll, she has the privilege of choosing a desk for the next month, but she cannot choose a desk in the front row, for "little girls were denied the satisfaction of sitting in the first seat of the first row of desks, even when their names were written high above the name of any little boy" (43). The democratic principles of the public Calhoun

Street School that her mother so feared did not extend, obviously, to the females in the classes.

When Katharine is fifteen, she is sent to the private Misses Washington's School so that she will be provided with a sufficient number of intimate friends from the upper class to invite her to the dinners and dances that will enable her to meet eligible young men with the proper backgrounds. The Misses Washington's School is a more "lenient" school where "the pursuit of knowledge" is "abandoned" in favor of training young women to be proper southern ladies, of "reducing" them "to a mental state which was likely to make them satisfactory partners for the members of the Piedmont Driving Club" (58–59). Thirty years later Katharine reflects that she was lucky to have been sent to Miss Washington, who "had felt her duty ended when she left the brains of her young ladies in a state of paralysis," instead of across the street to the Misses Rutherford's School, where "her brain would have been extracted in the process which the Misses Rutherford felt their duty to southern womanhood required" (58).

Realizing her youngest daughter lacks the beauty that is central to the success of a southern belle, Mrs. Faraday sends Katharine to Mrs. Randolph's School in Washington, D.C., to complete her education, hoping her duckling will be transformed into a swan by observing the wives of diplomats and learning more about charm and taste in clothing. Katharine Faraday, like the heroines in the novels of Johnston, Glasgow, and Glenn, is educated primarily in how to attract a husband and become a properly submissive wife. Intellectual pursuits are abandoned in favor of learning obedience and a thoughtless adherence to tradition, together with a smattering of literary knowledge, artistic skills, and the social graces with which to enrich the home.

Receiving an education similar to Katharine's, Johnston's Hagar attends Eglantine, Mrs. LeGrand's School for Young Ladies. It was founded after the Civil War when Mrs. LeGrand sought an occupation both "ladylike and possible" for the impoverished orphan of a southern statesman and widow of "a gallant officer" of the Confederacy (27–28). Mrs. LeGrand receives praise not for expanding the minds of her students but for her "guardianship of the young female mind . . . the safe and elegant paths into which she guided it, and . . . her gift generally for preserving dew and bloom and ignorance of evil in her interesting charges" (29). As her name suggests, Mrs. LeGrand is pretentious and concerned with appearances. Eglantine itself is a "sweet place" as its students, parents, and visitors attest, but Johnston satirizes this sweetness by having the French teacher call it "saccharine" and by undercutting the universal praise: "it was praised of all— almost all!" (57). The literature teacher, for one, scorns his position at the school, feeling that he "at the very least should hold a chair in some actual college for women"—Eglantine "was nothing but a Young Ladies' Seminary" (80). Later, Hagar wishes she had had the opportunity to go to an actual college instead of this traditional finishing school.

In *Virginia,* Glasgow is even more satiric than Johnston about southern schools for girls, which stress indoctrination rather than enlightenment. Like Mrs. LeGrand, Miss Priscilla, impoverished and without male support after the Civil War, "had turned naturally to teaching as the only nice and respectable occupation which required neither preparation of mind nor considerable outlay of money" (11). Her school is respected not for academic excellence but for its teaching conformity; it was "earnestly believed that no girl, after leaving there with a diploma for good conduct, could possibly go wrong or become eccentric in her later years." Miss Priscilla's educational philosophy is simple: "The less a girl knew about life, the better prepared she would be to contend with it." Her "ignorance of anything that could possibly be useful to her was supposed . . . to add to her value as a woman and to make her a more desirable companion to a man" (22). Glasgow emphasizes that this educational philosophy is not peculiar to Miss Priscilla but that the object of "every well-born and well-bred" southern woman's training "was to paralyze her reasoning faculties so completely that all danger of mental 'unsettling' or even movement was eliminated from her future" and she would agree totally with "the inherited mould of fixed beliefs" (22). Even Virginia cannot understand why her best friend Susan wants to go on to college, and when Susan asks her father for a loan to make this dream possible, he dismisses her without even taking her desire seriously. A generation later, Virginia's daughter Jenny does go to college, but whereas Virginia has claimed never to have bought a match without thinking about her son's future educational expenses, she still cannot understand "that it could possibly do a woman any good to go to college" and considers sending her daughter "a waste" (407). This sentiment is echoed by Gabriella's uncle in *Life and Gabriella*, who repeats his own father's attitude: "He didn't believe in all this new-fangled nonsense about the higher education of women— none of his daughters could do more than read and write and spell after a fashion, and yet look what wives and mothers they made!" (22).

Miss Habersham in Isa Glenn's *Southern Charm* similarly believes a college education to be the "ruination of feminine strength" (81); she has sent her daughters to Miss Cassandra's finishing school, where they have been indoctrinated in the proper behavior and ideas for southern ladies. Its full name— The Cassandra Toombs Seminary for Young Ladies—indicates its ineffectual ideas and deadly influence on young women. The school's curriculum is "complete," covering everything from "how to walk into a room" to "how to seem surprised at a proposal of marriage" and is noted for equipping young ladies for "the demands of polite society" (64–65). Of all the writers discussed, Glenn paints the darkest picture of the pernicious effect of the innocence perpetuated by the southern finishing school and the general upbringing of the southern belle, but she does it without the humor or sophisticated style of Newman.

Despite their limited and impractical educations and their cultural indoctrination, many southern women in the early twentieth century left the home to become involved in political activism or to work for wages; yet their opportunities were usually limited and in traditional women's spheres, and their activism was often described in domestic terms consistent with the image of the southern lady. Although lagging behind their northern sisters, southern women were involved in social reform and in securing the vote, even though they carefully maintained the public demeanor of ladies. George Britt wondered in 1930 whether southern women were even aware of social problems surrounding them (411), but Anne Firor Scott reveals that social activism among southern women during the late nineteenth and early twentieth century was much more prevalent than was apparent. Working through church missionary societies, the Woman's Christian Temperance Union, and later women's clubs, southern women developed leadership qualities as they pushed for various social reforms, including temperance, child labor laws, compulsory education, improved working conditions for women, and clean water and sewage systems. In addition, they organized or expanded schools, libraries, and settlement houses (A. F. Scott, "New Woman" 476–78, *Southern Lady* 177–78).[5] In 1926 Edwin Mims wrote admiringly of the accomplishments of women's clubs in the South, but he defended them as continued participants in the cult of true womanhood: "They have done for the state and for communities what others have done in the home. They do not lose their womanhood, nor their sense of motherhood" (237). This portrayal is reinforced by the advice given by a Mississippi leader to her group as they prepared to lobby the legislature: "An unpleasant aggressiveness will doubtless be expected from us. Let us endeavor to disappoint such expectations" (A. F. Scott, "New Woman" 479). Instead of defying the image of the southern lady, socially and politically active southern women were courageously expanding the definition of her appropriate sphere.

Southern white women were slower than their northern and western counterparts in organizing for suffrage, and southern white men were more vehement in their opposition, fearing to lose more status and comfort than they had already lost through the emancipation of slaves (A. F. Scott, *Southern Lady* 169–70). Many southern men argued that female suffrage would endanger white supremacy by changing election laws that effectively kept black men from the polls, and some feared it would be more difficult to keep black women from voting since white men might not be willing to use the degree of violence against black women that they routinely used against black men (Wheeler 17–18, 26). Ruoff quotes a South Carolina lawyer and historian, Conway Whittie Sam, as one who argued against suffrage on the basis of the eroding authority of white men in his book *Shall Women Vote? A Book for Men:* "Authority has declined far enough in this country. . . . About all that is left is domestic authority" (Sam). Defeated in war and aware of their poverty in comparison with northerners, white southern males clung to their belief in white male supremacy and to romantic illusions of the past. As could be expected, their arguments against suffrage, like those of their northern brothers, involved biblical injunctions about women's appropriate place as well as allusions to attributes of the true woman, which were incompatible with voting (A. F. Scott, *Southern Lady* 169). With his sense of "masculine identity eroded," the southern gentleman held "even more firmly to the dual image of woman as the lodestar of perfect southern virtue . . . and as the fragile and submissive lady who needed his help and his strength, and could not withstand the polls" (Jones, *Tomorrow* 19). Jones notes the irony of the southern patriarch's placing white women on a pedestal as exemplars of morality and yet considering them "too morally weak to vote" (17). However, a woman's moral strength was precisely what many of the industrialists and cotton men who lent "behind the scenes assistance" to the antisuffragist movement feared, according to Marjorie Spruill Wheeler. "Many antis were more afraid that enfranchised women would clean up politics, support prohibition, and crack down on the exploitation of women and child laborers, than that politics would despoil women" (27, 36).

Despite the exploitation of southern prejudices and fears by the antisuffragists, southern white women did organize for suffrage as well as for moral reforms, although, unfortunately, they sometimes used the argument of offsetting the votes of illiterate blacks and immigrants (Ruoff 175–78). Wheeler dates the revitalization of the woman's suffrage movement in the South at around 1910, and notes that many southern women joined the large group of suffragists marching in a parade on the day of Woodrow Wilson's inauguration in March 1913 (23). In Alabama, only two suffrage groups existed in 1910, but by 1917, the number had grown to eighty-one, and in North Carolina there was a tenfold increase in the single year of 1917. By 1916 even the Daughters of the American Revolution and the United Daughters of the Confederates endorsed suffrage (A. F. Scott, *Southern Lady* 180). Nevertheless, of the southern states, only Arkansas, Kentucky, Tennessee, and Texas voted for women's suffrage (184), and after suffrage was won, widespread opposition to women voting and being involved in political life continued (208–9), as these activities were still largely seen as inappropriate for "true women."

It was perhaps to disarm opponents to women's voting that Corra Harris protested the unnaturalness of women becoming involved in politics while paradoxically urging women to exercise their vote to enact social change. At first, Harris's 1923 article seems totally against women's voting as an unladylike pursuit: "We can amend the constitution, but it is my belief that we cannot change the nature of women by doing so. They belong to love, goodness, faith in all things and happiness. . . . They will never endure the revolting revelations of political life nor the fierce competitions of public life. They are only trying on a new-fashioned garment to see if it becomes them. It will not" (21). However, she continued: "My anxious hope is that we may stay in public service at least long enough to give the national household a cleaning up and establish a good many domestic reforms" (21). Harris concluded that women "must come back home presently and take up the ancient duties and pleasures of that place with some of this efficiency we have learned in public life" (21), but even her description of women's political activity is in domestic terms. Her seeming ambivalence about proper roles for the southern woman can be explained by Anne Firor Scott's observation that those women who were involved in significant social change found that they had to maintain "an outward aspect of the southern lady . . . as the necessary precondition for securing

a hearing"; even those who "impatiently called for an end to pedestals . . . found it effective to operate within the ladylike tradition" (*Southern Lady* 210).

After they had the vote, southern women continued to work
for federal and state child labor legislation (Britt 421) and for
minimum wages and maximum hours for women workers, and
they were instrumental in securing the Sheppard-Towner Act for
maternal and infant health (A. F. Scott, *Southern Lady* 188–91).
Yet, Anne Firor Scott finds from her extensive reading of primary
texts including letters and diaries that "in public, women continued to defer to men," even though "in their private correspondence they described their own efforts as more practical than
those of men" (191). Candidates for public office appealed to
women voters in language consistent with women's traditional
role as moral guardians. An article to "Women Voters of New
Orleans" in a January 1925 issue of *New Orleans Life* began by
declaring, "Woman is God's greatest work!" and assured readers:
"It is a part of the Divine plan of the Universe that she take her
place in the affairs of the world." It was women's "responsibility
to themselves and their children," the article continued, "to exercise extreme vigilance in the council chambers of the city to
see that they and theirs are protected in the health and safety of
their homes by officials possessing a high degree of civic consciousness!" The article concluded that a particular candidate for
mayor "stands for the welfare of women and the happiness of the
home" (Haardt 62). Earlier, the image of the southern lady had
absorbed the impact of the southern woman's active role during
the Civil War in running plantations and businesses (A. F. Scott,
Southern Woman 96–102). Although many white southern women
had felt incompetent and overwhelmed by their new responsibilities during the war and eager to relinquish them afterwards as
revealed in their letters and diaries (Faust 53–113), the image of
the southern lady after the Civil War included "the oxymoronic
ideal of the woman made of steel yet masked in fragility" who
was working for the welfare of her own family (Jones, *Tomorrow*
13). Similarly, in the twenties women's voting and social activism

Questioning Social Change

were incorporated into the image of the southern lady without substantially changing the image itself, and the southern patriarchy was thus not threatened.

Southern women were also struggling to support themselves at the beginning of the twentieth century. Most single upper-class working women were teachers, but some became writers and newspaper editors (A. F. Scott, *Southern Lady* 118–19). A few even became school principals and superintendents (Mims 232), although in the twenties fewer than 2 percent of the nation's cities had a woman superintendent (Chafe 60). Also, whereas a large percentage of teachers in the South were women (65 percent in 1900 and 82 percent by 1920), teaching jobs did not employ that many women—fewer than 61,000 in 1900 and 145,000 in 1920 (Ruoff 146)—and throughout the nation women teachers were concentrated in the lower grades with the lowest pay and the least status (Chafe 60). George Britt provides examples of a few southern women running their own insurance businesses or stores and documents strong membership in the National Federation of Business and Professional Women's Clubs in the South during the late twenties (417–18). However, Lois Banner indicates that with the exception of a few entrepreneurs who started successful businesses, women throughout the United States found few opportunities in business and advertising except as low-paid clerical workers (161–63), and during the first two decades of the century Mary P. Ryan finds evidence of few professional women, even graduates of schools like Bryn Mawr, "outside the limited domain of social housekeeping" (Ryan 232–33). Most employed southern women worked as domestics or in mill towns or on tenant farms, and most were black or foreign born, not upper-class white women (Chafe 57; Britt 413–14).[6] Only 4 percent of professionals in the South in 1900 were women versus 10 percent in the remainder of the United States (Ruoff 142), and whereas 16.4 percent of employed women nationally had white-collar jobs in 1910, only 7.4 percent of southern women had such jobs (Hall 169). Married women were not only discouraged from working, but they were considered to be working for "pin money" and often had no legal rights to their wages. In arguing for

80

a married women's property rights law in Texas, Jessie Daniel Ames met the resistance of a committee member who claimed that southern chivalry made such a right unnecessary and that the current law kept women safe and protected by their husbands (Hall 51–52).[7]

Like their counterparts in reality, heroines of white southern women's novels sometimes go against societal conditioning and expectations to work outside the home, but only Johnston's idealistic novel *Hagar* envisions a southern woman engaged in social activism, and she must leave the South to do so. Anne Delane of *The Gold-Fish Bowl* and Isabel Ramsay of *Dead Lovers Are Faithful Lovers* are librarians, and Gabriella, after a short stint as a shop girl in a department store, is in the dressmaking business like Laura of Glenn's *Southern Charm*. In becoming writers, Newman's Katharine Faraday and Johnston's Hagar join a profession an upper-class southern woman could undertake without economic necessity and still be considered a lady (Jones 41), and yet both, like Glasgow's Gabriella, leave the South to become successful. Despite their choices of occupations considered respectable and often even as extensions of women's traditional roles, most of these heroines must confront family and social disapproval for working at all, even when impelled by economic necessity, and of these novelists, only Johnston clearly envisions a woman working after she is married.

Newman's characters need not fight societal and familial disapproval in order to work as do the characters in earlier southern women's novels, but they are limited to conventional women's professions. Katharine Faraday in *The Hard-Boiled Virgin* becomes a dramatist, but she begins writing only after she relinquishes her search for a suitable husband and after she has left the South for New York, where she feels free to express her unladylike thoughts. Like Newman herself, Anne in *The Gold-Fish Bowl* and Isabel in *Dead Lovers Are Faithful Lovers* are librarians. Anne Delane begins work because of a reversal in fortune and her desire not to lose the family estate that she has inherited, but she also sees working as somewhat of a lark, an opportunity to play the role of the heroine in saving the estate or of a Cinderella waiting to be rescued by the right prince. The novel is written in the first person in a playful tone of mock seriousness, which is the tone Anne assumes in relaying her relatives' response to her working, as well as her own expectations: "The next day I was planning to disgrace the Delanes even more acutely than by having red hair. I was going to become a working-girl on Monday morning at nine o'clock and I saw no reason to suppose that I should ever again have either time or strength or spirit to wash my boisterous hair" (1). Her black "mammy" protests Anne's working as beneath her, especially since she will be waiting on "all those po' white ladies and gentlemen" who cannot afford their own books (18), but the Delane family itself seems quite reconciled to Anne's working although willing to support her. Her cousin Thomas, while offering her a place to live with his family, accepts her decision, calling work in a library "the nicest thing a woman can do"; still, he hopes to solve vague problems with her inheritance so that she need not work at all (23).

Anne herself thinks of working only temporarily and sees work as an opportunity to have interesting experiences: "After all, sensations are the thing, and if you can be paid real money for getting them, it's much better to put in the interregnum between incomes that way—leisure is so expensive to keep up" (20). During her first day, Anne continues to think playfully about her job; she is joining the other "priestesses" of the "temple of knowledge" (29), and her first task of helping high school boys find articles for a debate makes her feel "just like the beautiful third daughter of the fairy-tales when the witch gives her a few brief hours to separate all the beans from the ashes." Having no fairy godmother arrive to rescue her, she begins her task, "thereby showing more spirit than the princesses, who always trust to tears and who always get away with it" (39). Working is a game to Anne not only because she has sufficiently wealthy relatives to support her. She is also making enough money from leasing her ancestral home to live comfortably in a family cottage and thus can quit if it ceases to amuse her. When her friend Pelops tells Anne she is working in the library because she "wanted to do something to uplift humanity" after her husband died, Anne replies, "I came for the filthy lucre, myself, but I do find it very amusing" (58). Elsewhere Anne explains her choice of becoming a librarian as motivated by her love of books: "If you are born with a taste for reading novels, the most economical thing is to be a library assistant, for the same reason that it is well to be an assistant in a candy-shop if you're born with a sweet tooth" (84). As she dresses after work to serve tea at her aunt's party, Anne realizes that having both a work life and a social life is not so unusual—"After all, it's only what every mere man does" (87). However, there is no question of her working after marriage; her fiancé Stephen thinks she has "an extravagant sense of duty" even to go to work the morning after their engagement, and she reassures him, "but of course I'll give notice" (213).

Dead Lovers Are Faithful Lovers provides a more cynical look at working in a library. Isabel Ramsay is oppressed by the "bleak feminine atmosphere of the Carnegie Library" (187) directed by Miss Currier, who rules with "cautious malice" and "cautious envy" (180) as autocratically as a czar or pope or even Jehovah (173). Looking at two nervous new librarians, Isabel wonders if they realize they will be expected "to have something more than the wisdom of Pallas Athena and a good deal more than Pallas Athena's knowledge, and something more than the endurance of Hercules, and something more than the amiability of the founder of their own religion" for which they "might receive as much as one hundred dollars a month" (163–64). Pondering the few opportunities for advancement open to women, Isabel wonders why most people believe "that a man is suited to any official position he has managed to slip into," while believing "that even a woman is suited to her official position if a woman has managed to slip into it before" (192). Isabel need not fight family objections to her working since her parents are dead and in the urban setting no other relatives appear. She seems to take the necessity of working for granted, unlike many of the characters in other southern women's novels of the period, but she regrets that her options are so limited.

Newman also implies the lack of employment opportunities for southern women in having her character Evelyn Cunningham consider her only option as a young woman—besides marriage or being supported by her parents—to be the unrealistic one of becoming a landscape painter because of her talent in decorating place cards for her mother's dinners (95–96). Newman's characters are not involved in social activism, and indeed, in conforming to her society's verdicts about a woman's proper place, Evelyn agrees with Mrs. Abbott's conviction that women are not intelligent enough to vote (43).[8]

In Johnston's novel *Hagar,* Thomasine's mother, Mrs. Green, is the only member of the older generation who is not opposed to young women working and who understands the discrimination they face in trying to support themselves. "Girls have got to go out in the world and work nowadays, just the same as boys," she tells Hagar. "Food an' clothes don't ask what sect you belong to" (111). Yet when women try to earn money, she continues, "What they call 'Sentiment' fights them. Sentiment don't mind their being industrious, but it draws the line at their getting money for it" (112). In contrast, Mrs. LeGrand criticizes Thomasine's looking for a job as a store clerk even though her family is poor and needs her income, but she reserves her sharpest criticism for young women who leave home to work when their families could support them, declaring that whereas "gentlewomen in reduced circumstances may have to battle alone with the world . . . they do not like it," but instead feel that their position is "unnatural." For young women to choose to work is "positively shocking," an aspect of "the degeneracy of the times" (76). Despite having earned her own living for decades, she insists to Hagar that "we can surely trust everything to the chivalry of our Southern men," that "there is almost always some one" to support a young woman (117).

After Hagar wins a cash prize for a fairy tale, she decides to be a writer, and her grandfather is at first "indulgent." However, he does not take her ambitions seriously: "There have been women who have done very good work of a certain type. It's limited, but it's good of its kind," he tells her, adding, "of course, it isn't necessary for you to write, and in the Old South, at least, we've always rather deprecated that kind of thing for a woman"

84

(223). Yet as long as Hagar's stories remain harmless and are recreation rather than employment, her grandfather does not protest. When Hagar receives a letter from a friend in the Equal Suffrage League and discloses that she has decided to work for women's suffrage, however, her grandfather delivers the ultimatum that she desist from such activities or be disowned, and her horrified grandmother refuses to believe that she was "friends with those brazen women who want to be men" and threatens never again to speak to her (315–16). In *Hagar,* the South is seen as a place a woman must leave even to learn about social change and broader roles for women. Old Miss has seen a woman in bloomers in New York and Mrs. LeGrand has seen suffragists in Baltimore, but when an old school friend of Hagar arrives in New York in 1910 and is asked if she is interested in the suffrage movement, the friend replies, "We're so far South that as a movement it's all as yet only a rather distant sound." Southern newspapers, she explains, "chiefly confine themselves to being scandalized by the English Militants" (342). Hagar must leave the South to begin her work for social justice. Even so, her success as a writer seems too easily won to be believable, and while she is establishing her reputation, she is supported by her father, who has inherited a million dollars from his second wife and takes Hagar with him on his travels all over the world. Thus her own life seems almost as much a fairy tale as her first piece of writing.

Like Hagar, Ellen Glasgow's Gabriella and Isa Glenn's Laura find the freedom to live productive lives only after they leave the South, and Glasgow's other women characters are restricted in their roles outside the home. In *Virginia,* Glasgow is satiric about the societal attitudes concerning the kinds of work appropriate for upper-class southern women. Mrs. Pendleton felt that "to have been forced to train her daughter in any profitable occupation which might have lifted her out of the class of unskilled labour in which indigent gentlewomen by right belonged, would have been the final dregs of humiliation" (54). Similarly, Gabriella's family is horrified when she proposes working in a shop to help support her sister Jane and her children, and they all begin proposing alternatives—sewing, crocheting, making lampshades,

even teaching—"ladylike" work that would not threaten or interfere with her "social position . . . and having attention from
young men" (27). Her fiancé is similarly horrified, but Gabriella
is tired of being dependent and begins work at the town's pres-
tigious dry goods store after breaking her engagement. Despite
her family's sense that she has "step[ped] out of her class" (61),
Brandywine's is "an almost conventional shelter for distressed
feminine gentility" (62), and Gabriella's feminine taste in clothing and interest in her customers make her popular as a clerk.
Nevertheless, her mother remains unreconciled: "it was inconceivable to her that any girl with Berkeley blood in her veins
could be so utterly devoid of proper pride as Gabriella had
proved herself to be," and so she often refuses to speak to her
daughter for days but sits with a "countenance [that] implied
that she was piously resigned to disgrace as well as to poverty"
(78). Gabriella works only out of necessity, and after her sister
returns to her husband and Gabriella becomes engaged to
George, she quits her job. When he leaves her in New York City
with two children to support, she once again seeks employment
in a women's clothing establishment, not an outrageous choice
even at the turn of the century, and her rise in the business is
hard won. Although the issue of women working is not raised
as strongly in *The Romantic Comedians*, Annabel's mother regrets
having "wasted" her time as a young woman in seeking a marriage proposal instead of training herself for a career: "If I'd
spent my girlhood learning some useful pursuit, how much better off we should be by now" (112), she reflects. She encouraged
the judge's interest in her daughter and was pleased to have him
set Annabel up in her own business, but she responds to the news
of their engagement with "consternation" (113). "If I were Annabel," she comments, "I'd think twice before I gave up landscape
gardening for the richest man in the world" (112).

The only woman who works in Glenn's *Southern Charm* is
Laura, who had a job first in a beauty shop and is now importing
Paris fashions. Laura is proud of supporting herself and of competing with men in business; she tells her mother that she "out-
grew the parasitic stage" and "stopped running on charm" (271).

However, her mother is still surprised Laura has been able as a "fallen woman" to secure any employment besides prostitution. Laura had no family opposition to her working, since she was abandoned by her family when she was discovered pregnant; she made her own way through sheer necessity. Seeing her elegant, self-confident younger sister after twenty years, Alice May wishes she could support herself as well.

In their satirization rather than romantic idealization of the southern culture and traditions, Frances Newman, Mary Johnston, Ellen Glasgow, and Isa Glenn were flying in the face of the southern literary tradition. As late as 1925, in a review of the previous year's literature, Addison Hibbard remarked on the scarcity of satire in southern literature directed towards its own region, calling the "chief weakness" of its writers the "almost utter failure to face the materials about us," especially when writing in a satiric or critical vein (56–57). Yet Frances Newman and the other southern women writers discussed in this study squarely faced problems of their culture, especially concerning women's limited roles and subordinate positions in marriage, education, and work outside the home. Like Mary Johnston and Isa Glenn, Newman questioned the extent of social change for women in the South despite widespread discussion in the press of the emancipation of women during the 1910s and 1920s. Like Ellen Glasgow, she questioned the conservative southern attitudes towards race, class, and religion that reinforced the image of the southern lady, and she also indicated the difficulties for women who were caught between two expectations and standards of behavior. Some critics such as Malcolm Cowley have dismissed Newman's fiction because of her humorously satiric voice. Cowley groups her with other writers of the era who also found "life in general comic," calling their skepticism "mere snobbism" and their satire only "something to smile over" (86), instead of recognizing the serious social critique implicit in her writing.

Newman's social critique did not, however, escape the notice of the Southern Agrarians, who preached a return to the order and values of the "best" aspects of the past southern tradition, a tradition that Newman not only satirized but also revealed as demeaning and dehumanizing to the upper-class white women it idealized. According to Donald Davidson, one of the founders of the Agrarian movement, the purpose of the Agrarians was "to seek the image of the South which we could cherish with high conviction and to give it, wherever we could, the finality of art" (*Southern Writers* 60). It is ironic that the Old South that Davidson and his friends scorned as Fugitives became their symbol as Agrarians of a traditional rural society that fostered literature and the arts. In the mid-twenties, Allen Tate asserted in an article for the *Nation* that nothing in the culture of the Old South was useful to the writer, that it provided "no tradition of ideas, no consciousness of moral and spiritual values" (O'Brien 143), and Davidson agreed with this statement in his 1926 article "The Artist as Southerner" (782). However, as Agrarians, both later defended the Old South and its culture. In extolling a stable society as embodied in the Old South as the basis for art, the Agrarians pointed to the benefits of a leisure class free to pursue art and ideas and ignored or trivialized inequities and injustices and often even the dehumanizing slavery that had been its economic base. John Crowe Ransom championed the Old South as developing its culture on the European principle of hereditary inheritance "in order to put the surplus of energy into the free life of the mind," and, incredibly, he even defended slavery as "monstrous enough in theory, but, more often than not, humane in practice" ("Reconstructed" 3–5, 14). Similarly, to Allen Tate the antebellum South exemplified a traditional society, in which "the whole economic basis of life is closely bound up with moral behavior, and it is possible to behave morally all the time" (302–3).

The Agrarians' abhorrence of the industrialization and materialism of the modern South and their idealization of traditional southern rural life ran counter to the values and experience of many southern women and lower-class men. According to Jay Hubbell, Ellen Glasgow supposedly remarked after hearing John Crowe Ransom speak on agrarianism that "while she was out of sympathy with the crude industrialism that tends to dominate some sections of the South, she could not work up any enthusiasm over a rural civilization dominated by hookworm and fundamentalism" (181). Anne Firor Scott's discussion of the "new woman" in the South indicates that industrialization was sometimes a positive instead of negative force in women's lives in offering them economic options as well as in disrupting the image of the southern lady and the patriarchal culture. The "fluidity brought about by the immense social changes" that could be traced to industrialization "created a climate in which the restructuring of woman's role could more easily take place," she explains, noting that most "new women" in the South lived in towns where group activities and freedom from endless work were possible (*Southern Lady* 227–28). Anne Firor Scott's argument seems more applicable to middle-class white women for whom changing social roles brought opportunities for education and professional careers than for working-class women, whose positions as unskilled laborers in factories and textile mills brought them low wages (often based upon piece rates), long hours, and seasonal employment (Ryan 202–4). Nevertheless, even for them, the slave-owning Old South was not a lost utopia. It may have provided a leisure class of affluent white males with the time for artistic endeavors as the Agrarians asserted (although it is ironic that no critically acclaimed literature arose from the antebellum aristocracy), but for others in the society, the Old South meant powerlessness and even slavery, and they left it behind with no regrets.

The valuing of the land and of rural life, while valid and even praiseworthy in itself, also led the Agrarians to proclaim the rural landscape as the true source of art and thus to devalue art such as Newman's that did not spring from this source. In the introduction to *I'll Take My Stand*, the manifesto of the Southern Agrarians, Ransom proclaimed that "art depends, in general, like religion, on a right attitude to nature" (xv), and in an essay in that same book, Davidson maintained that the arts "have been produced in societies which were for the most part stable, religious, and agrarian . . . where men were never too far removed from nature to forget that the chief subject of art, in the final sense, is nature" ("A Mirror" 29). In their endorsement of a rural society as the basis for art, they defined the Southern Renais-

Questioning Social Change

sance as essentially agrarian, and Davidson lamented that even the rural artist "cannot escape the infection of the cities. . . . The skepticism and malaise of the industrial mind reach him anyway . . . and attack his art in the very process of creation. Unself-conscious expression cannot fully be attained" (57). Clearly Davidson's aesthetic values ran counter to Newman's, who championed skepticism and a highly conscious expression, and despite the roots of the Southern Renaissance in the skeptical, rebellious literature of the twenties that her novels exemplified, the Agrarians paid sparse critical attention to this literature—most of it negative—and relegated it to obscurity.

It is no wonder that men who ignored the inequities of southern life and even wrote as if slavery did not exist in the antebellum South—or as if it were basically a benevolent system that enabled the existence of a graceful, gentle, artistic leisure class—would be blind or indifferent to the psychological entrapment and powerless legal position of upper-class white women, which Newman and other southern women writers chose as their subject matter. In "The Profession of Letters in the South," Tate praised the South for retaining its "eighteenth-century amiability and consideration of manners" and its "patriarchal family still innocent of the rise and power of other forms of society" (*Collected Essays* 269). In contrast, Newman exposed these manners and amiability as often merely superficial codes of behavior in a society where "courageous convictions do not take precedence over politeness" (*Dead Lovers* 220) and the patriarchal family as leaving women at the mercy of their husband's continued pleasure or as considering them devalued if unmarried. Seidel notes that Newman's fiction is centered on the effect of a patriarchal society on individual women, a theme "not valued by critics like Donald Davidson," who as "a member of the Fugitive and Agrarian groups . . . would be expected to praise the order and stability of the male hierarchy endorsed by this milieu, rather than censure it" (*Southern Belle* 45–46).

To say Davidson did not value Newman's themes and writing is an understatement. He actively condemned her work for its skepticism about the celebrated old order and its satirization of

90

the values that he cherished. Demanding "an attitude of acceptance," Davidson believed the "positive transmutation" of southern values to be "the highest function of art" for a southern
writer, and he felt that "the Southern character, properly realized, might display an affirmative zest and abandon now lacking
in American art" ("The Artist" 783). Newman's questioning
southern values through her portrayal of a young woman continuously being disillusioned of her belief in traditional southern
ideals clearly disqualified her as a candidate for Davidson's approval or for the approval of those who shared his values. Instead
of displaying "affirmative zest," her characters, as Fay Blake notes,
"are so crippled psychologically by the education they receive
and the severe constraints of the society they live in that their
lives are shadowy half-lives and their loves unfulfilled half-loves";
they "thrash . . . impotently in a world that denies them independent recognition" (312–13). Davidson disapproved of "the
critical tendency, so marked in Frances Newman . . . and others,
[that] continued with little abatement throughout the nineteen
twenties, in various harsh or agitated studies of southern life"
("The Trend" 193), claiming that these southern writers, "over-
anxious to avoid the charge of sectionalism," assumed "too readily the journalistic damnations that were every day being pronounced against the South" (193).

Davidson apparently did not consider the possibility that Newman and these other critical southern writers were influenced
by their own experiences rather than the northern press, that
they themselves might have found the southern tradition lacking;
rather he found it "astonishing" that they should "contrarily write
like Northerners" ("A Mirror" 58–59). He attacked Glasgow's social realism as invaded by attitudes "imported, not native" in its
emphasis on weaknesses rather than strengths of the southern
tradition, and he found in Newman's novels and in some of Isa
Glenn's "the deliberate puncturing of pretensions thought to be
southern [that] smacks of a paying off of old scores." "The southern woman," he continued, "now intellectually as emancipated
as her northern sister, takes a dig at the tradition that would have
kept her in 'woman's' place" ("The Trend" 200–1). Newman, like

91

Johnston, Glasgow, and Glenn, in exposing the hypocrisies, pre-tensions, and injustices of the southern culture and its stultify-ing roles for women, wrote counter to the Agrarian's desire to "restore to Southern thought an image of the South that would be entirely relevant and valid, and defensible in modern terms" (Davidson, *Southern Writers* 46). Davidson attacked Newman's *The Hard-Boiled Virgin* specifically for having "hardly a page with-out its malignant intent of puncturing some convention, espe-cially the conventions of the Old South as represented in the St. Cecilia Society of Charleston and the aristocracy of Peachtree Street, Atlanta" ("Frances Newman" 28).[9] Instead of recognizing any validity in the critique of the southern society and tradition by writers such as Newman, Davidson concluded that "the south-ern tradition has evidently become inaccessible" to them: "It is not an intimate and immediate part of their understanding" ("The Trend" 202).

Davidson's next step was denying that these critical women writers were genuinely southern, a curious conclusion similar to the "odd" argument of American literary criticism discussed by Nina Baym that "only a handful of American works are really American" (127). In explaining that "all the writers of the Agrar-ian movement are for the Southern tradition and our heritage of Western civilization," Davidson added: "In the modern world there is no other way for the Southern writer to enjoy and use his rightful heritage and still be in any true sense a Southern writer" (*Southern Writers* 60–61). Defining the Agrarian position as the norm, Davidson could then exclude from the southern canon—as not characteristic of southern writing—any literature that did not follow its mythologizing and idealizing of the south-ern tradition. Ransom also defined southern literature as a "par-ticular kind of literature," asserting that "a writer may evidently have the juridical status of a Southerner without having the tem-per of one" and conversely that "some writers must impress us as having Southern quality . . . who are not physically of the South" ("Modern" 191–92).[10] Davidson even questioned the worth and artistic value of uncharacteristic southern writing in his article "The Trend of Literature": "I must ask of the new southern literature, not only whether it is modern or good, but whether it is characteristic, and work on the hypothesis that unless it is characteristic it is likely somewhere to fall short of being either truly modern or ultimately good" (184).

These literary judgments and aesthetic values of the Agrarians were influential in Newman's fall into oblivion since the Agrarians were instrumental in the establishment of the modern literature canon of the South through their association with New Criticism. It was Ransom who first articulated the ideas of New Criticism in his 1941 book *The New Criticism*, and Tate was also a central figure in the movement. Robert Penn Warren and Cleanth Brooks, who brought the ideas and methods of New Criticism into literature classrooms through their textbooks, were students of Davidson at Vanderbilt, and of these central figures only Brooks was not a Fugitive or Agrarian although he "worked closely with members of both groups and shared most of their views" (Cowan vii, 61–62, 67). Cowan asserts that "these Southern critics," in accomplishing "a major transformation in the study of literature," have used the "principles stemming from their Fugitive-Agrarian days" and that "the myth sought by the Agrarians, according to Donald Davidson, has been . . . achieved" (74).

The New Critics' contribution of their method of close textual analysis is important and should not be trivialized, but they were also responsible for constricting the concerns of literary criticism by excluding or at least deemphasizing sociological and historical considerations and for narrowing the canon. Henry F. May points out that the New Critics "found little to praise in the twenties," rejecting its "rebellious literature . . . as completely as they did the business civilizations of the era" (415–16). Fraya Katz-Stoker also links the New Critics with political conservatism, noting the simultaneous squelching of the "vigorous sociological approach" of the middle thirties and of the feminist movement because "both were seen as radical political movements which attempted to undermine and expose the ideology of established power relationships" (319–22). With their concern for a work of literature as a discrete object, studying it in isolation from its historical, cultural, and biographical context, the New Critics, Katz-Stoker argues, are guilty not only of "the sin of omission" but also "the sin of commission" in "perpetuating the status quo both by defusing the anti-social implications of art, and by participating in an education of the young" that limits ways of thinking by treating "certain writers and certain ideas . . . as if they were non-existent" (314–16). Davidson spoke for his group in "rejecting . . . the servile collaborationism of the modern Southern liberals," adding, "we were attacking, not retreating" (*Southern Writers* 51). Similarly, Ransom found the "militant liberal fiction which is given to preaching" rarely written in the South and not indigenous: "If Liberalism has invaded literature, it has made less inroad on the Southern variety, and it is essentially here an imposition" ("Modern" 193–94).

The New Critics' role in the definition of the canon was significant. In looking specifically to the South, John Bradbury observes that with the appearance of a number of anthologies of southern literature, "something of a canon has been established, with the result that a quite limited number of authors have been credited with total responsibility for the South's modern contribution to American letters." Bradbury includes Newman within "a strong and wide-spread liberal wing, covering both urban and rural subjects, [which] has been largely ignored," noting that "the canon includes almost exclusively that group . . . whose work fits the pattern prescribed by the South's New Critics" (5). This defining of southern literature remained essentially a male-oriented affair as late as the early 1970s. Not a single woman was among the two dozen scholars who read papers and spoke on panels at the 1972 conference on southern literature at the University of North Carolina at Chapel Hill. Rubin and Holman comment in their editing of the resulting papers that only one important person was missing, Jay Hubbell of Duke (*Southern Literary Study* xii), seemingly without any consciousness that the perspectives of women scholars might have been valuable.[11]

Newman's writing, then, and that of the other southern women writers in this study, suffered neglect in the hands of a dominant literary group that did not share their values or perspectives. Because Newman's values differed so much from those of the Southern Agrarians and New Critics, her work was attacked and trivialized and ultimately buried. Ironically, her fiction was characterized by the very concern for artistry that the Agrarians and New Critics applauded. Applying to her novels the methods of close textual analysis emphasized by the New Critics reveals Newman as a brilliant stylist worthy of extensive literary attention.

4

Revising Literary Conventions

IN HER BOOK *Women and Fiction,* Patricia Stubbs argues that "a genuinely feminist novel must surely credit women with more forms of experience than their personal or sexual entanglements" (xiii) and that until recently women in novels were " 'prisoners' of feeling and of private life" (x). She considers the envisioning of new roles for women the only valid expression of feminism and concludes that only contemporary novels can be "genuinely feminist." Yet a feminist critique is imbedded in the novels of Frances Newman, which reveal the restrictive conditions of women's lives and therefore implicitly call for an end to gender restrictions and strict gender roles. Responding to critics like Stubbs who "are strongly inclined to condemn the love-story plot as an arbitrarily imposed literary convention that worked women no good," Kathleen Blake urges them "instead of deprecating" to "explore the love story and come to recognize . . . the complexity of the critique that can arise within it" (xi). Women novelists like Newman can subtly question or undermine society's assumptions about proper roles for women even while writing within narrative conventions that prescribe limited roles for women.

Elaine Showalter divides American women's writing into three hierarchical as well as chronological categories: the "feminine phase" (1840–1880), in which women writers internalized male assumptions about women; the "feminist phase" (1880–1920), in which women protested or dramatized "the ordeals of wronged womanhood"; and the "female phase, on-going since 1920," in which "women reject both imitation and protest—two forms of dependency—and turn instead to female experience as the source of an autonomous art, extending the feminist analysis of culture to the forms and techniques of literature" (35–36). Although Showalter sees the first two phases as dependent upon the dominant male culture, she recognizes the critique implicit in protest literature, designating it as "feminist" and labeling "female" what Stubbs terms "feminist." Newman's novels bridge Showalter's feminist and female phases; all focus on love relationships, yet they subtly or overtly assess the limitations of women's roles and particularly the pervasive sexism of the southern society, and they often subvert the conventions of male literary forms to reveal the submerged female experience.

Newman's first novel, *The Gold-Fish Bowl,* illustrates how a woman novelist can follow a narrative convention filled with male assumptions about the nature of women and their proper roles and yet simultaneously question that convention. *The Gold-Fish Bowl* loosely follows the two-suitors or marriage plot convention discussed by Jean Kennard in her book *Victims of Convention,* but it also subtly subverts that convention and thus provides a critique both of it and of the assumptions underlying it. In her second novel, *The Hard-Boiled Virgin,* Newman revised aspects of the traditional *bildungsroman* to criticize a society that envisioned fulfillment for a woman only within marriage. Like other women writers, Newman revealed a young girl's aspirations as stunted rather than enlarged in the process of growing into maturity. Finally, in her last novel, *Dead Lovers Are Faithful Lovers,* as in her first short story, "Rachel and Her Children," Newman continued to portray women focusing their lives on personal relationships with men, yet here she inverted conventional literary images of women to create her feminist perspective. Newman was clearly within a tradition of southern women writers who satirized the southern culture and the role of upper-class white women in that culture, but she was more innovative than many in reshaping literary conventions to make her critique artistically powerful.

Revising Literary Conventions

In envisioning *The Gold-Fish Bowl,* Newman intended to "evolve the kind of lovelorn story that delighted elderly ladies" and, in her desire to write a best-selling novel, to write it "so wittily and so charmingly that it would delight low-brows and high-brows, and even medium-brows" ("Frances Newman Tells" 6). But instead of a simple romance, she later reflected that she wrote "a tale whose plot would have outraged the thousands of American library borrowers who are terribly annoyed by wisecracks, and who are happiest with a nice long dull book" (6). Newman's subversion of marriage plot conventions made potential publishers uneasy. Robert M. McBride rejected it as a "hybrid book," fearing that "the people who enjoy the sprightliness and frequent pungency . . . would not care for the innocuous romance" (H[olt], unpublished letter), and the novel remained unpublished until 1986, when it was edited by Margaret Manning Duggan as a doctoral dissertation. Duggan's interest in the novel, however, is as "apprentice fiction." She discusses it primarily as proof that Newman "could write respectably traditional fiction" and that her later highly sophisticated and complex style was not a personal eccentricity but "wrought by conscious design" (xxi). Duggan labels *The Gold-Fish Bowl* "a thoroughly competent, conventional romance in the most popular understanding of the term" (xx).

Like other marriage plot novels, *The Gold-Fish Bowl* centers around the period of courtship, that time when the heroine makes her most important life choice within the context of the genre—whom to marry—a decision that will "determine her rank and company for the rest of her life" (Zeman 16). According to Jean Kennard, the two-suitors convention is "fundamentally sexist" (10) because it postulates female maturity as consisting of submitting to the values of the proper male: "The wrong suitor embodies the qualities she must reject; the right suitor those which . . . make for the good life. The heroine's personality and development are thus defined through comparison with two male characters" (11). Newman undermines this convention of having the young woman's maturity depend upon eventually choosing the proper suitor and adopting his values rather than his rivals', even though she does not subvert the tradition to the extent of having Anne Delane's maturation consist of developing and insisting upon retaining her own values. The Englishman Stephen Eliott has no substantial rivals as a suitor to Anne De- lane. Ernest Crandall talks incessantly of the ginghams he manu- factures and thus bores Anne, and "poor faithful Randolph" is penniless and excites no ardor. Both have fruitlessly proposed to Anne numerous times and continue to do so throughout the novel, but her attention is riveted on Stephen Eliott, and the plot concerns less her choosing wisely than her managing to land her choice. She is certainly not tempted by the values of Ernest, who is obsessed with manufacturing and material goods, and al- though she appreciates Randolph, who is affectionate but dull, he seems to her a better match for the young widow Pelops, who is also affectionate but has plenty of money. These other two men serve primarily to make Stephen aware "that she is not entirely without swains" (52), and Anne does not hesitate to flirt with them and keep them dangling to ensure his interest. In addition to these three current suitors, Anne divulges an earlier infatu- ation with an admiring professor, who functions primarily to sati- rize the convention of an older and wiser suitor's serving as a guide to a young protagonist. The professor has taught Anne only such trivial information as the "learned name" for opos- sums, which she refers to as "nocturnal marsupial mammals" dur- ing an opossum hunt to impress Stephen (129).

Stephen Eliott's greatest rival as a suitor is the novelist Edward Hamilton, whom Anne thinks Stephen to be. Because of his slight resemblance to a photograph she has seen of Hamilton, she has convinced herself that Stephen is the British novelist living in- cognito to gather ideas for his next book. Anne must mature enough to accept a real relationship with Stephen over a fantasy relationship with the author of *Green Meads* and accept Stephen for who he is rather than for his imagined literary prowess or for the ego-gratification of having been chosen by a famous man.[1] Anne's need for clear vision, for the ability to see beneath surface appearances and to accept a realistic relationship rather than to cling to a fantasy, is an element of the marriage plot novel, as is the linking of maturation with choosing the proper suitor. However, the idealized Edward Hamilton becomes a foil to the more ordinary Stephen and undercuts Stephen's role as the right suitor. Stephen's conversation is not witty as Anne had expected of "the greatest English novelist" (75); she admits she has "never heard him say anything so very clever," realizing, "certainly he hadn't tossed epigrams about and he hadn't been in the least poetic" (110). Newman may be gently satirizing Anne's naive expectations of a novelist, but she is also pointing out the distance between the ideal and the actual lover.

Certainly Stephen is not the idealized suitor often found in conventional marriage plot novels. His lack of interest in fiction and his lack of cleverness are humorously presented as deficiencies, not virtues, even though Anne tries to rationalize them as examples of his superior taste and his reserve before she realizes his actual identity. She explains his lack of apparent wittiness to herself as his need "to save all the best things for his books" (110), and when it occurs to her it is "odd" that he never talks about novels, she quickly thinks of a justification: "probably he doesn't read many because it's tedious to read dull ones and annoying to come upon clever things that other people have outrageously thought of" (141–42). Here Newman is undercutting the two-suitor convention with its implication that the right suitor is "the repository" of commendable values and a guide for the heroine (Kennard 14–15). Stephen Eliott seems merely a likable, handsome man with a sufficient income and the added charm of a British accent, who falls in love with the heroine. Anne Delane's acceptance of him is not a rejection of what she had valued in Edward Hamilton. Although she accepts Stephen's true identity and his political rather than writing career, Anne proposes to surround herself with a "salon full of writing chaps" when her husband becomes prime minister (263); she, like Newman herself, values cleverness and wit. Instead of changing her values in accepting Stephen's suit, Anne simply realizes that the Edward Hamilton whom she had thought she was in love with was largely a figment of her imagination and never an actual suitor and that she had meanwhile fallen in love with the actual Stephen Eliott. Despite his shortcomings, Stephen is not an "inadequate embodiment of the virtues to be emulated by the heroine even though he is obviously intended to embody them," a weakness that Kennard finds in several marriage plot novels (14); rather, he is simply an attractive, kind man who, despite his imperfections, will be a good husband and, because of them, a more suitable companion than guide.

Newman also subtly questions the basic assumption behind marriage plot novels—that a suitable marriage is the proper resolution for a young woman's life—when Anne finally comes to what should be a mature recognition that she loves Stephen not for being the famous writer, but for himself. Her realization that she is "absolutely, inextricably, in love with him" (143) comes "in a horrible flash" (142), and she thinks: "So this was it . . . this was the end of everything . . . this was what I had heard of, what I had seen, what I had read of in a thousand tales" (143; ellipses are Newman's). The phrase "the end of everything" refers to the customary ending of marriage plot novels—when the curtain is drawn over the heroine's life—while also mocking such endings as unrealistic and suggesting that for a woman marriage is similar to death.[2] Patricia Spacks comments on this tendency of women novelists to discern not only the appeal of marriage to their characters but also its threat: "In their investigations of internal and external female experiences," she observes, women novelists "often question, overtly and covertly, marriage as a happy ending—even in the context of Victorian propriety" (77). In addition to questioning marriage as a happy ending, Newman subverts the conventional expectations of marriage for a young heroine, which involve her submission to her husband. When Stephen and Anne decide to marry at the end of the novel, it is not clear at all that the feisty Anne will be dominated by her rather mild-mannered Englishman since she has managed him quite well during their courtship, and he admits that although he expects her to be "an adorable wife," he also "suspect[s]" she will keep him "on tiptoe" (258).

Newman's gentle satirization of aspects of the marriage plot novel, even while writing within that tradition, is reminiscent of Jane Austen's *Northanger Abbey*, which playfully mocks conven-

101

tions of the gothic romance. Indeed, although Newman claims that the "prototype" of *The Gold-Fish Bowl* was the novel *Patricia Brent, Spinster* by Herbert George Jenkins (*Letters* 69), Jane Austen's novels instead seem her ultimate pattern, especially *Northanger Abbey.* Newman greatly admired Austen. In an interview with Ellen Glasgow, Newman was disappointed when Glasgow listed the six greatest English novelists and omitted Austen, but she was later pleased to learn that Glasgow shared her admiration of Austen's novels ("Having Tea"). Also, when Newman's mentor Cabell wrote of *The Hard-Boiled Virgin* that he could "think of no book ever written by any woman which I like better" (*Letters* 213), Newman remarked to Lamar Trotti, "He doesn't like darling Jane Austen, which explains the extravagance of his remarks" (214). She even named a newspaper column "Elizabeth Bennet's Gossip" "in honor of Jane Austen's heroine," "whose spirit," she modestly added, "has certainly not descended" on the namesake (*Letters* 161). Newman's admiration for Austen's writing is evident in *The Gold-Fish Bowl.* Assessing what she had learned from her first novel, Newman explained: "Apparently I had learned that no aspiring novelist should read any writer enough to be unduly influenced by him" ("Frances Newman Tells" 6), undoubtedly alluding to Austen's influence on the structure and tone of *The Gold-Fish Bowl.*

Kathleen Blake discusses *Northanger Abbey,* which "mocks the formula requiring that no young lady dream of a young man before he dreams of her" (121), in demonstrating how subtle critiques of romance conventions can arise within the genre of the love story. The gentle mocking of this formula while writing within it is one of the many parallels between Austen's novel and Newman's. When apologizing for breaking her engagement to walk with Henry Tilney and his sister, Catherine Moreland declares to him, "I had ten thousand times rather have been with you" (Austen 82–83). Like Catherine Moreland, Anne Delane of *The Gold-Fish Bowl* does not hesitate to pursue the young man of her choice; she even admits to him that she actively seeks what she desires rather than passively wishing for it: "At least I'll never die of suppressed desires, because when I want something I always take steps to get it instead of just moping about and having queer dreams" (124). However, she is less naive than Catherine and her pride is a restraint; she reveals that "its first principle is never, never to let any one suspect that I want the moon unless I see a sporting chance of getting it" (87–88), and so she manipulates situations rather than declaring her feelings outright. For example, in order to be alone with Stephen Eliott on a moonlit night, she arranges an opossum hunt and persuades her young widow friend Pelops to come to pair off with Randolph, Anne's faithful but penniless suitor. Later, when Stephen seems ready to propose but looks distressed at the news that Anne has recovered part of her fortune, she fears "he wouldn't quite fancy asking a newly-restored bourgeoisie to marry him when he had had two months to offer a glass slipper to a Cinderella" (153) and so makes an "ingenuous girlish speech" (156) to mollify his pride. Yet when she finally realizes that he is not Edward Hamilton and therefore had not deceived her but she has deceived herself, she is ready to pursue him directly and express her feelings openly. She sends him a telegraph immediately to apologize for having left without an explanation and decides to try to telephone him as well. Anne hopes to catch Stephen before he returns to England because "it would be dreadfully mortifying to have to pursue him across the Atlantic and beard him in the Lion's kingdom" (248), but she is willing to do so if necessary.

Also like Austen's Catherine, Anne has gotten many of her ideas about life from reading novels and must learn to perceive reality instead of a fantasy world. Catherine has been so influenced by gothic novels that she suspects General Tilney of having murdered his wife merely because of the abbey setting, and she misjudges Isabella's character. Kennard compares Catherine's early perceptions to John Thorpe's "inability to see the truth about others" and sees it as "no coincidence that in the novel John's first significant lie, which breaks Catherine's agreement with Elinor Tilney, is associated with a trip to the Gothic delights of Blaize Castle" (26). Anne Delane similarly ignores numerous details that suggest Stephen might simply be Stephen instead of Edward Hamilton in disguise to cling to her fantasy of a romance with a famous English novelist. His hair is styled differently from that in a picture of the novelist (80), he displays no distress over the mention of primogeniture although Edward's elder brother is dead (140), and he professes feeling "horribly inadequate" to discuss novels (141). As in *Northanger Abbey*, in which the suitor John Thorpe is only irritating to Catherine, Stephen Eliott has no actual rival for Anne's affections, and like Henry Tilney, Stephen is honest and kind. Rachel DuPlessis finds in most marriage plot novels "a contradiction between two middle-class ideas—gendered feminine, the sanctified home, and gendered human, the liberal bourgeois ideology of the self-interested choice of the individual agent" (14). Too often the independent young heroine must renounce the very qualities that have made her admirable to fit into the prescribed role of a wife. Yet Kennard asserts of *Northanger Abbey* that "there are no qualities or drives which Jane Austen has invited us to admire in the heroine which are irreconcilable with this marriage" (23). The same is true of *The Gold-Fish Bowl*.

Newman does not entirely subvert the conventions of the marriage plot, however. Despite her light satiric tone and gentle critique of aspects of the two-suitor convention, *The Gold-Fish Bowl* does retain aspects of this convention that Kennard found "fundamentally sexist." For example, Anne Delane is quite willing to relinquish a number of important aspects of her life to marry Stephen Eliott. Early in the novel she declares her determination to keep her ancestral home rather than sell it, and she "felt as heroic as Joan of Arc in the third act or Antigone in the first" (18) in working to save it. When she first becomes interested in Stephen Eliott/Edward Hamilton, Anne is cheered by the thought that writers can live anywhere, and later, when she learns that Stephen is a member of Parliament and realizes that he will certainly have to live in his own country, she thinks, "it is all very well . . . even to be madly in love. . . . But going off to England—to be an American in England—was something else" (180). Yet after Stephen proposes, Anne relinquishes her home and nation without a protest, declaring, "First I honoured you . . . and then I loved you, and so I suppose I shall end by obeying you, and liking it. And there's nothing else I want to do very much" (210). Anne also relinquishes her lifelong dream of a wedding at Clarendon for a quick justice of the peace ceremony, even though she wonders if they should be married in a church so the marriage will be considered proper by the English (257–58).

The Gold-Fish Bowl never raises the question, as Newman's later novels do, as to whether her heroine should marry but only considers whom she should marry and whether she can succeed in marrying him. Thus the patriarchal system, with the male at the center of a woman's life, is never seriously questioned. As Kennard suggests, "It is not the fact that the heroine marries which is significant but that the marriage acts as a conclusion to the novel and is to a large extent symbolic. It indicates the adjustment of the protagonist to society's values, a condition which is equated with her maturity" (18). The structure of the marriage plot novel itself to an extent does limit possibilities of meaning by defining the parameters of inquiry; as Marcia Lieberman asserts, a literary convention can be "the most subtle, pervasive level at which sexism affects literature" (326). DuPlessis sees an inherent contradiction in marriage plot novels in their promoting "growth, self-definition, community, insight" in the female characters but then limiting them to the domestic sphere where they have little if any autonomy (14); she concludes that "the romance plot, broadly speaking, is a trope for the sex-gender system as a whole" because it "valorizes heterosexual as opposed to homosexual ties" and "incorporates individuals within couples as a sign of their personal and narrative success" (5). Yet DuPlessis sees the possibility of "writing beyond the ending," of inventing "narrative strategies . . . that express critical dissent" (5), and to a limited extent, Newman has expressed dissent in this first novel through her subversion of elements of the romance plot. In her later two novels, however, Newman is much more critical of the assumption that marriage is the only meaningful role for women, and her narrative strategies themselves more directly criticize the southern patriarchy.

The Hard-Boiled Virgin contains autobiographical elements, including Katharine's physical description, her education, and her evolution into a writer. However, whereas Newman's pursuit of a career rather than marriage was a conscious choice, Katharine's early quest was for love, and her decision to write followed years of failing to attain importance by marrying a celebrated man. Thus her decision not to fit into the mold society had prepared for her contains the appearance of "accident," as discussed by Heilbrun in the lives of women "who wish to live a quest plot" (*Writing* 49). Yet Katharine's finally living an unconventional life, like Newman's, "may well be the forming of a life in the service of a talent felt, but unrecognized and unnamed" (Heilbrun, *Writing* 53), for despite her early longing for a suitable husband, Katharine alienated two potential suitors by rebuffing their tentative expressions of physical affection. In this novel, Newman avoids marrying the heroine to resolve the "contradiction between love and quest" (DuPlessis 3). Instead, she indicts a society that provides only limited acceptable roles for women by revising the traditional male *bildungsroman.*

Critics apply a variety of terms to a female *bildungsroman* or novel of development. Barbara White defines the novel of adolescence as a subgenre of the novel of female development that shares characteristics with the *bildungsroman* but focuses on a protagonist between the ages of twelve and nineteen. Annis Pratt reserves the term *bildungsroman* for novels in which the protagonist is under thirty and notes that in women's fiction *bildungsromans* usually concern social quest whereas in novels in which the heroine is over thirty, the quest is generally spiritual—thus her term *novels of rebirth and transformation.* Susan Rosowski refers to novels that focus on a sensitive, intelligent female protagonist engaged in self-discovery as *novels of awakening. The Hard-Boiled Virgin* concerns Katharine Faraday's adolescence, but it continues to show her development through her early thirties and thus encompasses aspects of all of these terms.

In her discussion of the novel of awakening, Susan Rosowski describes the direction of the female protagonist as "inward, towards greater self-knowledge and the nature of the world," but she concludes that "the protagonist's growth results typically not with an 'art of living' as for her male counterpart, but instead with a realization that for a woman such an art of living is difficult or impossible; it is an awakening to limitations" (49). Unlike the male protagonist in the traditional *bildungsroman* who learns to master the world, Katharine Faraday in *The Hard-Boiled Virgin* is initiated into a world of confinement and limited possibilities. At school she learns that not only can she not aspire to Congress or the White House, but by virtue of her gender she cannot even sit in the honorary front row of desks in her classroom, even though her marks are higher than any boy's. She realizes that her intelligence will win her no male admirers, that boys seldom have "romantic attachments for little girls who can spell words of five syllables and who can find the eighteenth term of an arithmetical progression" (46). At this early age she chooses not to pretend ignorance to win their approval, but her attempts to learn about the world are thwarted. As a sheltered young girl, Katharine has little access to knowledge except from unreliable sources such as slanted schoolbook accounts of Civil War battles, Victorian novels, advice columns to young girls, and magazine articles and stories. Occasionally she manages to piece together bits of information gleaned from these sources to gain valuable insight. From the mention of "childbirth pains" (28) in the novel *A Marital Liability,* she decides her friend's account of the birth of her sister was not "as improbable as golden gowns issuing from hazel-nuts or genii issuing from lamps" (22), as she had earlier thought. However, even with this bit of information she imagines a baby emerging when its mother's stomach bursts open (36); even occasional accurate information is so sketchy as to mislead rather than enlighten her.

Katharine Faraday's education is continued at a finishing school in Washington, D.C., where her mother hopes she will learn "a more ingenious method of doing her hair and . . . some information concerning methods of rousing ardent but honorable passions in young gentlemen" (59). Barbara White describes the heroine in a female novel of adolescence as "hampered both by the institutions designed to prepare her for a subordinate role and by her own inner conflicts and passivity" (137). Even more than Anne Delane in *The Gold-Fish Bowl,* Katharine Faraday follows the example set by heroines in the nineteenth-century novels she had read as a young girl in her desire to understand the world and her place in it.[3] She practices the art of *self-postponement,* the term coined by William Michael Rossetti to describe his sister Christina and adopted by Kathleen Blake in her discussion of Victorian love novels. Blake observes that the women in these novels "are waiting for love, as for salvation" (vii), and "if having to wait means postponement, making a habit of waiting amounts to self-postponement. The love vigil itself becomes a way of life" (viii). Throughout much of the novel, Katharine Faraday is waiting for love and "her destined husband" (79), and her thoughts and energies center around this quest for love. Having learned from her mother that "a woman should always persuade a man to talk about the subject he is interested in" (73), Katharine's reading is dictated by the interests of men she is currently seeing. She makes major decisions on the basis of the possible love relationships, deciding to leave Atlanta to attend lectures in New York since "she had begun to suspect that Atlanta was not likely to provide a satisfactory hero for the romance of Katharine Faraday" and hoping to meet a more sophisticated man "who might enjoy moulding a skeleton key to all knowledge" for her (194). In her world, not only are men the conveyers of knowledge, but also the possibility of a relationship with a professor supersedes the importance of what she might learn from him.

Katharine later decides to travel to Europe only to impress a young professor whose interest in her is waning: "She decided that she must take away the charms she was sure he had the ability to appreciate, and that she must increase her importance in his eyes by going to the countries in which he would have liked to be himself" (203). Until she is in her middle to late twenties, Katharine can imagine no other possibility for her life than attracting an interesting, important potential husband. According to Rosowski, this attempt of a heroine "to find value in a world defined by love and marriage" is a characteristic of the novel of awakening or female *bildungsroman,* which is also characterized by an inward movement "toward greater self-knowledge that leads in turn to a revelation of the disparity between that self-knowledge and the nature of the world" (49).

The greatest disparity that the heroine of a female *bildungsroman* must face is her own self-value and the lack of value that her society places on females in general and, in Katharine's instance, on intelligent females in particular. Anne Goodwyn Jones explains the effect of this disparity on Katharine.[4] If consonance exists between one's inner experiences and the perception of the self in an external world, a healthy self-image emerges, but "a radical contradiction between the messages from inner and outer worlds will impede the development of a self" (290). Katharine focuses on inner experiences in an attempt to protect her ego, yet she continues to seek experience in the external world, "whose learning can only teach her to devalue herself still further" (291). As a young girl, Katharine recognizes early that "the stupidest girl with a short upper lip and curly golden hair is born to a social situation much pleasanter than the social situation of the cleverest girl with a long upper lip and straight black hair" (30), and she "looked with mortification at the straight black braids of her own hair" (38–39). Katharine is devalued by her culture, her intellect seen as a liability rather than an asset. She is not popular at school, where recess becomes a half hour of torture away from the "easy triumphs of spelling and mental arithmetic" (20). When Katharine sees a portrait of George Eliot and reads about Eliot's "brilliant mind" on a book jacket, she momentarily questions society's judgment of her own worth: "She could not believe that there was any real good reason why no one had ever told her that she was surprisingly pretty for a girl who was as clever as she was" (41). However, she compares herself with her beautiful, popular older sisters, who epitomize society's standards, and hopes but is "not sure she could be right in suspecting that a woman's charms and her taste in hats sometimes survive intelligence and even education" (60).

Even though Katharine has not escaped internalizing her society's values, to an extent an authentic self does emerge. She begins to resurrect her childhood desire to be a writer and prove "her cleverness in print" (229), for the first time entertaining "the possibility of becoming important herself instead of waiting to find honourable favour in the sight of a man so celebrated that he could make her important merely by allowing her to use his names with a suitably apologetic prefix" (230). Her first published essay sounds her rebellion against society's view of marriage as the only fulfilling role for women in arguing that "marriage has a bad effect on a woman's writing" (235). Thus, although Newman illustrates the way in which society teaches women to devalue themselves (especially if they are intelligent instead of beautiful) and to focus their aspirations on marrying well instead of on their self-development, her resolution of the quest theme is not entirely negative, nor does it follow the pattern of many novels of female development. Ellen Morgan asserts that in *bildungsromans* by women even protagonists who achieve self-growth are generally "halted and defeated" before reaching "transcendent selfhood." In novels written before the current women's movement "they committed suicide or died; they compromised by marrying and devoting themselves to sympathetic men; they went mad or into some kind of retreat and seclusion from the world" (184). Newman resolves the conflict neither in marriage nor in death, and she also avoids the resolution of madness for her heroine. Instead, Katharine Faraday writes a successful first play, and, as Seidel observes, she "has rejected marriage as her goal, a rejection of the ultimate goal of the belle, for she has achieved her earlier dream of becoming a writer" (*Southern Belle* 43). The success of her own play enables her for the first time to be "bored by a celebrated man," and she reflects on the value of her own individuality instead of trying to conform to the interests of whatever man she is with: "She had begun to feel at last that a peg has at least as much right to be square as a hole has to be round" (281). This identification of herself with the Freudian male symbol can be seen as an indication that Katharine is valorizing herself as an active participant in life rather than as a traditional passive female.[5]

Katharine's emergence as a writer is significant. DuPlessis notes the importance of the woman writer or artist in fiction in emphasizing the conflict between quest and woman's prescribed role in society: "The figure of a female artist encodes the conflict between any empowered woman and the barriers to her achievement. Using the female artist as a literary motif dramatizes and heightens the already-present contradiction in bourgeois ideology between the ideals of striving, improvement, and visible public works, and the feminine version of that formula: passivity, 'accomplishments,' and invisible private acts" (84). In *A Portrait of the Artist as a Young Woman,* Linda Huf discusses the small number of *kunstlerromans* written by women, explaining that since women "have been encouraged to sacrifice themselves to others" rather than the reverse, the woman artist "has been caught . . . in a double bind": "In trying to be both woman and artist—that is, both selfless and self-assertive—she has been trapped in a no-win situation" (151). Thus many women writers fail to envision women characters with the degree of autonomy they themselves possess and, despite their own escape from the narrow confines of acceptable womanhood, affirm patriarchal patterns in their fiction (Heilbrun, *Reinventing* 71–72). Newman refuses to follow the approved script of society in *The Hard-Boiled Virgin.* In creating a female character with the autonomy to become a writer, Newman affirms self-assertion for women rather than self-sacrifice.

Seidel criticizes Newman for not envisioning the possibility of Katharine's combining a career of writing with marriage (*Southern Belle* 43), but Newman as well as her character recognized the difficulty of fulfilling both roles. In her essay "Silences," Tillie Olsen lists the large number of women writers in the past two centuries who have been unmarried or childless to create the time and space for serious writing and the very few with more than one child (106–7). Linda Huf discusses the "practical impossibility of being both selfless helpmeet and committed craftsman" (6), and Virginia Woolf's discussion of the difficulties facing women writers in *A Room of One's Own* is well-known. Newman herself intended to write a book about famous writers who never married to be entitled *Those Eminent Virgins.*

Many male critics have completely misread the resolution of *The Hard-Boiled Virgin* because it does not fit into their preconceptions of a woman's nature and role in life. As Annis Pratt comments, women's fiction sometimes "has a synthesis so alien to patriarchal culture that it is invisible to all but those already at odds with gender strictures" (177–78). Robert Drake, Jr., for example, labels Katharine's determination to write a best-selling play rather than to sublimate her creative urges in admiring male writers merely a "revenge" on the successful playwright with whom she has had her only sexual encounter. He considers her decision to be a writer a "tragedy . . . typical of that of many twentieth-century dislocations: in seeking the reality which will give her the greatest fulfillment as a person, she runs headlong from the only experience which can give her what she wants" (392). It is interesting that Drake apparently does not consider personal fulfillment an appropriate or even believable desire for women. His chauvinism causes him to misinterpret Newman's critique of the traditional subordinate role of the southern woman with its self-postponement and self-denial as well as Katharine's limited escape from some of its precepts. Instead, he concludes that she has discarded potential happiness and fulfillment in rejecting her traditional role as a wife and mother; her fears about a possible pregnancy that would curtail her writing career are "morbid fears of the very experience which would give her the fullest realization as a woman—motherhood" (392).

In noting that Katharine Faraday "recoils from motherhood and, eventually, the prospect of marriage itself," Louis Gallo observes that "*The Hard-Boiled Virgin* offended the prevailing social sensibility" because it "threatened" that sensibility: "Women were not *supposed* to think such thoughts" ("Frances" 278). Despite Gallo's understanding of Newman's "indictment of Southern gentility, of archaic ante-bellum mindsets" ("Notes" 93) and the threat that this indictment presented to her culture, he too projects his own values and expectations. He speculates that had Katharine been more beautiful and therefore desirable she would have gladly chosen marriage over a career: "if she had possessed those . . . [golden] locks and [watery blue] eyes, if the right man somehow appeared on the scene, and if her intelligence had proved only a slight bit more practical and compromising, she would have fit into the scenario [of love and marriage] beautifully" ("Notes" 93).

In portraying a young woman being initiated into a world of limitations rather than opportunities, Frances Newman joined other women writers in revising the traditional *bildungsroman* or novel of development to illustrate the extent to which southern society could thwart female development. Her resolution envisions some hope for women breaking out of society's confining roles, although not to the extent of Mary Johnston's hope in *Hagar*, in which obstacles to social change are naively ignored, or to the extent of Ellen Glasgow's in *Life and Gabriella*, in which Gabriella attains independent self-realization and also begins a marriage of equality with a good friend. In her growth towards a limited self-realization, Katharine struggles not only against the social institutions that limit her opportunities but also against psychological restraints and her own passivity. Yet she does finally end her cycle of self-postponement in waiting for the love of the right man and the marriage that her society insisted on as a woman's means of attaining dignity and importance.

In her last novel, *Dead Lovers Are Faithful Lovers*, Newman further questions marriage as a sufficient and satisfying goal for women. She also blurs the distinctions between two stereotypes, the selfless angel of the house and the other woman, and thus indicates actual women do not fit into the narrow definitions that literature affords them. Newman was, of course, not alone in this feminist revision of literary images. Annette Kolodny discusses "inversions" of "stereotyped, traditional literary images of women" as a recurring pattern in women's writing (43), and Gilbert and Gubar's *Madwoman in the Attic* concerns nineteenth-century women writers engaged in "deconstructing and reconstructing those images of women inherited from male literature, especially the paradigmatic polarities of angel and monster" (76). However, whereas Gilbert and Gubar explain the assault on traditional images of women as primarily unconscious or subtextual in the writers they examine, Newman's shattering of the myths of the ideal wife, the "angel in the house," and of the monstrous other woman lies at the center of *Dead Lovers Are Faithful Lovers* and its structure; it *is* the text.

Newman's shift from the point of view of Evelyn Cunningham to that of Isabel Ramsay in the middle of the novel to effect this inversion of expectations has been misunderstood by critics. Isabel Paterson faulted Newman for this shift in focus, listing as a "glaring" error that "the fragile thread of narrative breaks sharply in the middle" (3), and Ruth Suckow even more strongly criticized the novel for "its very bad construction": "It starts out to show the fears and vanities and jealousies of love in one lady, and arouses a certain amount of sympathy for her in spite of her triviality, and then it breaks in two and thereafter goes on to show exactly the same fears and vanities and jealousies of love, in exactly the same terms, and for the same man, but in a supposedly totally different lady." Similarly, Smelstor feels that "the symmetrical structure of the book makes it far too stylized" and thus "not nearly so effective as the less rigid format used in *The Hard-Boiled Virgin*," and from her perspective, the problem is that Newman "had originally intended to tell a sympathetic story from the librarian's point of view but entirely changed her plan and decided to have the wife be the heroine" (15). It is true that Newman's ideas about the novel changed as she was writing it. "I'm getting interested in the wife, with whom I'm beginning," she wrote to her niece, "and I didn't intend to" (*Letters* 269). However, her sympathy did not shift from the librarian to the wife but rather enlarged to include both. In creating sympathetic portrayals of both characters by writing from their perspectives in turn, Newman disrupts the expectations of a dualistic world of good/evil, right/wrong. Also, by making many of the feelings of Evelyn and Isabel similar despite their different situations and personalities, she underscores the commonality of women's experiences beyond the labels of *wife, mistress, other woman*.

In "Professions for Women," Woolf characterizes the "Angel in the House" as "intensely sympathetic," "utterly unselfish," and "pure." Sacrificing herself daily, "she never had a mind or a wish of her own, but preferred to sympathize always with the minds and wishes of others" (59). The angel in the house is thus another version of the true woman of the nineteenth century and her counterpart, the southern lady. Newman goes beyond satirizing this female image; she deconstructs it in *Dead Lovers Are Faithful Lovers.* Outwardly, Evelyn Cunningham embodies most of the characteristics of the angel of the house; she showers her care and affection on her husband, centers her life around his interests and career to the exclusion of all other interests, is kind and tactful even to rude visitors, and never expresses a dissenting opinion. Yet Newman portrays these characteristics not as the natural attributes of a happily married woman, but rather as a socially imposed facade of behavior that conflicts with Evelyn's inner life and creates not happiness but misery. Evelyn is not genuinely unselfish but rather narcissistic, and not from extreme self-regard but from a profound insecurity. Her obsession with her own appearance stems from her belief that her body "is all she has to hold Charlton" (Jones, *Tomorrow* 309).[6] She is so convinced that "beautifully disarranged hair and a flattering deference" are essential in pleasing men that she constantly scrutinizes her appearance in mirrors: "Even when her husband was eight hundred miles from the room where he could see her and touch her, Evelyn Cunningham always looked into her little blue-enamelled mirror until her voice had the courage to answer the voice which would call her name in three beautifully separate syllables" (110). Even on their honeymoon, she thanks her god for allowing her to wake before her husband so she can comb her tangled hair, arrange her ribbons, and apply her cosmetics "until the long mirrors could give her enough courage to slip back beside Charlton Cunningham, and to wait for his brown eyes to open into her brown eyes" (10–11). Preparations for his return home after a day's work and for their lovemaking become elaborate rituals before the dressing table.

The angel in the house is usually seen as a devoted mother as well as wife, but because of Evelyn's fear of losing her husband's love, she practices birth control. She is certain that her own mother "was not the only wife who had been transformed into a mere object of respectful veneration" (85) after having a first child. She wonders "if her husband would always go on loving her if her photographs always went on showing her sitting . . . coolly and serenely alone" (85), and although she calls to mind famous men who continued to feel passion for their wives or mistresses after the birth of a child, she feels almost certain that if she has a baby, "her husband could not possibly go on looking at her as if he were looking at a Cleopatra and a Mary Stuart and a Juliet" (86). Newman's subtle references to birth control include Evelyn's circling a date every month in a calendar she keeps hidden and almost regretting that as an Episcopalian she cannot thank the Virgin Mary "for the signal mercy of being able to draw the fifth circle she had drawn on a calendar" since she had married. However, she is grateful she is not Catholic because "she might not have been able to keep her first year of marriage to consolidate her position with her husband" (80–81), presumably because Catholics forbid birth control devices. Newman refers to birth control more explicitly in Evelyn's remembering the talk with her mother the night before her wedding about "the methods which had presumably kept her an only child during the years when such methods had apparently still been necessary" (84).

Kathryn Seidel interprets Evelyn's childlessness and desire to appear unruffled as signs of her dislike and avoidance of sexuality (*Southern Belle* 44). On the contrary, Evelyn considers the bedroom "the centre of her house" (*Dead Lovers* 124) because there she can touch and be touched by Charlton, and she wonders if other wives similarly long for the moment when they can be alone in bed with their husbands. Their physical relationship is so important to her that "she felt sure that even in a less corporeal heaven, her soul would still be married to a golden soul that she could see and that she could touch" (116). After twelve years of marriage, she can scarcely listen to a friend talking about her garden because her "whole back was quivering with consciousness of her husband," and she hears Mrs. Curtiss only through "the hot swift waves" of sexual desire (145). Evelyn also realizes the importance of sexual intercourse as a means of cementing her husband's love for her. Her desire for a sexual relationship with her husband and her reflection that "a baby is a strange result of an emotion like love" (56) contradict the myth of the sexually unresponsive southern lady who regards sex only as a duty and means of procreation.

Evelyn centers her life around her husband's not only in her obsessive concern with retaining his love through her appearance and sexuality, but also in spending her time entertaining wives of men who might be important to Charlton's career and in making "elderly and influential gentlemen show enough interest in her to make her seem important to her husband" (73). Again her inner nature contradicts her outward appearance as a charming, polite hostess. Inside she is seething, wondering "at all the things civilization can teach a woman to endure" (44), including a guest's catty references to Charlton's former interest in her daughter. After her visitor leaves, she mentally expresses exasperation at her changed status from that of a debutante entertaining admirers to that of a wife entertaining boring elderly ladies: "She wondered how a girl can be expected to walk up a church's middle aisle after seven years spent in making herself interesting to young gentlemen, and to stand for ten minutes before the church's altar and its rector, and to walk down the same aisle changed into a woman who can enjoy making herself interesting to elderly ladies whose unimportant marriages have gradually become important marriages" (46).

Evelyn's married life becomes a litany of waiting—waiting for Charlton to come home from the office, waiting after a social dinner until he has danced with the woman on his right and left and can ask her to dance without breaching social etiquette, waiting for a play or concert or opera to be over so she can once again be alone with him. Always insecure about her position, Evelyn fears one day her husband will love her less and eventually lose his love for her altogether. When she sees him flirting at a dinner party, she realizes fully how utterly dependent she is upon him for her very livelihood; the house she lives in, even the water she washes her face with, is not theirs but his. And so she recognizes that "she must assume that her husband's hour with Mrs. Jordon's dark-haired daughter was only prudent politeness to the daughter of a man who might some day be useful to the South-eastern Railway" (108). Her sweet submissiveness and patience are socially sanctioned patterns of behavior necessary, she believes, for survival. Ironically, her husband is planning to leave her in spite of her excessive devotion—not the expected reward for the faithful, loving wife.

Newman was not the first southern woman novelist to question the role of the angel of the house. Her portrayal of Evelyn Cunningham has some similarities to Ellen Glasgow's portrayal of Virginia Pendleton in *Virginia*. Yet Glasgow's Virginia *is* the angel in the house, and she envisions no other way to behave, whereas Evelyn only seems to be the stereotypic angel. Virginia never questions her role, nor do her thoughts reveal a subterranean life chaffing against societal restraints and definitions. Instead of viewing a wife's position with irony as does Evelyn, Virginia believes a woman's centering "her whole existence" around a man to be "divinely right and beautiful" (205). Virginia sacrifices her individuality first to her husband and then to her children, and even when her sacrifices cease to please either, she clings to traditional beliefs about motherhood and wifely duties: "Virginia's conception of duty was that she should efface herself and make things comfortable for those around her. The obligation to think independently was . . . incomprehensible to Virginia" (431).

Like Evelyn, Virginia is rewarded for her devotion as a wife by her husband's interest in a more independent, younger woman. However, Virginia has so internalized the role of the angel of the house that when she realizes Oliver is about to tell her he is in love with a New York actress, "the shame in his eyes awoke in her the longing to protect him, to spare him, to make even this terrible moment easier for him than he could make it alone" (488–89). When he has made the decision to leave her, "there was no rebellion in her thoughts, merely a dulled consciousness of pain" (494). Even though both Glasgow and Newman reveal the pain and ironic lack of reward for being an adoring, self-sacrificing wife, Newman's revelation of the distance between Evelyn's external conformity and her inner feelings was much more threatening to society. Isabel Paterson said of *Dead Lovers Are Faithful*

Lovers: "No man could have written it. Most men will be unable to read it. It says a good many of the things men have tried by every social and economic device to avoid hearing" (4). Perhaps what they have least wanted to hear is that beneath the exterior of a gracious, adoring wife is her discontent and her preference not to die herself (as Virginia wishes to when her husband leaves her), but for her husband to die rather than to lose his love.

Just as Evelyn Cunningham is not portrayed as an angel but as a frustrated, limited woman, Isabel Ramsay is not portrayed as a *femme fatale* but rather as a decent, intelligent young woman who falls in love with a married man. Isabel is not a voluptuous temptress but rather a chaste librarian accustomed to having men look at her "as if they were looking through a glass case at a Gutenberg Bible" (182). Her calm beauty is not threatening to women nor especially exciting to men. Isabel reflects on the contrast between herself and another librarian: "She was sure that every man who came into the library looked at Clare Garrard . . . and she wondered if a man's glance fell on Clare Garrard as the hot sun fell on a border of petunias, and if the perfume of a hundred remembered kisses rose from Clare Garrard's lips and her cheeks and her throat and her arms to tell him that Clare Garrard was remembering all the difference between her body and the body of the man who was looking at her" (201). In contrast, both men and women enjoy looking at Isabel's "serenely parted black hair," her classic profile, and her grey eyes like those of "grey-eyed Athena," Greek goddess of wisdom and the arts, but none of these physical attributes cause any envy in the feminine Carnegie Library's "envious staff" (202).[7]

When Evelyn Cunningham sees Isabel for the first time, not suspecting the young woman's relationship to her husband, "she felt that the girl's grey-eyed beauty was too calm and too quiet and too cool for a man to feel that it was an encouraging beauty" (148). It is Charlton rather than Isabel who encourages their relationship. When Isabel first met Charlton Cunningham in the library, "she had seen only the face of a man who could endure Mrs. John Prince Abbott's conversation" (166). Yet at a dinner party at the Abbott's, his eyes are continuously on her, and she notes his wit and beauty as well as his looking at her "as if she were a woman instead of a Holy Bible" (202–3).

Rather than condemning Isabel for her love for a married man, Newman creates sympathy. Like Evelyn, Isabel is continuously waiting for Charlton, even though she has her job as a librarian to fill her hours. She realizes that "even if a man loves a girl after he has stood before a clergyman and a congregation with another woman, the girl can only have a few of the little crooked scraps which are left when the scissors have cut around the pattern of his life" (150). Not only does she wait to see him through months "of ugly heavy minutes" (269), but even when she is with him, "her whole body was still a waiting body" for his touch (253). Recognizing that Charlton is already committed to another woman causes her pain so intense that it seems physical. When Isabel remembers seeing his wife Evelyn, "she felt as if her whole memory had been cut across by a hot jagged knife. . . . And when she dragged her mind away from that flower-scented picture, she felt as if her whole mind and her whole memory were tearing as helplessly as wet squares of paper" (190). Newman uses crucifixion imagery in describing the pain caused by Isabel's passion for a married man: "She looked down at the aching palms of her hands with surprise that the pain in them had not left its stigmata" (151). Later, after meeting the mail and not finding a long-expected letter from Charlton, Isabel again feels crucified: "She wondered . . . how she could go on walking down the iron stairs while she felt that two long icicles had been struck through the aching palms of her hands, and while she felt that her green skirt would barely cover the two icicles which were burning just under its hem" (162). It is her twenty-seventh birthday and she wonders how she can turn the calendar page to the day's date "against which she would feel that the four icicles had nailed her . . . because she had lived a month for the letter she had been almost sure she would open" on that morning (162).

When finding a romance significantly entitled "Angel" for a library patron, Isabel makes the astute observation thát "writers of old-fashioned love-stories seem to punish a villainess for wanting the very things with which the writers are preparing to reward a heroine for not wanting" (215). Instead of following this pattern of old-fashioned love stories and punishing Isabel at the end, Newman erases the sharp line between the heroine and the villainess. Both women are instead major, sympathetic characters in her novel. Newman creates understanding for both women by providing access into both of their minds and revealing parallel thoughts and observations. For example, when the two first see each other, Isabel wonders "if Mrs. Charlton Cunningham could possibly feel as calm and complacent as she looked" (149), but we know not only that Evelyn does not feel complacent but also that she had wondered the same thing about Mrs. Curtiss a few minutes before, and in almost exactly the same words (146). Both enjoy hearing Charlton say their names "in three beautifully separate syllables" (110, 229), and when he begins his verbal love-making to both by saying that "human speech is not one of the languages of love" (108, 253), each thinks she is the only one he truly loves. In drawing parallels between their thoughts, feelings for Charlton, and experiences of waiting, Newman links their subterranean lives and thus revises the traditional images of the devoted wife and the wicked mistress.

In revising traditional literary images of women, Newman structures not only the two halves of the story but also its ironic, unconventional ending. Annette Kolodny explains that the "inversion" pattern can "even structure the plot, by denying our conventional expectations for a happy ending and substituting for it an ending which is conventionally *un*happy, but which, in terms of the particular work, pleases or satisfies nonetheless" (43; emphasis is Kolodny's). *Dead Lovers Are Faithful Lovers* ends with a grieving widow, but, despite her grief over her husband's death, Evelyn Cunningham feels simultaneously victorious. Her marriage has not ended with a dreaded divorce but with "a beautiful memory" intact, "a memory over which she was dropping the victorious curtain of her very long black crape veil" (294–95). Throughout the novel, Evelyn has thought that death would be preferable to her husband's waning love or unfaithfulness. At first it is her own death that she considers. Barely returned from their honeymoon, she is convinced that "she already loved her husband more than he loved her" (45), a position her mother warned against, and she fears that "she might live long enough to die on the day when he did not love her at all" (46). But soon Evelyn recognizes that she would rather have Charlton dead than to lose his love. When her husband is twenty minutes late from work, she wonders if he has stopped at the club for a drink instead of rushing home to her. Concluding that if he did so he could no longer love her, she decides that she would rather learn that he has been found prostrate across his desk, clutching her picture, or that he has been struck by an automobile while bringing home flowers (59).

The ending of the novel is foreshadowed when Mr. Perryman, the Southeastern Railway's most important vice-president, dies and Evelyn ponders whether all the losses that his widow sustained "could quite weight down Mrs. Perryman's calm consciousness that her marriage was victoriously ended, and that a husband in a black morning coat and striped grey trousers was safely waiting for her in the soil of the most aristocratic town in North Carolina" (120–21). Unlike Mrs. Perryman, who had no "consequence" (119) of her own and had therefore been condescended to even while married (41–42), Evelyn is from an aristocratic Virginia family and will continue "being a great lady in Richmond" (293) even though her husband is dead. Evelyn has ambivalent feelings about the death of her husband; she grieves but also feels a sense of release. As she rides the train with Charlton's coffin back to Richmond, "the pain rushed through every one of her nerves again as she lifted her hand to her little hat" (294), the symbol of her widowhood and Charlton's death. However, she also feels relief; no longer need she fear losing her husband's love, and "her social status is no longer at risk in a world in which her husband's infidelity would have been read as her fault" (Jones, "Foreword" xxii). Although she envisions a life "decorously emptied" (293), she still has her memories, safe from warranted fears of Charlton's possible desertion. Newman also implies Evelyn's repossession of her own life in the contrast between her earlier realization that the house she lived in and everything in it belonged to her husband and her thoughts about a future in which she will walk "into a house which was her house" and look "at her father across her mahogany table and her bowls of white iris and white lilies and white camellias" (294). Newman transforms the conventional tragic ending of the death of a beloved husband into an unconventional happy ending, since Evelyn never suspects her husband's love for Isabel and retains both her happy memories and her position as a "great lady."

The story of the easily consoled widow is ancient, as is the ironic twist at the end of a story. It is the topic of one of the earliest short stories, "The Widow of Ephesis" by Petronius, which Newman had translated for the opening story of her collection *The Short Story's Mutations* to illustrate the antiquity of the "Reversal of the Situation" attributed to Maupassant.[8] But whereas the ancient story questions woman's fidelity and thus makes a misogynist statement, *Dead Lovers Are Faithful Lovers* makes a feminist statement. It can be compared to an earlier short story by Kate Chopin, "The Dream of an Hour" (later renamed "The Story of an Hour"), in which Louise Mallard's uncontrolled sobbing at the reported death of her husband is interrupted by a sense of release, of freedom. "Free! Body and soul free!" she whispers repeatedly. She realizes she will weep again, yet she welcomes "a long procession of years to come that would belong to her absolutely," years when "there would be no powerful will bending hers." When her husband returns home, his reported death an error, she dies from a heart attack, not from unexpected joy as her husband and aunt believe, but from the shock of the sudden loss of her new-found freedom.

Newman had similarly revealed the hidden reality of the apparently sorrowful widow in her first short story, "Rachel and Her Children." The main character, Mrs. Overton, in her thick veil, is the very picture of a grieving widow who has also been bereaved of her children. But behind her concealing veil she is instead reliving the constant constraints of her past life and the relative freedom and importance she had assumed while her daughter was in the hospital. Once again she had poured the coffee "from her own silver urn," carried the household keys, done the marketing, and received visitors (51). When a hymn is sung, she shivers rather than being consoled by the thought that her domineering mother and husband are angels in heaven waiting for her: "Mrs. Overton had no doubt that Mama, tulle cap, black bombazine, and all, and Colonel Overton, beard, temper, and all, would be smiling among those angels, and the idea was not cheering" (48). Sally Overton had hoped after her husband's death at last to be able to do as she pleased, "to talk to the people she wanted to talk to about the things she wanted to talk about" (50). However, her desire was thwarted by her domineering daughter's concern for what was "correct" (49). Acting the proper role first of a wife and then of a widow prevented her from having a life of her own.

Now, instead of grieving at her daughter's death, Mrs. Overton is looking forward to assuming her daughter's place of importance in the home, being asked to dinner by sympathetic friends, and arranging parties for her grandchildren. Her reverie is abruptly halted when she notices a young widow's "decorous look of heartfelt sympathy" directed towards her son-in-law. She suddenly realizes that most of the women who had come to cheer her were also young widows whose daughters—unlike her own—would not discourage them from remarrying. Seeing her future too clearly "back to the side of another Mrs. Foster's table" (52), who this time would not even be her daughter, Mrs. Overton finally begins to weep bitterly. Newman frames her story with the cultural expectation; at both its beginning and end, the townspeople see Mrs. Overton only as "Rachel weeping for her children" (45). But in creating her portrait of Mrs. Overton, Newman has inverted this customary image of the grieving mother and widow. Mrs. Overton is instead a woman lamenting the culturally imposed limitations of her own life.

In her book *Reinventing Womanhood*, Carolyn Heilbrun discusses the rarity of a woman writer creating autonomous roles for her female characters (71–73, 133). Most women writers have portrayed the passive female role as inevitable or have projected action and autonomy onto male characters (139). Frances Newman refused both to accept passive female roles as inevitable and to focus on male characters in her fiction. Instead, she envisioned female characters internally rebelling against male values and moving towards autonomy—without minimizing the difficulties, including the imprint of social codes upon the psyche. In her fiction, Newman subverts, revises, and inverts literary conventions to undermine or question patriarchal attitudes and assumptions about women and their appropriate roles.

5

Experimenting with Novelistic Devices

AN EARLY CHAMPION OF James Joyce and an admirer of Dorothy Richardson, Katherine Mansfield, and Virginia Woolf, Frances Newman was similarly interested in revealing the inner lives of characters, to capture, in Woolf's famous words, "life," which "is not a series of gig lamps symmetrically arranged," but rather "a luminous halo, a semi-transparent envelope surrounding us from the beginning of consciousness to the end" ("Modern Fiction" 150). Explaining the form of *The Hard-Boiled Virgin*, Newman wrote: "I wanted to paint a truthful picture, and I wanted to paint it with strokes which would make it the charming picture I wanted it to be. Therefore, I realized I could not paint it truthfully except by giving a truthful impression instead of an inaccurate photograph—that I would have to go far below the surface of my scenes and of my characters" ("Frances Newman Tells" 6). As Anne Goodwyn Jones notes, Newman was "highly conscious herself of form, and was familiar with—in fact considered herself and was considered part of—the experimental avant garde of the period" (*Tomorrow* 284). Recent critics compare Newman with other modernists, but without offering a close analysis of her style. Kathryn Lee Seidel wrote that Newman's "stylistic innovations paralleled the work of Virginia Woolf and James Joyce" (*Southern Belle* 41), and Joseph Flora cites Woolf as "the major influence on her, especially Woolf's emphasis on small moments and her attention to form," noting Newman's appreciation of "Woolf's ability to reach beneath surfaces" (281).

Newman's concern for the life beneath the surface is especially similar to that of Mansfield and Woolf in her stated desire "to express things only as a woman—as distinct from a man—could express" (Hardwick ii). Sydney Janet Kaplan discusses the "vital link between experimentation and the need to express a definite sense of women's reality," in writing about Katherine Mansfield and Virginia Woolf (120). Woolf's essay "Women and Fiction" asserts a change in women's fiction that is true of Newman's two published novels as well as of her own and Mansfield's fiction: "Women are coming to be more independent of opinion. They are beginning to respect their own sense of values. And for this reason the subject matter of their novels begins to show certain changes. . . . Women are beginning to explore their own sex, to write of women as women have never been written of before; for, of course, until very lately, women in literature were the creation of men" (49). Like Mansfield and Woolf, Newman experimented with novelistic devices in an attempt to capture the essence of women's lives rather than their surface appearances, to express the truth about women's experiences. She once wrote to her publisher Horace Liveright that she thought *The Hard-Boiled Virgin* was "about the first novel in which a woman ever told the truth about how women feel" (*Letters* 205), and she continued her experimentation with novelistic devices in portraying women's inner lives in *Dead Lovers Are Faithful Lovers*. In both novels Newman experimented with narrative structure, point of view, sentence structure, and language. In doing so, she questioned narrative forms themselves; like the twentieth-century women writers discussed by Rachel DuPlessis in *Writing Beyond the Ending*, Newman invented "strategies that sever the narrative from formerly conventional structures of fiction and consciousness about women" (x). Although Newman shared with the writers DuPlessis examines the desire "to change fiction so that it makes alternative statements about gender and its institutions" (x), her narrative strategies differ from those DuPlessis considers.[1]

Experimenting with Novelistic Devices

After writing *The Gold-Fish Bowl*, with its conventional structure and narrative stance, Newman decided the form of the novel that she had inherited from nineteenth-century novelists was not the proper vehicle for portraying the truth of a woman's experience. She was dissatisfied with the structure and style of her first novel, seeing it as merely "a bit of experience" (*Letters* 48), an apprenticeship during which she had learned "that every aspiring novelist must write in the way that is naturally his, but that he must write in the greatest possible perfection of his natural style" ("Frances Newman Tells" 6). In a letter to a friend she was even harsher in her criticism of her first novel, calling it "absolutely untrue to myself in any way, or to any of my ideas" (*Letters* 297). "It is originality and individuality which count today" (Essig), she later advised aspiring writers. Although she was too harsh in her condemnation of her first novel, Newman developed her own unique voice in her second novel by experimenting with novelistic devices and became the "important prose stylist" Reginald Abbott champions in "A Southern Lady Still" (50). The structure of *The Hard-Boiled Virgin* is original, but Jones's observation in *Tomorrow Is Another Day* that "no critics have yet paid the novel's structure the attention it deserves" (284) has continued to remain accurate. This novel contains no chapters or dialogue but instead a series of long episodic paragraphs of 350 to 1800 words (Crawford 148), which reveal the developing consciousness of the central character, Katharine Faraday. Newman's decision to omit all directly quoted conversation from this novel stemmed from her desire to reveal the truth of her characters' lives: "I tried to show my characters as they were," she explained, "and I didn't dare let them speak," for "we practically never say what we think" ("Frances Newman Tells" 6).

Newman chose short episodes rather than long chapters to avoid drawing out incidents unnecessarily, making "every episode as long as I felt that its importance to Katharine Faraday justified" ("Frances Newman Tells" 6). Even the significance of details is measured through Katharine's eyes, and thus her dress is described only when she is concerned about her appearance. Events may seem trivial or even nonexistent; they are important not in themselves but in how they shatter yet another illusion of the sheltered and innocent protagonist. In describing the progress of her novel to Frank Daniel, Newman recounted events described in the newly written portion of the novel but emphasized the minor role that the actual action plays: "Katharine Faraday has had her heart broken three times. . . . She is now in the Blue Ridge Mountains discovering that one may be born in the South and still write something, and she has just read Carnival. One of her brothers has died and left her four thousand dollars and she will shortly be embarking for the Mediterranean. All of that may sound like an Action Story, but I hope and believe the action is well hidden" (*Letters* 196).

The episodes deemphasize action; they have the effect of being complete entities loosely joined together, glimpses into a life rather than one long continuous narration of action. Through making each episode a single long paragraph, Newman hoped "to get a perfect sequence, and—if possible—a perfect sequence of the reader's attention." She objected to the insertion of numbers for the episodes by the typesetter, explaining that each episode should "begin quite low on the page, exactly like a long chapter . . . so that there won't be such an effect of solidity" (*Letters* 210–11). Joseph Frank describes Proust's method of letting characters disappear and then reappear, changed by time (239), and in some ways, Newman's episodes have this effect, although there are no intervening descriptions of other characters or narration of events. Frank claims Proust's "reader is confronted with various snapshots of the characters 'motionless in a moment of vision,' taken at different stages in their lives" (239). The effect of Newman's episodes is similar. The first "snapshot" of Katharine Faraday is of her learning at the age of eight that "the horrifying felicities of the holy bonds of matrimony sometimes follow the horrors of connubial fury" when she has been sleeping in her mother's room because she is ill and witnesses her father's return home after a night of debauchery. The second "snapshot" finds her abandoning her first novel at age ten because her reading has made her "hopelessly Anglomanic" and she has "realized that her own novel must necessarily be an American novel" (13–14).

Experimenting with Novelistic Devices

As these examples illustrate, Newman is making no attempt at
reconstructing a complete history of her character; rather, she is
providing scenes that reveal the developing consciousness of a
young girl.

Unaided by a continuous thread of narrative to provide cohe-
sion to her novel, Newman instead repeats particular phrases
or incidents, sometimes slightly modifying them to indicate a
change in the character's insight or view of the world. Like the
experimental substitution of episodic paragraphs for chapters,
repetition is used to reveal the inner life of her character and the
psychological importance of trivial events. It also discloses dis-
crepancies between what the protagonist has been taught and
the reality she confronts. The first repeated phrase is the injunc-
tion Katharine has read in countless advice columns "that no girl
can allow any man to touch so much as her pocket handkerchief
until he has humbly begged her to become his wife, and that she
cannot allow him to touch anything very much more intimate
than her pocket handkerchief until she has become his wife"
(27). Katharine Faraday remembers this advice when she is seeing James Fuller eight years later, although she has amended "no
girl" to "no southern lady," and she has also learned that "no
gentleman ever thinks of kissing any one except a disreputable
girl until he has asked her to marry him." At this stage in her
life, she presumably does not question these dictates of the genteel tradition, and she remains so innocent that "she did not
think about the occasional touch of his assisting hand, and she
did not think of finding her gloves too warm so that his hand
might touch her arm instead of her long white glove" (116).
Later with Edward Cabot, she "had just discovered that propriety
allowed her to slip her grey glove off her right hand" (144), but
she does not yet suspect that a kiss might be a spontaneous sign
of affection rather than an insult: "She knew that if Edward
Cabot could offer her the insult of an unbetrothed kiss he did
not love her" (151). The pocket handkerchief appears once more
to emphasize the distance she has traveled in her relationships
with men by shifting its reference from a woman's purity to her
intellect: Katharine remarks to Doctor Howe "that he was the

first man who had ever talked to her as if his mind and hers were not the relative sizes of their pocket-handkerchiefs" (199). The slow development of Katharine Faraday's understanding of male/female relationships is also seen through her series of "scientific discoveries," the first when she is kissed by Henry Brown and realizes that she "must have smiled up at Edward Cabot very much as she had smiled up at Henry Brown": "She was feeling all the satisfaction of a scientific discovery because she realized how much her future life might be influenced by the knowledge that if a girl sits down and smiles up at a man who is looking down at her, he will certainly kiss her if he takes either an honourable or a dishonourable interest in her" (186–87). But later when she realizes that something is going wrong with her evenings with Doctor Howe, she does not realize that it involves sitting at his feet or "how to get up and sit down by his side . . . so that he could raise her to his knee" (202). The *leitmotif* of sitting down and looking up at a man continues with Katharine Faraday's observation that the significantly named, more sophisticated Virginia Wise sitting opposite her on a matching chesterfield "seemed to be giving Max Boeckman the feeling that she was sitting at his feet and by his side and on his knee at the same time" (249). This *leitmotif* not only unifies the work by reminding the reader of earlier occurrences but also emphasizes the simultaneous roles women were expected to play—they should at the same time seem to be inferior admirers, equal companions, and sexual enticers. Numerous relationships later, when Katharine fears that "her virtue was probably intact only because Samuel King had breathed so noticeably," she is nonetheless once again "feeling all the satisfaction of a scientific discovery," this time "because she realized how much her future life might be influenced by the knowledge that if a woman tells a man she is hopelessly virginal, he will almost immediately try to prove that she is mistaken" (253). Katharine's "satisfaction" in the two instances comes from learning through her own experience rather than uncritically accepting what she has read in novels or been told. Her eventual movement from a series of relationships in which she is trying to please and impress important men to a relationship in which she is instead the celebrity is noted in a simple reversal in the sitting-down-and-looking-up pattern. With Philip Cobb, "she began to suspect that she might enjoy having him sit at her feet and by her side at the same time" (283). Unfortunately, while the change in this *leitmotif* emphasizes Katharine's growth in self-confidence and power, she is still trapped within the confines of the same pattern of behavior between the sexes.

Other repetitions of parallel situations continue to underscore changes in Katharine Faraday's perceptions of reality and propriety while providing a sense of unity among the short episodes. As a young woman waiting five days for a letter from James Fuller, her adolescent exaggeration of the difficulty of the suspense is seen in her thought that "she was only less unhappy than she would have been if she had been justly accused of murder, and if a jury had deliberated her fate for a hundred and twenty hours" (106). The next time that the agony of suspenseful waiting is portrayed so dramatically—"she realized that for two weeks she would have to endure a suspense less bearable than the suspense she would have felt if she had been justly accused of murder, and if a jury had deliberated her fate for something like three hundred and thirty-six hours" (274)—it has the more reasonable cause that she fears she might be pregnant. Making the two incidents clearly parallel emphasizes Katharine Faraday's maturing sense of proportion.

Similarly, a shift in Katharine's exaggerated sense of propriety is handled through a series of parallel encounters with men who are strangers and a repetition of phrases. When Katharine Faraday and Margaret Cameron accept an invitation to have tea at the New Willard Hotel with two young men to whom they have not been formally introduced, Katharine "felt as publicly depraved as Hester Prynne standing on her scaffold and holding her baby against her scarlet letter" (66). Years later in Versailles, "she suffered the same hot untidy feeling she had suffered when she went to tea at the New Willard with two compatriots who had not been properly introduced to her" (213) when she viewed the fountains with a young man from Mobile. But as she becomes more sophisticated, it takes a famous writer's suggestion that losing her virginity will help her style of writing and his invitation to accompany him to New York to become his mistress to give her "the same hot untidy feeling" (246). Finally, when she meets the playwright Alden Ames in Germany, not only does she "not suffer the hot untidy feeling she had supposed she would always suffer when she talked to a man who had not been properly introduced to her" (270), but she immediately thinks of completing with him the drama she had begun with another writer, her euphemism for finally becoming sexually involved. The repetition of the "hot untidy feeling" emphasizes both how bound she is to propriety and her eventual escape from some of its dictates.

Another narrative strategy that creates structural unity and questions the importance of social success for women through relationships with men is Newman's development of a story or drama motif, and this was the aspect of the novel that most pleased Newman herself. "All of Katharine Faraday's masculine admirers were only actors playing in different acts of the same drama she was writing for herself by living her own life," she explained in an interview ("Frances Newman Tells" 8). Even in the throes of her first infatuation with an older married man, Katharine thinks of her relationship as "the story of Katharine Faraday and Robert Carter" and fears she is "the heroine of a story as sad as the story of the little mermaid and the prince with golden hair" (76). She has read so many romance plot novels that she thinks of her own romantic involvements as stories and makes comparisons with novels she has read. While visiting a friend, she elicits from a young man "a declaration as flaming and as respectful as any declaration . . . Lucy Feverel ever heard" (79).[2] The young man's ancestors, unfortunately, do not meet the approval of her friend's mother. However, after rejecting his advances, Katharine can contentedly read "with complete satisfaction his description of his uncomfortable emotions when . . . the curtain of his life went down on an empty stage" (80), because she sees this conquest as an attainment of the first sign of social success, a "flaming but respectful love letter" (79). The young man's possible feelings have no reality for her, although he is obviously engaged in overdramatization as well, especially since their acquaintanceship has been brief.

Katharine next progresses from merely thinking of her romances as stories to creating romantic stories about the men in whom she is interested. Even before she meets the West Point cadet James Fuller, who is her date for a West Point hop, she has "composed the first episode of the story of Katharine Faraday and James Fuller" (86). After their successful evening together, she "began to compose a more romantic and more carefully punctuated episode in the story" (89). Katharine's creation of fictitious episodes effectively captures the spirit of romantic fantasies of adolescent girls.[3] Simultaneously, it foreshadows Katharine's later career as a dramatist, suggesting her ability to transform experience into art.

Newman presents another version of the story/drama motif through the narrator's viewpoint, emphasizing a more mature and worldly wise perspective than the young protagonist is capable of having. All of the male characters begin to be seen by the narrator as replaceable actors in the various plays of Katharine Faraday's life—the part of the military hero or famous writer can have one actor in the first act and another in the second or third, and as the frequency of her brief encounters with eligible or ineligible men accelerates, a number of men can act in scenes of a single play. When Katharine meets Edward Cabot at her friend's wedding, she does not "realize that this James Monroe back-drop was set for the third act of the play which had begun beside the tall rubber-tree in the drawing room of the West Point Hotel, or that Edward Cabot was playing the part of the martial hero whose more youthful scenes had been played by James Fuller" (125–26). Even after the protagonist has "begun to suspect that Atlanta was not likely to provide a satisfactory hero for the romance of Katharine Faraday" (194), she knows neither the kind of man she is seeking nor that he will only be another transient actor "who could carry on the role whose prologue had been elegantly played by Robert Carter and whose first act had been very badly played by Henry Brown" (195). Thus, when she meets

Doctor Howe, "she did not think of him as the third actor who had played the role of the hero in the romantic drama of Katharine Faraday and the scholarly gentleman" (195).

By the time Katharine is engaged in "the cynical comedy of Katharine Faraday and the eminent author" (249), the male actors begin to overlap. The same day she receives a letter from the author David Hofmann praising her writing style, she forgets to mail a letter she has written to the celebrated writer Frederick Thomas, whose proposal to make her his mistress she has surprised herself by not definitely refusing. But although this letter from David Hofmann releases her from "suffering from her belief that she was in love" with Frederick Thomas (248), she becomes involved with the dramatist Samuel King before she ever meets David Hofmann. Amidst this frequent change in heroes, Katharine wishes that the play would not keep rushing so rapidly towards the climax of sexual involvement that she fears. Just as she had "wanted to linger in the second half of the first act" while "Frederick Thomas had wanted to get on to the third act" (247), so she emerges "shivering from the evening which would have been the scene-a-faire if she had really been playing the third act of the cynical comedy of Katharine Faraday and the celebrated author" with Samuel King (253). Her decision to complete the third act by becoming sexually involved with the playwright Alden Ames is motivated by her desire to make the married David Hofmann suffer as she has suffered from the news of his having become father of another son. The very night she meets Alden Ames, "she was sure that she would be able to finish the play which would make David Hofmann understand what he had lost" (271). Only her fear of pregnancy finally jolts her into a fuller understanding of the potential consequences of her actions and gives her a stronger sense of the reality of her own life.

The drama motif highlights the artificiality of the life of a southern society woman whose primary preoccupations are with form and appearance. What is important is to have a socially desirable man at one's side between the hours of eight and twelve in the evening, because to appear at the theater or a concert or even a restaurant without one is unthinkable. Thus the men who

Experimenting with Novelistic Devices

play the roles in Katharine Faraday's life are interchangeable; she
may have the illusion of being in love with each one in turn, but
the very way in which she thinks of them as characters in the
dramas of her life and the ease with which she transfers her desires from one to the other demonstrate her lack of emotional
investment. Her growth as an individual is seen in her realization
finally that she would rather go to a play alone or with another
woman or not at all rather than to go with a man who could so
totally misunderstand Pirandello's *Six Characters in Search of an
Author*.[4] Newman's choice of a drama to bring Katharine to this
irritated conclusion is significant. To an extent, Katharine finally
stops searching for the author in the play of her life, the famous
man who will give her life meaning and importance, and starts
to become the author of her own life by deciding to become famous and important in her own right through writing plays.

The significance of Katharine's decision has often been ignored
or misunderstood by critics. Louis Gallo defines Katharine's "momentous emancipation" only as her overcoming "her rather in-
explicable chastity" (93), deemphasizing her decision to become
a writer and concluding that if she were only more beautiful she
would have married and "thrived" ("Notes" 93). Although her
initial motivation for beginning her play "No Sheets" was "to
show Alden Ames that she could write a better play than he had
written" (276), after the play is produced her sense of self-worth
and accomplishment is not tied to the approval of men with
whom she has been involved: "She was sure she did not care
whether either Alden Ames or David Hofmann agreed with the
men who said that she had written a brilliant play" (281–82).
Instead of continuing her misguided search for a husband who
would become the author of the rest of the drama of her life,
Katharine decides to have a series of relationships with men,
hoping her new fame as a writer will compensate these men for
her refusal of sexual involvement, which might bring with it the
entrapment of motherhood and the end to her new writing career. Significantly, when she meets Philip Cobb, she does not have
her usual illusion that she is in love for the first time, but rather
she "began to think that at last Georgia was providing another

136

hero for the romance of Katharine Faraday" (282–83). Their first evening together she imagines their last, when "she supposed she would tell him she had been mistaken when she thought she had found a man who had a soul, and when she had hoped that her small celebrity would take the place of her body" (284). Jones sees this relationship with Philip Cobb as undermining Katharine's "belief that she has attained confidence and a sense of identity" in that whereas the roles have been reversed and the young man will sit at her feet, the play remains the same: "there is no way out of the utter predictability of the relationship" (*Tomorrow* 298). Newman does offer little hope for male/female relationships to be open, honest, and equal partnerships; instead, she illustrates that such relationships are difficult if not impossible within the rigid codes of behavior of southern society. It is nonetheless significant that Katharine has been able to reverse roles.

Newman's development of a drama motif throughout her novel and her use of repeated incidents and phraseology provide more structure and unity to her experimental novel than has been previously recognized. *The Hard-Boiled Virgin* is not merely a series of episodes loosely held together, "a jumble of impressions and ideas, based on what the girl hears and sees, and what she feels emotionally" (Hansen), but rather a tightly structured novel that reveals the inner experiences of a woman seeking romance yet managing to avoid a serious commitment, which would lead to a further loss of independence.

Dead Lovers Are Faithful Lovers has a more conventional plot structure than *The Hard-Boiled Virgin,* but Newman's critique of prevailing stereotypes of women and their limited roles in society continues to be reinforced by narrative strategies prompted by her desire to express the reality of women's experience. This novel does contain chapters and dialogue, although the dialogue is kept to such a minimum that it nearly disappears. However, the novel does not follow a simple time sequence of events. Jones notes, "it takes a careful reader to sort out the chronology, and one must be on one's toes even to recognize that Charlton Cunningham . . . never actually completes a sexual relationship with

137

his supposed 'mistress' " (*Tomorrow* 300). Time's passing is noted only within the thoughts of the two major characters. Evelyn Cunningham measures time at first by how many months she has managed not to get pregnant and later by how many years she has been able to retain her husband's affection and thus her respectable married state. Isabel Ramsay measures time by how many ugly minutes and hours and days and months she has cut out of her own body while waiting for a visit from Charlton Cunningham. Thus time itself is seen as revolving around the man whom both women love, and especially for Evelyn he effectually becomes her standard in all things simply by being her husband. Evelyn's father makes this link between time and authority explicit: "You reckon from Charlton Cunningham exactly as the rest of the world reckons from Greenwich" (53), he tells his daughter. Similarly, changes in locale are seen only through the two women's minds as they notice details surrounding them, and often a reference to time follows several pages after the narrator begins to reveal a remembered incident so that it is difficult at first to orient oneself fully.

Although this novel does have a slender thread of a plot, even more than its predecessor it focuses on daily occurrences in women's lives and their interior responses. In this way, it resembles Woolf's *To the Lighthouse* and Mansfield's "Prelude" and "At the Bay," which Newman admired. (She even borrowed the name Isabel Ramsay from Woolf's novel.) After reading *To the Lighthouse,* Newman called Woolf "an extremely intelligent and an extremely feminine writer of fictions—one of the increasing number of women who realize that a woman must write the things a woman feels," and she recognized Woolf's indebtedness to Mansfield in writing *Mrs. Dalloway* ("Review of *To the Lighthouse*"). Although the first half of *Dead Lovers Are Faithful Lovers* covers eleven years, it does so by revealing representative incidents and their corresponding memories through Evelyn Cunningham's mind instead of narrating a series of causally connected events leading inevitably to a climax. Most of the second half of the novel concerns a single day in Isabel Ramsay's life, as she is hoping to receive a birthday letter from Charlton Cunningham and her memory tortures her with flashbacks to earlier scenes with him and to endless scenes of waiting for him to call or visit or write a letter. The climax of the novel—Charlton's death—is withheld for the last sentence and disclosed indirectly through Evelyn's "black crape veil" (295). Newman was pleased with this indirect revelation of his death; she wrote to Lamar Trotti, "I *do* hope you'll think the ending is neat—it's all in the very last three words" (*Letters* 304). Because of her indirectness and oblique revelations, some critics like Donald Davidson have said that the novel lacks logical development and "tells no story" ("Frances Newman"), but Isabel Paterson, while attacking the novel in many ways, commends Newman for the "candor of her revelation of a woman's point of view," which is not only honest but also "an artistic merit" in that "it integrates the work, supplying the structure which is usually derived from that interrelation of action which constitutes a plot" (3).

While she was in the process of writing *Dead Lovers Are Faithful Lovers,* Newman described its basic structure to a friend: "It's a story of a woman who was so much in love with her husband that she spent her whole married life dreading the day when he would love her less. And of course the day came. The second half . . . is in the mind of the girl he falls in love with after about eleven years, and it goes back to the wife when he is dead and she is triumphantly widowed" (*Letters* 277). Lamar Trotti, to whom Newman had written while working on this "modulation" from one mind into the other (*Letters* 278), compared this movement from Evelyn Cunningham's mind to Isabel Ramsay's with a musical composition and credited her with a new technique in fiction ("Tragic Love"). Hansell Baugh also made an analogy with music in discussing this shift; he reported that Newman "conceived the viewpoints" of the two women "as being in different musical keys, and she effected the change of key musically by finding a common chord" (256). Although the musical analogy seems more an idea of Newman's reported by her two friends than an integral aspect of the structure, the transition from one character to another is deft. The viewpoint shifts from Evelyn to Isabel as Evelyn looks across roses into the eyes of a beautiful young woman and wonders that "the girl should be looking at roses instead of at a lover or at a husband who was still a lover" (148), not realizing that this young woman is involved with her own husband who is standing next to her. Just before Evelyn's eyes meet Isabel's for the first time, Evelyn notices the waving green lines in her husband's forehead that indicate sexual excitement and thinks that he must have seen Mr. Curtiss admiring her as she had hoped and that his jealousy has rekindled his waning love into a "bridal love" (141). After the narrative moves into Isabel's mind, the reader quickly learns that she and Charlton are in love, and suddenly what had seemed a confirmation of his continued attraction for his wife becomes an indication that he had caught a glimpse of Isabel before his wife met her eyes. Evelyn has also just wondered if Mrs. Curtiss, whose husband has been flirting with her in front of his wife, "could possibly feel as complacent as she looked" (146), and as the viewpoint shifts to Isabel, who is looking across the roses "into the brown eyes she knew were the eyes of Charlton Cunningham's wife," she is "wondering if Mrs. Charlton Cunningham could possibly feel as calm and as complacent as she looked" (149). Not only does this passage provide a smooth transition from one viewpoint to another, it also links the two women together in their feelings and perceptions, emphasizing the subterranean lives of people, who may be acting calmly while momentous events are happening internally. In countering Grant Overton's assertion that Newman's details are "irritatingly incongruous and irrelevant," H. E. Dounce argued: "Those particulars are sometimes . . . essential for a valid purpose, which is to do in a strict, formal way of her own a thing the stream-of-consciousness writers do in their free and 'incoherent' way—to present simultaneously the doldrums surroundings or trivial acts of her characters, and the emotions that preoccupy them, the memories or anxieties that are breeding typhoons within them."

In addition to Newman's experimentation with the structure and form of her novels, she also experimented with narrative viewpoint in her desire to recreate, like Mansfield and Woolf, a woman's world of daily occurrences, in which what happens is not as important as how her central characters respond to what is happening. In 1927 Newman recommended Percy Lubbock's *The Craft of Fiction* to an aspiring writer as "the only intelligent book on the subject that has yet been written" (*Letters* 263). *The Craft of Fiction* stresses point of view as fiction's most crucial aspect: "The whole intricate question of method, in the craft of fiction, I take to be governed by the question of the point of view—the question of the relation in which the narrator stands to the story" (251). Newman shared Lubbock's conviction about the centrality of point of view. In explaining her writing theories, she said that the writer "must be painfully careful about choosing his point of view and sticking to it" (*Letters* 263).

Newman's narrative stance in her first novel, *The Gold-Fish Bowl,* was not appropriate to her new determination to capture the essence of a woman's experience, nor was it entirely satisfactory in conveying her social criticism. She did not create the intimacy usually associated with first-person narration; the witty and clever narrator Anne Delane is playing a role so self-consciously, and she is so satiric and distanced in describing her own emotions, that a sense of her deeper self is never developed. She reveals to the reader only the surface personality that she reveals to the other characters in the novel. The sense of her playing an expected role can be seen when she returns to Clarendon for Christmas and realizes she is in love with Stephen Eliott but pretends a passionate interest in dull conversations to avoid looking at him and betraying her feelings. She compares herself to a heroine in a novel when she is offered a cup of tea: "Like the exhausted heroines, I was very 'glad of a cup', and I professed a most unfelt interest in Mrs. Birch's Greenwich Village village" (144). Later when she is thinking of possibly marrying Stephen and thus moving to England, she again describes herself in a very distanced, lightly satiric manner as playing an expected role while she is in the very act of privately thinking: "So I lay distractedly in General Delane's bed considering the pros and cons as sensibly as a love-lorn maiden may be supposed to consider such things" (180). This dramatization of her own experiences and thoughts, the way she plays a role rather than revealing her actual feelings, can especially be seen when Anne misses the trolley on her first day of work as a librarian: "That was too much and I collapsed on the bench by the road-side feeling worse than the children of Israel beside the waters of Babylon. Like those temperamental children, I wept. I wept large tears of rage and nervousness and red-haired temperament and if the waters of Babylon or even the Chilhowee River had been more convenient I should probably have sought a watery grave at once" (22).

This overdramatization involves both self-satirization and distancing and has somewhat the quality of an older narrator looking back on youthful experiences with a more mature perspective. Yet often Newman's first-person narration in this novel has more the quality of an outside observer, as when Anne is given a party upon moving into the little cottage on her property and is embarrassed to find herself crying over the generosity of her friends: "And to my own great horror and the consternation of the assembled company, two tears that felt like rather larger Niagaras burst their moorings and dropped on the apple-green crepe jersey" (96). The first-person narrator evokes sympathy and identification, yet Newman undercuts this sympathy and identification with satiric, detached observations. Later, having decided that the man she loves is deceiving her because he has not revealed his actual identity as Edward Hamilton, Anne can describe herself as feeling "as gloomy as a newly-emptied whiskey bottle looks" (221), and when she finally realizes that Stephen Eliott is not the famous writer and that her leaving town without an explanation after their engagement may be an irreparable error, she can toss in a witticism about New York as she enters her friend's house to try to call him: "When I had rung the bell, I was rather sorry that I had come in. Troubles are so much worse indoors, even in New York which hasn't any proper outdoors" (249). As Margaret Manning Duggan explains in her introduction to Newman's novel, " 'The Gold-Fish Bowl' vividly observes the characters and conventions of its time and place, but they are rendered from the outside although, ironically, the narrator is the consummate insider in her circle" (lviii). Anne has been portrayed as extremely clever and witty, but this degree of objectivity and distancing from her own emotions seems implausible. The narrative voice is inconsistent and unsuited to Newman's desire in her later novels to convey the inner lives of her central female characters.

In her later novels, Newman experimented with narrative viewpoint. Believing that "conversation is nothing . . . except surface" and desiring to reveal the essential nature of her characters ("Frances Newman Tells" 6), Newman was interested in writing a novel with "no dialog, no immediate scene, nothing at all but a diffused and purely subjective impression" (A. F. Scott, "Foreword" xv). Anne Firor Scott observes that this "vision of a novel" was "very much like that of Virginia Woolf, who was her exact contemporary" (xv). In fact, a number of critics have commented on similarities between Newman's narrative strategies in *The Hard-Boiled Virgin* and those of Woolf and Joyce, even to the extent of labeling her work stream of consciousness. Gallo asserts that *The Hard-Boiled Virgin* "belongs to the 'modernist' mode, in that its creator utilizes a crude stream-of-consciousness to capture the reflections of her protagonist" ("Notes" 93), and Seidel credits Newman with extending the *bildungsroman's* "narrative boundaries by using the stream-of-consciousness technique" (*Southern Belle* 46). Nelson Crawford suggests the presence of stream-of-consciousness material in comparing her narrative perspective to those of Joyce and Richardson (148). Yet despite Newman's interest in the inner life of her main character, her experimentation with narrative devices followed a different path than the experimentation of Richardson, Woolf, Mansfield, and Joyce in their representations of the stream of consciousness. Unlike much of their fiction, her novel does not attempt to recreate subconscious, nonverbal states of the mind.

Because of the revelation of Katharine's most intimate thoughts, even many of those critics who do not identify these thoughts as stream of consciousness have mistaken Katharine Faraday for the narrator. For example, Harry Hansen described Newman's "task" as being "to reflect what goes on in this mind without seeing it from the standpoint of an adult on the outside looking in." Although he credited her with being "more successful than most writers on the subject," he saw as a weakness the intrusion of "an adult viewpoint," an "ironical sizing up of people and customs . . . too shrewd for even so conscious a worker as Katharine Faraday." Thomas Cadett raised the question of "whether or not Miss Newman has invested the doubts and self-searchings of an undoubtedly clever child with all the subtlety that later came to her" and then concluded that "in this respect . . . the author reveals a quaint inconsistency."

Newman's narrative stance in *The Hard-Boiled Virgin* may seem inconsistent because it does not fit neatly into the traditional categories of point of view, but as Wayne C. Booth observes, when we consider the variety of narrative techniques used in fiction, "we soon come to a sense of the embarrassing inadequacy of our traditional classification of 'point of view' into three or four kinds, variables only of the 'person' and the degree of omniscience" (149). The novel is written in the third person, without any dialogue or dramatic scenes, and since Katharine Faraday's thoughts primarily are revealed, the point of view at a superficial glance might seem to be third-person center of consciousness (Booth 153). Yet whereas the narrator does provide countless insights into Katharine Faraday's mind, the narrator also comments on these thoughts, on the naiveté of the protagonist, and on aspects of the society she lives in. Even in the beginning of the novel, when the perspective presented is primarily that of a young girl with all her misconceptions and discoveries, the narrator explains that when Katharine was eight, "the prestige of double beds and double standards was not seriously diminished" (9), an observation clearly not that of the young Katharine herself. Similarly, when evening is falling on the last night of Katharine's second weekend with James Fuller, we first see Katharine's thought and then the narrator's: "She realized the propriety of his gloomy reference to a bugle-call named Taps, and she was even unhappier than the occasion required" (120). It is the narrator, not Katharine, who realizes the disproportion of the unhappiness. Newman constantly provides this dual perspective of the naive girl or young woman and the older, more worldly wise narrator. Often the narrator explicitly points out what Katharine

144

does not yet consciously realize or question about herself or society. For example, in a scene with Edward Cabot, Katharine is described as enjoying "the public isolation of a darkness she did not think about as a screen for the possible touch of Edward Cabot's experienced hand" (126). Similarly, vacationing with her family in an isolated spot in North Carolina, Katharine "did not know that she disliked being alone because she liked conversation more than any other human diversion" (69). Later when she plans to be the guest of Mildred Cobb and her mother so that she can attend West Point dances with James Fuller again, "she did not know she disliked being a guest because the number of people who could publicly neglect her, and who could see her publicly neglected, was necessarily exactly as large as the number of people with whom she could talk" (113). Didier Coste discusses negation in narration as helping to define the narrator (104–5). In these and numerous other passages negation emphasizes the narrator's wisdom and insight in contrast to the protagonist's naiveté. It creates distance between the narrator and character as in traditional satire, yet the scapegoating often found in satire (Bloom and Bloom 128–29) is absent. Whereas the reader is invited to share the narrator's insights, the gentle tone of the satire invites the reader to identify with the protagonist as well in remembering his or her own youthful foibles. In discussing narration, Gerald Prince has referred to "all the events that *do not* happen but nonetheless appear in the narrative text" as the "disnarrated" (Coste 103–4).[5] In keeping with her focus on the interior life rather than external action, Newman's use of negation is somewhat different. She relates what a character is not thinking or realizing rather than an event or action that fails to happen.

According to Anne Goodwyn Jones, "all of the action comes to the reader not just through the point of view of its heroine, Katharine Faraday, but through the voice of an omniscient but circumlocutory and ever-apparent narrator" (*Tomorrow* 283). The narrative point of view is not simple omniscience, however, even though thoughts of characters besides Katharine are disclosed. These glimpses into the minds of other characters are so brief

Experimenting with Novelistic Devices

and superficial that it is easy to read the entire novel without realizing the narrator has been inside any mind but her own and
Katharine's, especially since these thoughts of others always concern Katharine. When Katharine is fifteen, we learn that her
mother "had decided that the increasingly democratic sympa-
thies of her god would not enter the sphere of women before
Katharine Faraday was nineteen years old" and thus "that even
the necessities of Eleanor Faraday's wardrobe must give way to
the necessity of providing Katharine Faraday with several intimate friends whose great-grandfathers had given their names to
the counties of the more distinguished southern states" (57). Although it is conceivable that she might reveal such a thought to
Katharine, the idea is not filtered through her daughter's perspective but through the narrator's. Later the narrator uses the
same device she has used with Katharine of revealing what the
mother has not thought, thus implying access into her mind; however, again, what is revealed concerns only Katharine: "Since her
mother had never suspected that Katharine Faraday might ever
be interested in any subject a man could be interested in, she had
told her that a woman must always expect to be bored" (73–74).
When the narrator reveals Katharine's brother's thoughts, it is
to satirize his reasons for never talking to her: "Since Arthur
Faraday was sure men would never publicly admit that they had
seen their best days by inviting women into the polls women had
nothing at all to do with inventing, and since he did not think
Katharine Faraday was likely to charm votes out of his enemies,
he never conversed with his youngest sister" (158). These infre-
quent glimpses can be seen as a violation of Newman's narrative stance, but they are consistent with the narrative function of
presenting the primacy of a character, which Seymour Chatman
labels "centering" (147–48). They also contribute to the development of a sophisticated narrator who looks with amused detachment at the characters and at southern culture and social mores.
By not limiting her perspective to that of her main character,
although still focusing solely on her life, Newman has created
a narrative stance that enables her to develop the feelings and
inner experiences of a young woman growing up in the South

146

while satirizing both the restrictive society she is in and her naive beliefs in the myths that it perpetuates.

Dorrit Cohn's section on "Consciousness in Third-Person Context" in her book *Transparent Minds: Narrative Modes for Presenting Consciousness in Fiction* is helpful in further distinguishing Newman's narrative viewpoint and in comparing it to Mansfield's and Woolf's. Cohn describes three methods for this presentation of consciousness in third-person narration: psycho-narration, quoted monologue, and narrated monologue. Psycho-narration involves "the narrator's discourse about a character's consciousness"; quoted monologue, "a character's mental discourse," either introduced or not; and narrated monologue, "a character's mental discourse in the guise of the narrator's discourse" (14). Whereas Mansfield and Woolf use a combination of these three techniques of presenting a character's consciousness, Newman exclusively uses the first. Her character's thoughts are always presented through the perspective of the narrator. Never is there the sense of having entered directly into the stream of consciousness of a character as Mansfield does in "Prelude" and "At the Bay." For example, in "Prelude," when Beryl is preparing for bed, only the individualistic language used to reveal Beryl's thought patterns indicates that a recurrent fantasy is being disclosed:

> She shut her eyes a moment, but her lips smiled. *Her breath rose and fell in her breast like two fanning wings. The window was wide open; it was warm, and somewhere out there in the garden a young man, dark and slender, with mocking eyes, tiptoed among the bushes, and gathered the flowers into a big bouquet, and slipped under her window and held it up to her.* . . . She turned from the window and dropped her nightgown over her head.
>
> "How frightfully unreasonable Stanley is sometimes," she thought, buttoning. (63; italics added)

Here, casual readers may be at first disoriented by the representation of the stream of consciousness and come to the quoted monologue before realizing that the preceding scene was wholly within Beryl's mind and not actually happening. This passage moves from descriptive narration to a narrated monologue (in italics) back to narration and finally to a quoted monologue. The narrated monologue remains in the third person and past tense but uses Beryl's idiom to suggest a rendering of her consciousness; it creates a sense of immediacy and allows Mansfield to weave in and out of Beryl's mind without transitions. The narrator is present but fades into the background as Beryl's fantasy is represented. In contrast, Newman's narrator is ever-present, reporting the character's thoughts and feelings and even commenting on what the character does not know. Katharine Faraday fantasizes about meeting a romantic young man, just as Beryl does. But instead of recreating the immediacy of Katharine's fantasy of meeting and marrying an English diplomat, Newman's narrator reports it: "She knew that unless she sprained an ankle in Rock Creek Park within the next six weeks, and unless a tall young Englishman rode by on his devoted horse very soon after she had sprained her ankle, she would not be likely to find an English husband, since tall young English diplomats do not often ride down the streets of Atlanta" (89). Here Newman is characteristically presenting her character's inner life through psychonarration. Since psycho-narration is the least direct means of rendering the consciousness of characters in third-person narration, it creates a distance from the characters appropriate to Newman's satiric voice. In its gently mocking tone, Newman's revelation of Katharine Faraday's thoughts is similar to Woolf's presentation of Mr. Ramsay's thoughts about his own mind in *To the Lighthouse*. Woolf moves from narrator statement (with a hint of light sarcasm) into a representation of his thoughts through both narrated and quoted monologue: "It was a splendid mind. For if thought is like the keyboard of a piano, divided into so many notes, or like the alphabet is ranged in twenty-six letters all in order, then his splendid mind had no sort of difficulty in running over those letters one by one, firmly and accurately, until it had reached, say, the letter Q. He reached Q. Very few people in the whole of England ever reach Q. . . . He dug his heels in at Q. Q he was sure of. Q he could demonstrate. . . . 'Then R . . . ' He braced himself. He clenched himself" (53–54). Woolf's juxtapo-

148

sition of the narrator's perspective with that of her character creates an irony comparable to Newman's; Mr. Ramsay does think of himself as having a splendid mind, and yet the narrator simultaneously gently mocks his sense of self-importance. Similarly, Newman lightly satirizes Katharine's naive trust in whatever she has read and her reasons for enjoying conversation with a young married professor in the following passage:

> Katharine Faraday had never conversed with a man who gave lectures about English literature, and American fiction still painted such respectful portraits of American professors that she had no reason to doubt either their erudition or their intelligence. . . . No sensible girl ever damaged her fragile reputation by talking to a man through the bars of matrimony. But she could not resist the consoling ease of talking to a man who could not possibly suppose that she wanted him to ask her to marry him, and who could not possibly mortify her by interrupting a courtship with the announcement of his engagement to a girl who could hardly be as clever as she was. (184–85)

Although Newman's tone is similar to Woolf's, again Katharine's thoughts and feelings are reported rather than represented; they are filtered through the consciousness of the narrator.

Despite Cohn's assertion that psycho-narration is "rarely used simply to follow consciousness through its paces" rather than to take advantage of its flexibility in compressing, expanding, or arresting time (34–41), Newman uses the technique extensively throughout her novel, capitalizing on its advantage of allowing the articulation of thoughts that remain unverbalized or even unrealized by a character. As we saw earlier, Newman is interested as much in what Katharine Faraday does not know as in what she does know, and much of the witty, sophisticated humor arises from the ironic distance between what the narrator (together with the privileged reader) realizes and what the naive young Katharine fails to recognize. This distance between the narrator and Katharine further distinguishes the narration as *dissonant* in Cohn's terminology and implies the narrator's "superior knowledge of the character's inner life" as well as a "superior ability to

149

present it and assess it" (Cohn 29). In psycho-narration, attention is focused on the narrator's "own articulate self: a discursive intelligence who communicates with the reader about his character" (Cohn 25). In *The Hard-Boiled Virgin,* the narrator is such a strong presence as to seem almost a character in the story.

Although Newman's narration does not represent the stream of consciousness of her characters, she, like Mansfield and Woolf, uses free association to link seemingly unrelated subjects together. In Mansfield's "At the Bay," while Linda enjoys her aloneness when the family is at the beach, she thinks a recurrent thought, "Was there no escape?" The word *escape* transports her to the veranda of her childhood home with her father promising, "As soon as you and I are old enough, Linny, we'll cut somewhere, we'll escape" (115). Similarly, in *Mrs. Dalloway,* Clarissa thinks of her husband dropping a hot-water bottle and then remembers a scene with Sally Seton that reveals her deep and erotic love for her friend. Two pages later, Clarissa is remembering holding a hot-water can and "saying aloud, 'She is beneath this roof. . . . She is beneath this roof!' " (39). The mental image of hot water has triggered old memories and draws the reader into the stream-of-consciousness passage. In both of these instances, the association of past images or words with present ones makes the stream-of-consciousness passages psychologically realistic. In Newman's novel it is the *narrator's* thoughts rather than a character's that sometimes move by free association and provide coherence within an episode. In one episode, the narrator moves from thoughts about social status and obligations to thoughts about flowers through the observation that "Katharine Faraday's mother had lived most of her well-bred life before gardening succeeded charity as the social ladder with the smoothest rungs" (188). The narrator next reveals that Katharine's mother's "impersonal" admiration for flowers led her to discharge social duties by readdressing boxes of flowers she received "as soon as she had observed the name and colour of the flowers she must mention in the note of thanks" (188). The topic turns to the gardenias an admirer has sent Katharine for her birthday, which are put on display by the mother as "visible evidence of her youngest daughter's attractions" (189), and then to the red roses sent by Neal Lumpkin to Katharine, some of which she puts in a vase and the rest of which she takes to Sarah Rutledge. As Jones notes of this passage, "Such a structure has in fact an organic unity perceptible after close reading. Newman was very interested in stream of consciousness" (284). Jones stops short of actually calling this or any other passage of Newman's stream of consciousness although Newman's narrator does reveal the innermost thoughts of her main character, Katharine Faraday.

In *Dead Lovers Are Faithful Lovers*, Newman again tells her story through a third-person narrator, but this narrator is not as distanced or satiric as that in her previous novel. As in *The Hard-Boiled Virgin*, Newman experiments with narrative viewpoint in delving beneath the surface of expected behavior to reveal the inner reality of women's experience, although she does not directly represent the stream of consciousness of her characters. Yet her shifts in time and oblique references to past events through her character's memories, even though these rememberings are announced, do have the effect of dislocating the reader and compelling a close reading.

Although Charlton Cunningham is a major character in *Dead Lovers Are Faithful Lovers,* he is seen entirely from the outside. Newman explained why she had presented him from the minds of the two women who love him rather than from inside his own mind: "It would be absurd for me to write about a man's mind, or a Northern woman's mind, or a European's mind. I think writers should stick to the things they really know" ("Woman's Mind"). Her concern remains with the interior lives of her female characters, and she is sympathetic to both. Whereas satire effectively emphasized the ridiculousness of roles and codes of behavior for women in *The Hard-Boiled Virgin,* the sympathetic portrayal of the dependent wife striving desperately to retain her husband's love by carefully tending her body and by playing all the games her culture has taught her makes the same point in a different manner. Newman creates a greater identification with the plight of her characters by refraining from the distancing narrator comments that so characterized *The Hard-Boiled Virgin.*

Experimenting with Novelistic Devices

Instead, the psycho-narration in this novel is *consonant* in Cohn's terminology; the narrating voice "yields to the figural thoughts and feelings even as it reports them" and somewhat "fuses with the consciousness" presented (Cohn 31, 26). For example, it is Evelyn Cunningham and not just a more astute narrator who realizes that her husband scarcely knows more about her than what could be learned from a photograph:

> And she fell to thinking that if Charlton Cunningham had received her from the protection of a fat eunuch with a curved sword instead of from the hand of John Rolfe Page, and from the folds of a black Egyptian veil instead of from the folds of Chantilly lace . . . , Charlton Cunningham could hardly have begun his wedding-night with a woman who was less known to him. And while she was shaking all of her very light brown hair to the top of her head, she was thinking that he had done something very much like pulling her out of a Jack Horner pie by a frequently photographed head. (54–55)

Evelyn's recognition that Charlton was primarily attracted by her beauty leads her to reflect that it may be more difficult to keep him than it was to attract him, because he might some day wake before she has had time to repair to the bathroom to straighten her curls and lace and apply fresh cosmetics. Also, marriage affords a much narrower stage for drama than did courtship: "Her two breasts quivered with the realization that marriage is a drama played in dressing-rooms without footlights and in visible wings oftener than it is played behind the footlights which drawing-rooms and ball-rooms and motor cars provide for courtships, and that it is a drama on which the curtains of propriety do not close at the same convenient intervals" (46–47). Evelyn is not the naive young girl that Katharine Faraday was; she is the successful debutante become wife. The narrator need not emphasize the insights she lacks or the illusions she holds. Instead, the character clear-sightedly examines her position and determines a course of action. The drama of her life is not a series of fantasized relationships with men but rather an attempt to make herself continuously interesting to her husband in the only ways available to her—by remaining childless and beautiful and arousing his passion and by making herself important in his eyes by attracting the attention of important men. Only on a few occasions does the narrator comment on what Evelyn does not realize: once when she does not know that her thoughts about love making with her husband are reflected in the smile she is giving to her husband's colleague (89) and once when she prepares to act interested in an opera "since she had never heard that Giacomo Puccini was not a composer whose music should be admired or even enjoyed" (95). These departures from Newman's usual narrative voice in this section of the book are, however, slight enough not to detract from the sense that we are viewing what is happening through Evelyn's consciousness, even though it is reported rather than represented.

Isabel Ramsay is similarly sympathetically portrayed, usually through a revelation of her thoughts, although at one point the narrator does intervene to explain what she is not thinking or feeling, as the narrator did continuously in *The Hard-Boiled Virgin*. Until she sees the envelope with Charlton Cunningham's handwriting, Isabel is conscious of her every thought and her every attempt to keep her mind active so it will not keep remembering past experiences with Charlton; she is "feeling that she could not go on enduring the consciousness of her own consciousness, and that she could not go on cutting her mind and her body into such ugly heavy minutes" (211), minutes representing the time that she has been apart from him. Earlier, when she remembered seeing Charlton's wife, Isabel felt "as if her whole memory had been cut across by a hot jagged knife, and as if her whole memory and her whole mind and her whole soul were wet with the scarlet drops that were falling from the jagged wound the hot red knife had left" (190). Yet after she receives Charlton's flowers and touches her name on the accompanying envelope, "she did not realize that she felt them burning a quick narrow passage from her knee to the very centre of her body" (225). Newman's shift from an unobtrusive narrator to one that begins commenting on Isabel's unrealized thoughts and emotions creates the sense that Isabel is overwhelmed by her emotions, which have superseded her characteristic analytical thought. Thus, the shift in narrative voice is not a distancing device but one to suggest Isabel's emotional state. Later, as Isabel "was thinking of all the careful ministrations she was about to give the body she was sure Charlton Cunningham would not see," she walked through her house without looking out the window at her flowers and "without realizing that she did not know when her own body had become more important to her than roses and iris and tulips" (233). She can think only of the near future when she will see Charlton, and the suddenly highly visible narrator spends several pages explaining what Isabel is uncharacteristically not remembering or not suspecting about herself.

Except for these few instances of narrator comment on Evelyn's or Isabel's not knowing or remembering, the narrator reports almost exclusively what these two characters are thinking or feeling or observing. Even descriptions of their appearances are handled primarily through their own self-inspections in mirrors or when bathing and through their brief viewing of one another. These reported thoughts and feelings have the effect of bringing the reader into the consciousness of the characters, even with some of the lack of seeming rational order that characterizes stream of consciousness. For example, when Isabel looks at the librarian Miss Currier while remembering seeing Charlton's wife in the gardens in New York, it takes a close reading to understand that this is what is happening and that her view of Miss Currier is not obscured by a literal picture: "And while she was looking at Miss Currier through a flower-scented picture of two sun-burned hands holding a coat towards the black velvet shoulders which led up to a very white throat and a very white face, she walked on up towards the room where Miss Currier was waiting" (170–71). The clue to this glimpse into Isabel's memory is the "very white throat" and "very white face"; Isabel repeatedly remembers Evelyn's white throat and face when she thinks of her, and this scene is etched into her memory and reoccurs in her mind numerous times. Newman is quite close to representing the stream of consciousness here, but more often her narrator summarizes her characters' thoughts, using the same language for both instead of creating idiosyncratic, identifying language for each character as Mansfield does in "Prelude" and "At the Bay" and as Woolf does occasionally in *To the Lighthouse*. Both characters use the same language in describing Charlton's evidence of sexual excitement—Evelyn sees the "green veins that had waved their forked lines up Charlton Cunningham's forehead and across to his temples" (143) as a sign that he is still in love with her after eleven years, and shortly thereafter, Isabel remembers the first and second time "she had seen two forked veins wave their green lines up his forehead and across to his temples" (189). The passages are nearly identical, even though we are seeing Charlton from two different characters' perspectives. Similarly, as we have seen, each enjoys hearing him say her name "in three beautifully separate syllables" (110, 229). Newman sacrifices to an extent the effect of actually being within each character's mind in order to underscore the similarity of their feelings for Charlton and to erase distinctions between the two women.

Newman's complex sentence structure and her use of language in her two published novels, like her experimentation with narrative structure and point of view, are directed towards her revelation of the interior lives and experiences of southern women. Her style of writing is indirect in dealing with such taboo topics as menstruation, the size of the male phallus, birth control, sexual desire, and venereal disease—topics that her female characters ponder but are unable to inquire about or discuss openly. Newman once flippantly remarked that the "necessity of circumventing" the censors of the *Atlanta Constitution,* in which her articles appeared regularly, was responsible for her dense style of writing (*Letters* 144), and the necessity of escaping the censor's pencil by indirectness in fiction is exemplified by one of the passages deleted by T. R. Smith from the first proofs of *The Hard-Boiled Virgin.* The young Katharine, accidentally seeing her older brother naked, never again wishes to "go over to a sex which could be positively identified only by such hairy legs and by a russet reptile whose horrifying shape and size must surely be the result of some disease like the disease Mildred Cobb said was responsible for her Aunt Ellen's increasingly enormous nose"

("Two Passages"). The reptilian phallic symbol was considered too obscene by her editors to be published, even though in *Dead Lovers Are Faithful Lovers* Newman was able to mention "a young man who was not murmuring his desire to know whether or not the Carnegie Library owned any books on phallic worship" (217).

Newman's imbedding and concealing meaning through the complexity of her sentence structure and through figurative language and allusions is also influenced by her conviction that "inferences are pleasanter than statements" (*Letters* 161). She admired Henry James for "his pleasant habit of taking his readers with him on his long journey towards the point of his sentence instead of giving them merely the point" (*Short Story's Mutations* 169), a technique she adopted in her own writing. However, she was also well aware of the danger of imitation, the necessity of making certain "every phrase is your own," and the importance of sharing "your innermost emotions" in writing fiction (*Letters* 258). Novelists, she felt, must be true to their own experience and search deeply within themselves for the substance of their fiction (*Letters* 263).

Newman was determined to get beneath the facade of the southern lady to reveal the inner life, regardless of how "unladylike" it was. A reviewer of *The Hard-Boiled Virgin* asserted that while its author "doesn't believe she knows any more about the minds of women than other women do," Newman herself had commented that "[o]ther women are just afraid to tell all that I told in the 'Virgin' " ("Woman's Mind"). Thomas Cadett remarked that Katharine Faraday's "less creditable thoughts are recorded with a fine courage and a faithfulness that deserve nothing worse than surprise and certainly not disgust, since we all have them," but other contemporary critics were offended because many of these thoughts center on reproduction and sexuality. John Macy complained that *Dead Lovers Are Faithful Lovers* was "*fresh* in the wrong slang sense of the word" (432), and William Langfield described *The Hard-Boiled Virgin* as "hover[ing] between the unseen and the obscene," calling Newman "scientifically frank in frequent references to certain biologic facts

Experimenting with Novelistic Devices

of feminine anatomy and physiology," despite her indirection. Newman herself felt that since sexuality had been recognized by psychologists as "one of the fundamental instincts of life" and since it "plays such an important part in the lives of human beings, consciously or unconsciously, then the literature which deals with human beings must take cognizance of sex" (Rothermel). She explained that whereas earlier books had avoided mentioning sex "because it was not considered polite to mention it or to be conscious of such a force existing," she felt "it far better to tell the truth about life from the beginning and thereby avoid disillusionment" (Rothermel).

Newman's preference for indirection and implication rather than "flat-footed declarations" (qtd. in Overton 225) can be seen in her description of Katharine Faraday's first menstrual cycle in *The Hard-Boiled Virgin*. Because "her chest was flatter" than her two closest friends' were, Katharine "felt her defeat when Mildred Cobb . . . explained her absence [from school] with consciously reticent references to her mother's unwillingness to have her feet wet," because she realized the absence "could only mean that Mildred Cobb had become a woman" (54). When Sarah Rutledge "refused to wade because her mother thought the water was likely to be too cold, Katharine Faraday recognized the same conscious reticence" (54). Her own initiation into womanhood is anticlimactic since she, unlike her two friends, is not an eldest daughter, and "regular recurrence had naturally lessened" her friends' interest:

Katharine Faraday's mother did not lay down her comb when she received the announcement of an event which Katharine Faraday would have found alarming if her acquaintances had allowed her to live fifteen years in the state of innocence her mother thought good breeding required. She assured Katharine Faraday that the state of her health did not require the interruption of her education for even one morning, and she did not mention the possible consequences of wet feet. Since the day and the Misses Washington's garden were completely dry, Katharine Faraday was saved from the necessity of exaggerating

157

her mother's concern, but she was obliged to abandon reticence sooner than either she or Mildred Cobb thought good breeding allowed. (54–55)[6]

Newman was not merely conforming to conventional morality or displaying a stylistic preference; her allusive language is consistent with her indirect narrative stance towards a girl who is learning and unlearning southern artifice.

Sometimes Newman's references to taboo topics are more direct, as when Katharine learns about birth control from her friend Sarah, who shows her a "little grey box" on her wedding day and tells her it "would delay the advent of Rutledge Simpson until he could be born in the quarters of a first lieutenant" (127). When Katharine later visits her friend, Sarah finally abandons a "conscious reticence about the illness which had not allowed her to cross the harbour" to meet Katharine (145) and tells her reluctant listener about "the probable reasons why the contents of the little grey box . . . had not prevented the probability that Rutledge Simpson would be born in a second lieutenant's quarters in July" (149). Although the allusions to birth control and pregnancy are unmistakable, Newman never uses these terms.

Perhaps the most circumlocutious of Newman's handlings of taboo topics in *The Hard-Boiled Virgin* concerns the mysterious cause of the death of Katharine's older brother. Katharine cannot help wondering about "the strange circumstance that Arthur Faraday had apparently died without having any good reason for dying." In response to her "well-bred questions" about his death, her sisters "retreated either into their grief or into their wedded dignity"; newspapers provide no account of its cause, and even her mammy will divulge no information, so Katharine has to puzzle out the mystery herself (167). She remembers overheard conversations about "some unfortunate gentleman . . . suffering or dying or dead from a disease of a private nature" and about the unheeded warnings of her aunt to a "tired young woman . . . against the only man who wanted to marry her," and she reflects on the woman's subsequent death after the death of her infant (168–69). Pondering these incidents, Katharine decides to research the matter, and when she finds her mother in the library she pretends she wants to read about the Smithsonian Institution to explain her choice of the *S* volume of the encyclopedia. Finally the hints pointing to syphilis culminate in Katharine's reflections on a disease spread by Columbus's crew: "Ten minutes later, she was meditating on her discovery that the amorous Latin natures of Christopher Columbus's mariners had introduced Europe to a disease which did not actually follow the law of the sea far enough to respect the frailty of women and children, but which provided men with a consequence of polygamy and even of monogamy that seemed to be nearly as uncomfortable as a baby" (170–71). Newman hints of abortion even more obliquely: in reading medical texts because of her interest in an admiring young surgeon, Katharine realizes "that newspapers were evidently wrong when they politely ascribed all operations to appendicitis," and when her young surgeon is "suspected of an operation which was not for appendicitis," she looks elsewhere for a lover (232).

Newman's indirection is accomplished through complex sentence structures that realistically capture the way in which sheltered young women in the South received information about taboo topics. As Marjorie Smelstor observes, "Newman's technique suggests that the search for truth is not a simple process and that an author must employ stylistic devices to indicate the intricacies of the search" (15). Ninety-five percent of Newman's sentences in *The Hard-Boiled Virgin* are complex or compound-complex, and her average sentence length is sixty-seven words, with a range of five to 165 words.[7] These complex, lengthy sentence structures mirror the complexity of the search for truth in a society that continuously erects facades and "polite fictions" and sees innocence and reticence as characteristics of the well-bred. Nearly half of Newman's sentences in this novel begin with a conjunction, creating the effect of a continuity of thought and the mind's associations and often reflecting Katharine's assimilation of bits of information in her attempt to understand the world more fully. For example, the description of Katharine examining her undeveloped body in a mirror after a bath and then reflecting on how babies are born illustrates Newman's use of complex sentence structures and coordinating conjunctions to convey Katharine's circuitous, accumulative quest for understanding:

> Between her flat chest and her thin legs, she notices a line she had never noticed before—a delicate line which was slightly browner than the area she thought was her stomach, and which began just below the curious little dent her mammy called navel. And she had a sudden revelation that when her first child—of whose advent she had so little doubt that she had already baptized her Violet, with Diana reserved for her younger sister—came into the world, the part of herself which she thought was her stomach would burst along the delicate brown line, and that she would naturally shriek, and that her daughter would dart into the world like Pallas Athena darting from the brain of Zeus, and that a doctor would then give her ether and sew her up. (35–36)

As in *The Hard-Boiled Virgin*, in *Dead Lovers Are Faithful Lovers* Newman alludes to potentially objectionable topics, not to shock readers but to reveal women's actual thoughts and concerns. A woman's menstrual cycle is alluded to in Evelyn's circling a date every month on a "little calendar hidden in her olivewood desk" (80) and being grateful for continuing to be able to do so, since she wishes to remain childless. Lesbianism is referred to in "the unbelievable rumours that some peculiar women preferred the society of other women even in the later hours of the evening" (137) and in Isabel's overhearing "the reasons why so many women were preferring to exchange affections with other women instead of with men who were not feeling what women were feeling" (276). Some implications are more oblique, like the possible reference to condoms in the "alarmed" reference librarians' discovery of "a round aluminum box which contained three round objects no member of the department's staff had ever seen before, but which no member of the department's staff apparently had any difficulty in recognizing" (197).

In this novel, Newman begins sentences with coordinating conjunctions to suggest a continuousness of thought, sometimes in combination with lengthy, complex sentences that reveal the inner life Evelyn wants to keep hidden from her husband. In the following passage, the repetition of coordinating conjunctions also emphasizes Evelyn's obsessive concern with her marital relationship:

> She was sure she had married the man whom she loved most. And she was sure she had not married the man who loved her more than any man who had loved her. And she could not forget the mornings when her mother had sat beside her and told her that a wife's love always grows and a husband's love always lessens. And she did not want her husband to suspect that during all the minutes between nine o'clock and five o'clock, she might listen politely and talk politely, and drink tea with one lump of sugar and slice of lemon, and embroider her four initials on napkins of unmistakably Austrian damask, and say three no-trumps and then prove that she had been justified in raising her partner's bid, and dip dark green artichoke leaves into yellow hollandaise sauce, and read the biographies of all the most celebrated enchantresses of history—but that she was waiting for him during all those eight hours, and waiting just as consciously as she had been waiting since she had looked down at the little blue clock and seen that at last the shorter hand was pointing to a silver five, and the longer hand was pointing to a silver twelve. (57)

Newman's multiple negatives also contribute to the density of her prose. Sometimes these negatives simply indicate a character's preferences or inclinations, as in the following sentence: "She did not want to discover that he suspected her of an attachment he had not invited her to conceive, and even when she met him under the amorous influence of a party and of Saint Valentine's Day and of a game called Clap in and Clap out, she did not want him to offer her the indignity of a kiss" (*Hard-Boiled Virgin* 46). Often, however, negatives indicate the distance between the narrator's knowledge and a character's innocence or emphasize the prohibitions of the restrictive southern society:

> Since she had known for three years that no gentleman ever thinks of kissing any one except a disreputable girl until he has asked her to marry him, she did not think of what she might feel

if James Fuller's lips touched her lips, or of what she might feel
if his cheek touched her cheek. . . . When she walked with him
in front of the panoramic back-drop of Flirtation Walk, she did
not think about the occasional touch of his assisting hand, and
she did not think of finding her gloves too warm so that his
hand might touch her arm instead of her long white glove, and
she did not think about what he might be feeling when she sat
beside him. (116)

As we saw, Newman uses negatives less extensively in *Dead Lovers Are Faithful Lovers* to indicate a lack of awareness in her characters, as when "Isabel Ramsay did not know that her mind was
shut in between the hot high walls of waiting" (249). However,
in this novel Newman's negatives also emphasize women's subterranean lives, the private thoughts they cannot reveal to others
because these thoughts are not socially acceptable. For instance,
when asked to speak in a library staff meeting, Isabel "knew she
would not say" that soon "she would no longer have to look at
fifteen other feminine members of the Carnegie Library's staff
every day" or "that her memory was bleeding. . . . And she knew
she would not say that she wondered how she could have become
civilized enough to sit still in her brown chair" when Charlton at
that moment might be trying to reach her by telephone or tele-
gram (205). Similarly, Evelyn realizes that she will soon have to
think of something to say to the elderly and influential Mr. Perryman but that she cannot voice her actual thoughts: "But she
could not ask him if he was wishing that he was back in a room
where he could see Mrs. Perryman's wrinkling blonde smile.
And she could not ask him if he was wishing that he could kiss a
mouth which was growing thin and narrow and pale from the
passing of fifty years" (72–73).

In both novels, Newman indicates sexual arousal through figurative language. Newman's allusions to Katharine Faraday's sexual feelings involve "a fountain [that] rose and fell and dropped
its electric spray through her thin body" (75), and Frank Daniel
explains somewhat euphemistically himself that Katharine's "last
name is that of the discoverer of the principle of the dynamo,

because falling in love has an electrical effect" on her ("Frances Newman's Novel Draws"). Although the image remains essentially the same throughout the book, the spray is sometimes "radiant" (79, 107) or "a rainbow spray" (259, 263), and once it more explicitly rises "up from under her delicate brown line" that she had first noticed below her navel during puberty (107). At first Katharine associates this sensation with being in love, but finally "she did not think the rising and falling of her fountain was caused by the emotion she called love" (247). Newman's imagery may have been influenced by Virginia Woolf's description of Mrs. Ramsay's psychic and sexual energy, her "delicious fecundity, this fountain and spray of life," which Woolf also describes as "a rain of energy, a column of spray" (*To the Lighthouse* 58).

Katharine Faraday finally associates "her rainbow fountain" with sexual desire and feels "she understood herself at last" in enjoying its rise and fall as Alden Ames holds her hand and plays with her sash during a performance of *Tristan and Isolde*. However, she is sadly disappointed with her sexual initiation: instead of feeling "everything Isolde had ever felt for Tristan," or "the melting of the hard little core of consciousness" within her as she expected, the sexual act itself seems "much more remote than a kiss" (272–73). Intellectual attraction remains more erotic to Katharine than physical, especially when combined with the added flattery of being considered important herself, as suggested by the sexual innuendoes in a passage describing Katharine's earlier lunch with a famous writer:

> She did not have to act an interest in a monologue which such an eminent author addressed exclusively to her, and before she had reached the climax of her artichoke she was sure that she was in love with the celebrated Frederick Thomas. When she went to lunch with him the next day, she was pleased that he held her hand tenderly after he had two glasses of white wine, but she was more pleased that a restaurant satisfactorily full of people saw her lunching with an author who had penetrated American Literature as a banana penetrates a box of sandwiches. (245)

Experimenting with Novelistic Devices

For Evelyn Cunningham in *Dead Lovers Are Faithful Lovers*, sexual desire for her husband becomes a "heavy golden shell of pain [that] broke in the very centre" of her body, "a pain which was not caressing, and which rushed through every one of her nerves" because she fears the lessening of his love and desire for her, especially after overhearing him say to a young, unmarried woman at a dinner party that he hoped they would have artichokes because "they're the only food that has its best bites at the bottom. . . . Exactly the opposite of love" (130, 103). Earlier that evening she was thinking of the moment when she would take off her gown and her husband would put her on his lap "and slowly and gently slip off one golden stocking and then slowly and gently kiss every beautifully tended inch it had covered, and slowly and gently slip off the other golden stocking, and less slowly and less gently kiss every inch it had covered" (89). However, now she fears his desire does not match hers: "For the first time, she did not want to be back in a room where Charlton Cunningham could touch her, and where he could prove that he did not want to touch her" (106). Similarly, Isabel Ramsay's sexual desire for Charlton is mingled with pain. When she first felt attracted to him, "that warm realization had struck against the quick hot arrow which had shot up to meet it in the very centre of her body." She feels the same way whenever she thinks of him: "She felt everything she had felt when a warm caressing pain had fallen through every nerve in her body" (185).

Despite her indirect handling of sexuality and other related taboo topics, Newman was denounced and her novels labeled shocking and depraved because she revealed women thinking about sexuality, bodily processes, and human anatomy. "During her lifetime," her contemporary Lamar Trotti remarked, Newman "was too revolutionary to enjoy any widespread endorsement. . . . America—particularly a hypersensitive Georgia . . . could see in her works only that which its own mind labels as shocking and indelicate" ("Work"). Even Rebecca West, whom Newman admired but was disappointed in because of her departure from women's concerns, unjustly attacked Newman for a sensationalism that Newman was careful to avoid through her indirection. Newman "hurls the sexual facts of life around like custard pies," West charged, describing the indirect disclosure of Katharine Faraday's brother's death from syphilis as "a facetious account . . . which has the romping moronic quality of a tabloid front page" (327). Newman was upset by West's response to her fiction, and she considered another critic libelous in accusing her of "deliberately trying to shock people" (*Letters* 228). Instead of wishing merely to shock, Newman was determined to be truthful about women's thoughts and experiences. "Fiction, if it is worth anything," she explained in an interview, "must tell the truth about one's own emotions and what one is able to observe in the life and emotions of others" (Rothermel).

Newman's valorization of female experience in writing about the body was a courageous act. Male modernists like Lawrence and Joyce are celebrated for breaking the Victorian strictures against writing about the body. However, in male fiction, women are usually the object of the male gaze rather than the subject of the narrative, and it was more taboo for women to write about the body than for men. As Virginia Woolf explained in her essay "Professions for Women," even after a woman writer was able to kill the angel in the house who urged her always to be sweet and charming rather than truthful (59), she still had to confront taboos imposed by men against women writing honestly about sexuality, passion, and the body (61–62). She admitted never having solved the problem of "telling the truth about my own experiences as a body" and doubted that "any woman has solved it yet" because of the severe condemnation directed against any woman daring to exhibit such freedom of expression (62). Living in a more restrictive social environment than Woolf, Frances Newman somehow summoned the courage to write about women's bodily experiences, their menstrual cycles, and sexual arousal, despite the fierce attacks that resulted.

Newman also exhibited courage in mocking the precepts of the patriarchal southern society and subverting literary tradition. Her characters may not often escape the dictates of their society, but they revolt internally and celebrate some victories, such as Katharine Faraday's resolution to become an important

writer rather than to marry one and Evelyn Cunningham's triumphant resumption of independence as a widow. Newman's
modernist fiction, like that of other women, was "constructed not
just against the grain of Victorian male precursors . . . but as an
integral part of a complex response to female precursors and
contemporaries" (Gilbert and Gubar, *The War* 156). She admired
Jane Austen, Katherine Mansfield, and Virginia Woolf, and their
influence can be traced in her work, but she developed a highly
signatured voice of her own. She appreciated the feminist ideology of Mary Johnston, Isa Glenn, and Ellen Glasgow and their
stands against the southern patriarchy, but she was determined
to develop a more sophisticated writing style. She maintained
friendly and supportive relationships with other women writers,
offering encouragement and advice to Eunice Coston, Sylvia
Bates, and Edith Stern and writing friendly articles about Ellen
Glasgow and Isa Glenn.[8] Newman's alternate boldness and insecurity in the face of the male literary establishment suggests her
awareness of the marginalization of women writers, especially if
they refused to conform to dominant male values, yet she chose
to focus on women's inner experiences and urged other women
novelists to keep female characters at the center of their fiction.

Newman's emphasis on interior experience, her subversion
and inversion of literary conventions, and her linguistic innova-
tion and complexity clearly align her with the early modernists,
but she was more specifically helping to create a feminist version
of modernism.[9] Sandra Gilbert and Susan Gubar move towards
a definition of feminist modernism as distinct from masculinist
modernism in their introduction to the *Women's Studies* volume
on "The Female Imagination and the Modernist Aesthetic," a
subject that they later explore fully in their three volumes of criticism, *No Man's Land: The Place of the Woman Writer in the Twentieth
Century.* Newman's fiction demonstrates the characteristics they
find central to feminist modernism: an exuberance rather than
dismay at the disbanding of traditional structures, an empower-
ment from female literary predecessors, and a valorization of female nature and experience.

NOTES

Preface

1. Like Newman, Evelyn Scott also experimented with language and focused on women's lives from a feminist perspective, but she turned from the South to the Northeast for the characters and settings of her early novels, so I have not included her in this study.

2. When one considers the themes of the prominent southern women writers King names—Flannery O'Connor, Carson McCullers, Katherine Anne Porter, and Eudora Welty—but decides against discussing, it is difficult to understand his claim that they "did not place the region at the center of their imaginative visions" (9). He fails even to mention southern black women writers like Zora Neal Hurston.

3. Ben W. Fuson's 1952 study of American literature anthologies found only six women among seventy writers frequently covered; as few as 3.2 percent of the writers in some anthologies were women, with an average of 8 percent (Lauter 22–23).

1. Living as a Southern Lady and Literary Rebel

1. Linda C. Dowling discusses Wilde's ideas on the correlation between writing style and personality in *Language and Decadence in the Victorian Fin de Siècle* (188).

2. Newman probably identified with Wilde as a writer whose work was unjustly censored. In *Dead Lovers Are Faithful Lovers*, a librarian protests the restricted circulation of Wilde's *Salome* since the only objectionable language reminds her of that she has heard in church.

3. *Twentieth-Century Authors* incorrectly lists the date as September 13, 1888 ("Frances Newman" 1018).

4. Possibly responding to this description provided by Baugh, Anne Firor Scott describes Newman as "a dark, homely child in a family of beautiful blond sisters" and comments: "In a society that prefers women to be beautiful, homely girls take refuge, if they can, in the life of the mind, or they retreat into the arts" (Foreword vii).

5. Mencken was responsible for introducing Newman's work to

Clark. He had written a letter to Clark suggesting the person who had written an "excellent article on Cabell" in the Atlanta Public Library bulletin as a potential contributor to the *Reviewer,* and the author was Newman (Clark 112).

6. Ironically, in 1925 Newman received the O. Henry award for her short story "Rachel and Her Children." In a letter to Hansell Baugh she called the award "the world's record joke" but disclosed that she had accepted it on the advice of Cabell and her publisher (*Letters* 151).

7. In a letter to Edith Stern, Newman questioned her friend's choice of male, rather than female, protagonists in her novels (*Letters* 326–27).

8. In her article "On the State of Literature in the Late Confederacy," Newman indicated those writers published in the *Reviewer* whom she considered "eminent," including Cabell, Hergesheimer, Mencken, Van Vechten, Glasgow, Lowell, Galsworthy, and Firbank (1).

9. In a letter to Emily Clark on May 1, 1924, she reassured her friend that she was feeling better but added, "I still look like Lincoln and barely weigh a hundred pounds, and I still have to lie down two hours after each meal, which makes it frantically hard to accomplish anything" (*Letters* 120). Newman was especially susceptible to influenza whenever she visited New York in the fall or winter. In December 1924, she again wrote to Clark: "I have practically decided not to try New York because of the weather. I can't face another cold, after two terrific attacks this fall. . . . This is the high peak of my book [*The Short Story's Mutations*], I suppose, and the time I should go, but I don't see how I can" (Clark 208–9).

10. Baugh's introduction to her letters dates the writing of "Atlanta Biltmore" (113).

11. Despite her state of health, Newman generously offered to write a review of Crawford's new book, if he thought it "might be of some use."

12. Newman was probably referring to Nicola Sacco and Bartolomeo Vanzetti. In 1928, Albert and Charles Boni published Upton Sinclair's *Boston: A Novel,* based upon the Sacco and Vanzetti trials. Horace Liveright had been associated with Albert Boni since 1917, and they had established the publishing firm Boni and Liveright in 1918 with Liveright as president. Although Boni soon retired, the firm retained its joint name until 1928 when it was changed to Horace Liveright, Inc.

13. Quite possibly this young man was Lamar Trotti. After her death he sent only extracts of their correspondence to Hansell Baugh and Newman's sister Margaret Patterson, explaining that many of his letters "were of a more or less personal nature, and I know Frances would not want those published" (Unpublished letter to Mrs. Patterson). In an

unpublished portion of a letter to Mable Gieberich, Newman confided, "Lamar will be here for Christmas, but that's not so important now as it was last Christmas, though I'm still very fond of him" (Letter to Mable). The letter continued, "Apparently the Virgin has worked love out of my system." Newman also credited Trotti with providing the emotion for the book and in a letter to him explained that when writing an episode, "poor Katharine Faraday's fountain [Newman's symbol for sexual arousal] set mine off, and I couldn't calm down until I went out and walked in the woods and got bitten by mosquitoes" (Unpublished letter to Trotti, 14 July 1926).

14. Perhaps sensationalists seized upon the theory of Veronal since its name is taken from Verona, probably in an allusion to the sleeping potion in Shakespeare's *Romeo and Juliet*.

2. Demythologizing the Southern Lady

1. Malcolm Cowley traced the pervasive optimism of the genteel tradition to opportunities created by western expansionism (11–12), but this understanding of opportunity failed to encompass the declining opportunities for women as well as the status of immigrants and minorities during the nineteenth century. For a discussion of the declining opportunities for middle-class women during this era, see Alice Rossi, "Social Roots of the Women's Movement in America," in *The Feminist Papers* (241–81). Rossi argues that opportunities prevalent in the Jacksonian era for education and political participation as well as for substantial work outside the home were denied to women, and as work was separated from the home, women's opportunities for significant work decreased along with their value as producers.

2. Frances Cogan, in her book *All American Girl*, establishes a coexisting, competing ideal, which she labels "Real Womanhood." Her study of advice and etiquette books, domestic novels, popular magazine articles, and short stories written in the United States between 1840 and 1880 yields an ideal of womanhood that included the virtues of physical activity, robust health, intelligence, and self-sufficiency, together with a strong sense of duty for others within an expanded version of the woman's sphere. Yet this ideal of real womanhood "vanished as an identifiable entity sometime after 1880 and has never been seen again, except in fragments" (257). Cogan explains its disappearance as a result of its own influence on the rise of the "New Woman" ideology of the 1880s and 1890s, which lost popular support because it advocated careers based upon personal fulfillment rather than family need and disregarded or disdained domestic duties and a separate sphere for

women. Real womanhood advocates became advocates either of the new woman or the true woman and the earlier compromise position was lost (257–61).

3. These aristocratic pretensions are especially ironic since the proprietors of the Virginia Colony had brought over young women to be sold for their travel expenses as wives to planters. One hundred ninety women were supplied as wives by the proprietors in exchange for tobacco between 1620 and 1622 (Clinton 3).

4. Daniel Singal discusses the "Cavalier myth" and the myth of a stable aristocracy as persisting despite the rapid white social mobility that resulted from the invention of the cotton gin. The myth was important psychologically precisely because of the social chaos and because the South was a decentralized rural society with few social institutions. For upper-class white southerners, the myth was needed "to prevent the South from disintegrating into a social jungle" and to allay misgivings about the South as a civilized society (13–17).

5. In *Love and Death in the American Novel*, Leslie Fiedler traces the American literary development of the "Fair Maiden" and the "Dark Lady" back to Shakespeare's sonnets and explains the appeal of these images to "the primeval terror of darkness, the northern fear of the swarthy southerner, the ingrained European habit of identifying evil with blackness" (297). The fair maiden is Anglo-Saxon, while the dark lady is usually either of African or Mediterranean roots (301). She is both a "sinister embodiment of the sexuality denied the snow maiden" and the Protestant male's "projection of the fear and longing for the flesh" (296, 299).

6. Charlotte Hawkins Brown, founder of the Palmer Memorial Institute and the final black speaker at a conference of church women from all across the South at Memphis in 1920, argued that despite the prevalent idea that lynching was necessary to protect white women, their danger was minute in comparison to the danger of black women being abused by white men: "I want to say to you, when you read in the paper where a colored man has insulted a white lady, just multiply that by one thousand and you have some idea of the number of colored women insulted by white men" (qtd. in Hall 93).

7. Nevertheless, the prevailing idea among white people at the time was that lynchings were performed primarily as punishment for violent sexual assaults. In a 1924 article in the *American Mercury*, Gerald Johnson defended the South's lynching of blacks in 1922 by comparing it to the lynching of nonunion miners in the North who were only "trying to earn an honest living" whereas all of the blacks were "suspected on strong evidence of having committed infamous crimes" (76).

8. Between 1914 and 1928, 693 people were lynched in the South versus thirty-three in other parts of the country, and of this number, 628, or more than ninety percent, were blacks. In addition, twice as many lynchings were threatened as performed during the twenties, but many times hasty "trials" were substituted at the insistence of the mob and the death penalty inflicted. The proportion of lynchings that occurred in the South increased from eighty-two percent of all lynchings in the country in the 1890s to ninety-five percent in the 1920s, and the percentage of victims who were white decreased from thirty-two percent to nine percent (Hall 133–34).

9. Anne Goodwyn Jones and Anne Firor Scott agree that the image of the southern lady continued to influence southern thinking into the 1920s and beyond, but by then, Scott indicates, "not as a complete prescription for woman's life but as a style which as often as not was a facade to ward off criticism of unladylike independence or to please men" (*Southern Lady* 225).

10. Mencken labeled the Old South "a civilization of manifold excellences—perhaps the best that the Western Hemisphere has ever seen" ("Sahara" 137), ignoring that it was founded on slavery, and attributed the South's current cultural barrenness to the ascendency of "the poor white trash" (139) in whose veins "the worst blood of western Europe flows" (147). He exposed his racist assumption that the rape of black women improved their race; unlike the blacks, the "poor whites went unfertilized from above, and so missed the improvement" of aristocratic blood (149). Thus whereas Mencken was widely known as an iconoclast and delighted in assaulting and shocking proponents of the genteel tradition—Paul Carter remarks that he was "admired for his opposition to many of the things the radicals of his day also disliked," including religion, Prohibition, and Victorianism (20)—in many respects he was quite conservative and traditional in his views.

11. When an opportunity to help in a specific case presented itself, Newman took a more direct action than her characters. One incident involved a black man who pled guilty to burglarizing three houses, one of them Newman's—from which he stole sixteen cents. Newman appeared in court to plead for mercy, but succeeded only in having the sentence reduced to three years' imprisonment. She wrote to a friend that she "was ill for three days from the sight of *justice*" (*Letters* 320–21).

12. It may have been one of the articles she was still planning to write at the time of her death, but I have been unable to find another reference to it.

13. Newman also directed satire towards the tenets of Christianity itself. Katharine Faraday had never been able to believe in the central

doctrine of the sacrificial death of Christ for the remission of sins, but as a child she was surprised not to be struck dead for her blasphemy of taking communion without believing. However, as a young woman, "she was able to believe that she had been right and that all the rest of her world had been wrong" (53) about "a god who admired flesh and blood sacrifices so much that he had felt obliged to make himself a son of flesh and blood and then to drive three large nails in the son before he could let her off from the blazing hell he had felt obliged to make long before" (200). Katharine begins to gain confidence in her own ideas and to express them instead of saying what she thinks others want to hear. She takes pleasure in calling Christianity "a sadist's religion" and in criticizing American clergy for confusing patriotism with religion during World War I and thus "reducing their own god to a tribal deity" (226).

14. Newman also exposes the South's anti-Semitism in "Atlanta Biltmore," even though it is a northerner who initiates the cruel anti-Semitic practical joke at its conclusion.

15. Kathryn Lee Seidel's article "The Comic Male: Satire in Ellen Glasgow's Queenborough Trilogy" discusses narrator distance and the movement of Glasgow from Juvenalian to Horatian satire in her trilogy.

16. Jean Starr Untermeyer challenged Brewer's conclusions in a letter to the editor, offering as examples of female experimentation the works of Rebecca West, Gertrude Stein, Dorothy Richardson, H. D., Amy Lowell, and Frances Newman (480–81).

17. In an exchange of letters with Cabell over this article, Newman disputed Hergesheimer's insistence that a male literature would necessarily be better than a female literature. "If not an American woman could read, I think our novels would be different, but probably no better, which I call the war camp libraries to witness" (*Letters* 59), she replied to Cabell's defense of the article. Likewise, Frances Noyes Hart rebutted Hergesheimer's article by naming several excellent women writers including Willa Cather, May Sinclair, Edith Wharton, and Dorothy Richardson and by asserting that most men prefer detective stories, western stories, and love stories to experimental fiction.

18. In her collection *Pulling Our Own Strings: Feminist Humor and Satire*, Gloria Kaufman mentions a feminist humor tradition in the suffrage movement and in the flapper era (16), and both the tradition itself and Newman's place within it merit further study.

19. Leonard Feinberg asserts that satirists rarely attack basic problems of societies or economic and political structures but instead focus on hypocrisy, snobbery, and personal folly (256–58), and Edward Bloom and Lillian Bloom agree that the satirist often "rejects the destabilization of institutions and manners as a threat to social order" (246), even

though the latter characterize satire as adaptable to "circumstance and intention" (15).

3. Questioning Social Change

1. For a discussion of this period see Gerald Critoph, "The Flapper and Her Critics"; Freda Kirchwey, *Our Changing Morality;* James R. McGovern, "The American Woman's Pre-World War I Freedom in Manners and Morals"; George E. Mowry, ed., *The Twenties: Fords, Flappers, and Fanatics;* Mary P. Ryan, *Womanhood in America: From Colonial Times to the Present;* Nancy Wolock, "Cross-Currents: The 1920s"; and Kenneth A. Yellis, "Prosperity's Child: Some Thoughts on the Flapper."

2. The life of the most famous flapper of all, Zelda Fitzgerald, reinforces Jones's statement. Immortalized by her husband's fiction, Zelda was opposed by him in her own writing efforts and commanded not to use the material of their lives together as the basis for her fiction as he had done: "I am the professional novelist, and I am supporting you. That is all my material. None of it is your material. . . . Think of my interests. That is your primary concern, because I am the one to steer the course, the pilot" (qtd. in Milford 328).

3. The southern writer Evelyn Scott wrote three novels during this period that depict marriage as miserable for both men and women (*The Narrow House, Narcissus,* and *The Golden Door*), but since they are set in New England and do not involve southern characters, they are not relevant to this study.

4. Britt notes that even in 1930, not a single women's college in the South had an endowment of two million dollars or more (413).

5. John Ruoff asserts that only a small number of southern women were actually involved in the social reform movement, and he accuses Scott of overemphasizing the activism of southern white women (136). Yet the presence of women's activism in an area so characterized by tradition and conservatism cannot, perhaps, be overemphasized, and Scott's work is ground breaking in reclaiming this forgotten aspect of southern women's history.

6. Women comprised forty-eight percent of agricultural workers in the South in 1900, whereas they made up only 4.6 percent of farm workers in the rest of the country. In contrast, that same year, only nine percent of manufacturing jobs were held by women in the South, whereas thirty-two percent of such jobs were held by women in the rest of the country (Ruoff 142). Ruoff provides more specific information on women working in the South than most sources, but unfortunately most of his information does not go beyond 1900.

7. Ames's response was that, since unmarried and widowed women could own and manage property, in the law's eyes a woman was "feeble-minded" as long as she was married, "but just let the husband die and she gets her sense back" (qtd. in Hall 51–52).

8. Newman satirized club women's frivolous voting decisions in her column "Elizabeth Bennet's Gossip": "One . . . didn't like Mr. McAdoo's mouth. Another one voted for Mr. McAdoo because she thought Senator Underwood had a mouth like a fish. . . . They all agreed . . . they would never vote for a man with a stingy mouth like President Coolidge's" (27 Apr. 1924). Elsewhere Newman does, however, address the issue of suffrage more seriously. In her "Library Notes," for example, she calls the "anti-suffragist ladies" "those incredible people" and indicates that while women probably "neither saved the country nor destroyed it" in exercising their right to vote for the first time, "they . . . felt an extraordinary sense of heightened vitality" (2 Aug. 1920). Despite assertions that southern women would lose their femininity with involvement in the rough political process, when "the women of Atlanta came down from their handsome but inconvenient pedestals with great pleasure," they "found no resemblance between the polls and a prize fight or a circus except the sawdust on the floor."

9. Ironically Davidson managed to exonerate male writers who did not show the southern culture in an entirely positive light; he excused T. S. Stribling for taking "a more amused and detached tone" than Newman and Glenn ("The Trend" 201), apparently missing Newman's humor and narrative distance, and Cabell and Faulkner as "simply afflicted with the malady of the moderns and . . . prone to take a melancholy view of life in general, not of southern life in special" (205). Davidson praised Faulkner for his "objectivity" and his lack of "animus toward the South" (193), and Faulkner also fit into the myth-making tradition promoted by the Agrarians.

10. To illustrate how narrow the definition of southern literature has often been, Louis Rubin tells the story in his article "Southern Literature and Southern Society" of wanting to write a dissertation in the early 1950s on Thomas Wolfe as a southern writer, but being told by a "distinguished professor" to which he made his proposal that Wolfe was not southern but midwestern (5).

11. In 1931, Caroline Gordon had not been invited to the Southern Writers Conference in Charlottesville, Virginia, but came only as Allen Tate's spouse, even though her first novel, *Penhally*, had already been published (Makowsky 104–5). Gordon's continuous exclusion from the serious discussions of the circle of male writers, which included her husband, was admitted by Malcolm Cowley in a 1984 interview with Veronica Makowsky: "In our discussions we were the boys. The boys always got

174

together and the girls [Caroline Gordon, Josephine Herbst, and Katherine Anne Porter] weren't asked to join them" (72).

4. Revising Literary Conventions

1. Margaret Manning Duggan convincingly argues that Edward Hamilton was patterned after Compton Mackenzie, whose writing Newman admired. For a discussion of similarities, see pages liv through lvii of her introduction to the novel.

2. This is not the only place that Newman juxtaposes marriage with death. In her short story "Rachel and Her Children," the protagonist Mrs. Overton "belonged to a generation which believed that dreaming of a funeral was a sign of a wedding, and that dreaming of a wedding was a sign of a funeral" (46), and in *The Hard-Boiled Virgin*, Katharine's friend Sarah Rutledge was married in front of a white marble mantle that her grandmother "considered a fitting background for brides and for coffins" (125).

3. Reginald Abbott discusses Katharine Faraday's reading as an indication of her character in his article "A Southern Lady Still: A Reinterpretation of Frances Percy Newman's *The Hard-Boiled Virgin*." He particularly notes Katharine's failure to understand the encoded texts of women writers concerning male/female relationships (67–69).

4. In her discussion, Jones draws upon writings on narcissism by Vivian Gornick and Ann Douglas.

5. Newman expressed a preference for novelists who understood that "Freud and Tchekhov have crossed the ocean and who try to see below the surfaces of their characters" ("American Short Story" 190). However, she deplored the heavy-handed use of Freudian psychology by some American writers such as Evelyn Scott, commenting that "unless one be a genius like Mr. D. H. Lawrence . . . it is better to take one's Freud cheerfully or leave him to the generation that is not yet knocking on our door" ("Literary Complexes" 7).

6. Jones agrees that Evelyn's narcissism is motivated by insecurity instead of "exaggerated self-esteem" (309), and she also discusses narcissism in relationship to *The Hard-Boiled Virgin*, quoting Vivian Gornick's definition of narcissism in "Female Narcissism as a Metaphor in Literature" as "that paradoxical condition of self-regard in which the self speaks to an absence of the self" (Jones, *Tomorrow* 290).

7. While this portrait may seem autobiographical, Isabel is apparently modeled on someone else. Like Isabel, Newman was a librarian at the Carnegie Library, and she initially looked forward to a new job at the Georgia Tech library. Also, Isabel's complaints about the "bleak feminine atmosphere of the Carnegie Library" (187) echo Newman's

comment in a letter from Europe to her sister that she "simply can't go back to the awful atmosphere of the library" (94). But in a letter to Hansell Baugh, she muses that Isabel may not be the type of woman to go to New York, "so evidently she's not very like her model." She significantly adds: "And not at all like me." Obviously Newman drew on her experiences as a librarian in the library scenes as she notes in her letter: "I really think I've invented nearly all of these people except those in the library" (*Letters* 296).

8. Newman also includes the story to illustrate her theory that the origin of the short story was the male bragging of sexual conquests: "The fondness for recounting their amorous conquests, which was probably no less indulged between the first two men than it is today, was perhaps the origin of a literary form whose history is also the history of the relations between men and women" (8).

5. Experimenting with Novelistic Devices

1. DuPlessis discusses such narrative strategies as "reparenting, invented families, fraternal-sororal ties . . . bisexual love plots, female bonding, and lesbianism" (xi).

2. Lucy is a character in George Meredith's novel *The Ordeal of Richard Feverel.*

3. Newman divulged her own habit of creating stories involving herself: "All of my life, I have gone to bed and invented charming anecdotes about possible adventures for myself—I still do it. And those adventures always went through my mind a good deal as I wrote down Katharine Faraday's adventures in her story" ("Frances Newman Tells" 8).

4. Newman had seen this play when she was in Europe in 1923 while working on her first draft of *The Hard-Boiled Virgin.* She described herself as "enchanted with its pure cleverness" (*Letters* 96) and later remarked, "I bow whenever I mention Pirandello's name" (*Letters* 276).

5. Coste is quoting from a paper presented by Prince at the Twentieth Century French Studies Colloquium at Duke University in March 1987.

6. Kathryn Seidel describes Katharine as "completely shocked by her first menstrual period" (42), but although Katharine is supposed to be totally innocent, she has learned through her friends' experience and probably even earlier through her older sisters' experience since she guesses what her two friends are "reticent" about.

7. Statistics are from a computer-assisted analysis of the text of the *The Hard-Boiled Virgin* using AT&T's professional version of "Writer's Workbench."

8. In her article "Having Tea with Richmond Celebrities," Newman

called Glasgow "the very first literary lady of distinction I ever had the pleasure of beholding," adding "I am a little afraid that I have begun with the most charming woman writer." She described a visit to Isa Glenn in New York in her article "Atlanta Woman's Bungalow," calling Glenn "an important personage in the literary world . . . because she is charming as well as clever." Even though she did not appreciate Julia Peterkin's fiction (Clark 199), Newman assisted Peterkin in finding publishers for her work (*Letters* 275), and she similarly tried to help Bates find a publisher for her novel *Another Glory* (297). Her relationships with women writers are revealed primarily through her letters (293, 297, 306, 310, 323–25, 326, 337).

9. Stanley Sultan discusses various definitions and debates about literary modernism in the chapter "Our Modern Experiment" of his book *Eliot, Joyce and Company,* but like many male critics of modernism, he fails to significantly address women writers of the period. In *Makers of the New,* Julian Symons similarly ignores women modernists except for Djuna Barnes, mentioning Katherine Mansfield and Virginia Woolf only in passing. Sandra Gilbert and Susan Gubar comment that a means of dispelling the anxiety men feel in the twentieth century about women who are consummate literary artists has been to reconstruct a literary history marked by the absence of women (*The War* 153–54). Even Bonnie Kime Scott's critical anthology *The Gender of Modernism,* which works to correct this absence of female writers, includes no woman writer of the southern United States except Zora Neale Hurston.

WORKS CITED

Published Works by Frances Newman

"The Allegory of the Young Intellectuals." *Reviewer* 1.12 (1921): 359–65.

"The American Short Story in the First Twenty Five Years of the Twentieth Century." *Bookman* 63 (Apr. 1926): 186–93.

"Atlanta Biltmore." Introd. Reginald Abbott. *Southern Review* 25 (Summer 1989): 633–43.

"Atlanta Woman's Bungalow on a Roof." *Atlanta Journal* 7 Sept. 1924: 5.

"Dark Laughter." Folder 18, Frances Newman Papers, Archives, Library and Information Center, Georgia Institute of Technology.

Dead Lovers Are Faithful Lovers. New York: Boni and Liveright, 1928. Fwd. Anne Goodwyn Jones. Athens: Brown Thrasher Books, U Georgia P, 1994.

"Elizabeth Bennet's Gossip." *Atlanta Journal* 27 Apr. 1924: 6.

"Exit Mr. Castle and Mr. Williamson" ("Carnegie Library Notes"). *Atlanta Constitution* 24 Oct. 1920: G2.

"Five Years of American Fiction." *Carnegie Library of Atlanta, Georgia Bulletin* 15.2 (Sept. 1922): 3–7.

"Frances Newman Tells How She Writes." *Atlanta Journal* 1 Apr. 1928: 6, 8.

Frances Newman's Letters. Ed. Hansell Baugh. New York: Horace Liveright, 1929.

"Freud and the Flapper." *Library Literary Notes.* Folder 17, Frances Newman Papers, Archives, Library and Information Center, Georgia Institute of Technology.

The Gold-Fish Bowl. Ed. Margaret Manning Duggan. In *"The Gold-Fish Bowl": Miss Newman's Five-Finger Exercise.* Diss. U South Carolina, 1985. Ann Arbor: ULMI, 1985. 8518022.

The Hard-Boiled Virgin. New York: Boni and Liveright, 1926. Fwd. Anne Firor Scott. Athens: Brown Thrasher Books, U Georgia P, 1993.

"Having Tea with Richmond Celebrities." *Atlanta Journal* 27 Jan. 1924: 6.

"Herd Complex." *Reviewer* 3 (May 1922): 427–33.

"Library Notes." *Atlanta Constitution* 2 Aug. 1920: 5.

"Literary Complexes." *Carnegie Library of Atlanta, Georgia Bulletin* 10.2 (Oct. 1921): 3–7.

Works Cited

"Literary Independence." *Saturday Review of Literature* 4 Apr. 1925: 641–42, 645.

"On the State of Literature in the Late Confederacy." *New York Herald Tribune Books* 1.48 (16 Aug. 1925): 1–3.

" 'Quiet Interior' and the Woman's Novel" ("Library Literary Notes"). *Atlanta Constitution* 3 Apr. 1921: C2.

"Rachel and Her Children." *American Mercury* 2 (May 1924): 92–96.

Rev. of *To the Lighthouse*, by Virginia Woolf. [*Atlanta Journal*]. Folder 18, Frances Newman Papers, Archives, Library and Information Center, Georgia Institute of Technology.

"The Rising Age of Heroines" ("Carnegie Library Notes"). *Atlanta Constitution* 4 Apr. 1920: G2.

"Short Stories of 1925." *New York Times Book Review* 7 Feb. 1926. Folder 18, Frances Newman Papers, Archives, Library and Information Center, Georgia Institute of Technology.

The Short Story's Mutations. New York: BW Huebsch, 1924.

Six Moral Tales from Jules Laforgue. (Ed. and trans.) New York: Horace Liveright, 1928.

"Three Episodes for the Hard-Boiled Virgin." *Reviewer* 4 (Oct. 1924): 341–43.

"With One Year's Subscription." *Reviewer* 3 (Apr. 1922): 372–76.

Unpublished Works

Battey, Adrienne. Letter to Auntie. 23 Oct. 1928. Adrienne Battey Collection. Hargrett Rare Book and Manuscript Library, University of Georgia Libraries.

Daniel, Frank. Draft of article on Newman's death, ts. Adrienne Battey Collection. Hargrett Rare Book and Manuscript Library, University of Georgia Libraries.

———. Letter to Adrienne Battey. Friday night [Oct.? 1928]. Adrienne Battey Collection. Hargrett Rare Book and Manuscript Library, University of Georgia Libraries.

———. Letter to Adrienne Battey. Saturday afternoon [Oct.? 1928]. Adrienne Battey Collection. Hargrett Rare Book and Manuscript Library, University of Georgia Libraries.

———. Letter to Adrienne Battey. 30 Oct. 1928. Adrienne Battey Collection. Hargrett Rare Book and Manuscript Library, University of Georgia Libraries.

H[olt], G[uy]. Letter to Newman, 20 July 1921. Folder 2, Frances Newman Papers, Archives, Library and Information Center, Georgia Institute of Technology.

Works Cited

Mencken, H. L. Letter to Mrs. Harris. 27 Oct. 1928. Julian LaRose Harris Collection. Special Collections Department, Robert W. Woodruff Library, Emory University.

Newman, Frances. Letter to Sherwood Anderson. 6 Nov. [1925]. Folder 29, Frances Newman Papers, Archives, Library and Information Center, Georgia Institute of Technology.

———. Letter to Sherwood Anderson. 29 Mar. 1926. Folder 29, Frances Newman Papers, Archives, Library and Information Center, Georgia Institute of Technology.

———. Letter to Mable [Mrs. Oscar Gieberich]. 30 Nov. [1926]. Folder 11, Frances Newman Papers, Archives, Library and Information Center, Georgia Institute of Technology.

———. Letter to Mrs. Julian LaRose Harris. 1 Mar. [1928]. Julian LaRose Harris Collection. Special Collections Department, Robert W. Woodruff Library, Emory University.

———. Letter to H. L. Mencken. Undated. Folder 8, Frances Newman Papers, Archives, Library and Information Center, Georgia Institute of Technology.

———. Letter to Margaret Patterson. July 1922. Folder 1, Frances Newman Papers, Archives, Library and Information Center, Georgia Institute of Technology.

———. Letter to Margaret Patterson. 19 Apr. 1923. Folder 1, Frances Newman Papers, Archives, Library and Information Center, Georgia Institute of Technology.

———. Letter to Lamar Trotti. 14 July 1926. Folder 9, Frances Newman Papers, Archives, Library and Information Center, Georgia Institute of Technology.

———. Letter to Lamar Trotti. 26 Nov. 1926. Folder 9, Frances Newman Papers, Archives, Library and Information Center, Georgia Institute of Technology.

———. "Two passages from *Virgin* which had to be omitted." [Both from copies at the Houghton Library at Harvard University.] Folder 29, Frances Newman Papers, Archives, Library and Information Center, Georgia Institute of Technology.

Trotti, Lamar. Letter to Mrs. Patterson. 30 Mar. 1929. Folder 9, Frances Newman Papers, Archives, Library and Information Center, Georgia Institute of Technology.

Books, Articles, and Other Publications

Abbott, Emory Reginald. *Purple Prejudices: The Critical Writings of Frances Newman.* Diss. Vanderbilt U, 1992.

Works Cited

———. "A Southern Lady Still: A Reinterpretation of Frances Percy Newman's *The Hard-Boiled Virgin.*" *Southern Quarterly* 27.4 (Summer 1989): 49–70.

Austen, Jane. *Northanger Abbey.* 1818. London: The Folio Society, 1975.

"Authoress Dies of Poison: Frances Newman Victim of Veronal." *New York Journal* 25 Oct. 1928: 1–2.

Banner, Lois W. *Women in Modern America: A Brief History.* 2nd ed. New York: Harcourt Brace Jovanovich, 1984.

Bartlett, Irving H., and C. Glenn Cambor. "The History and Psychodynamics of Southern Womanhood." *Women's Studies* 2 (1974): 9–24.

Baugh, Hansell. Introductory Notes. *Frances Newman's Letters.* New York: Horace Liveright, 1929.

Baym, Nina. "Melodramas of Beset Manhood: How Theories of American Fiction Exclude Women Authors." *American Quarterly* 33.2 (Summer 1981): 123–39.

Beach, Joseph Warren. *American Fiction 1920–1940.* New York: Macmillan, 1948.

Blake, Fay M. "Frances Newman: Librarian and Novelist." *Journal of Library History* 16 (1981): 305–14.

Blake, Kathleen. *Love and the Woman Question in Victorian Literature: The Art of Self-Postponement.* New Jersey: Barnes and Noble; Sussex: Harvester Press, 1983.

Bloom, Edward, and Lillian D. Bloom. *Satire's Persuasive Voice.* Ithaca: Cornell UP, 1979.

"Books of the Month: Best Sellers of the Past Month." Mar., Apr., May, June, 1927. Scrapbook, Frances Newman Papers, Archives, Library and Information Center, Georgia Institute of Technology.

Booth, Wayne C. *The Rhetoric of Fiction.* 2nd ed. Chicago: U Chicago P, 1983.

"Boston Bans Sale of Nine Recent Books." *Herald Tribune* 11 Mar. 1927. Scrapbook, Frances Newman Papers, Archives, Library and Information Center, Georgia Institute of Technology.

Bradbury, John M. *Renaissance in the South.* Chapel Hill: U North Carolina P, 1963.

Brewer, Elizabeth. "The Flapper's Wild Oats." *Bookman* 57 (Mar. 1923): 1–6.

Brickell, Herschel. "A Vehement Spirit." [Rev. of *Frances Newman's Letters.*] *Saturday Review of Literature* 22 Mar. 1930. Folder 23, Frances Newman Papers, Archives, Library and Information Center, Georgia Institute of Technology.

Britt, George. "Women in the New South." *Woman's Coming.of Age.* Ed. Samuel D. Schumalhausen and V. F. Calverton. New York: Horace Liveright, 1931. 409–23.

Works Cited

"Cabell's New Book Reveals Dedication to Frances Newman." *Atlanta Journal* 25 Nov. 1928. Folder 16, Frances Newman Papers, Archives, Library and Information Center, Georgia Institute of Technology.

Cadett, Thomas. "Hard-Boiled Virgin Neither Mediocre Book or a Classic." *Atlanta Constitution.* Scrapbook, Frances Newman Papers, Archives, Library and Information Center, Georgia Institute of Technology.

Carter, Paul A. *The Twenties in America.* New York: Thomas Y. Crowell, 1968.

Cash, W. J. *The Mind of the South.* New York: Alfred A. Knopf, 1941.

Chafe, William Henry. *The American Woman: Her Changing Social, Economic, and Political Roles, 1920–70.* New York: Oxford UP, 1972.

Chatman, Seymour. *Coming to Terms: The Rhetoric of Narrative in Fiction and Film.* Ithaca: Cornell UP, 1990.

Chopin, Kate. "The Story of an Hour." 19 Apr. 1894. *Images of Women in Literature.* Ed. Mary Anne Ferguson. 4th ed. Boston: Houghton Mifflin, 1986.

Clark, Emily. *Innocence Abroad.* New York: Alfred A. Knopf, 1931.

Clinton, Catherine. *The Plantation Mistress: Women's World in the Old South.* New York: Pantheon, Random House, 1982.

Cogan, Frances B. *All-American Girl: The Ideal of Real Womanhood in Mid-Nineteenth-Century America.* Athens: U Georgia P, 1989.

Cohn, Dorrit. *Transparent Minds: Narrative Modes for Presenting Consciousness in Fiction.* Princeton: Princeton UP, 1978.

Cole, Paul B. "Southern Author: Frances Newman." *Cajoler* 1 (15 Mar. 1929): 19–22.

Coste, Didier. *Narrative as Communication.* Vol. 64 of *Theory and History of Literature.* Ed. Wald Godzich and Jochen Schulte-Sasse. Minneapolis: U Minnesota P, 1989.

Cowan, Louise. *The Southern Critics: An Introduction to the Criticism of John Crowe Ransom, Allen Tate, Donald Davidson, Robert Penn Warren, Cleanth Brooks, and Anthony Lytle.* Irving, Texas: U Dallas P, 1971.

Cowley, Malcolm, ed. *After the Genteel Tradition: American Writers 1910–1930.* 1937. Rpt. Carbondale: Southern Illinois UP, 1964.

Crawford, Nelson Antrim. "Frances Newman, American Ironist." *Midland* 8 (May 1927): 146–50.

Critoph, Gerald. "The Flapper and Her Critics." *"Remember the Ladies": New Perspectives on Women in American History.* Syracuse: Syracuse UP, 1975. 145–60.

Curtis, William. "Some Recent Books" (Rev. of *The Hard-Boiled Virgin*). [*Town and Country.*] Frank Daniel Collection, Special Collections Department, Robert W. Woodruff Library, Emory University.

Dabney, Virginius. *Liberalism in the South.* Chapel Hill: U North Carolina P, 1932.

Works Cited

Daniel, Frank. "Frances Newman's Novel Draws From Atlanta Life." *Atlanta Journal* 13 Nov. 1926. Scrapbook, Frances Newman Papers, Archives, Library and Information Center, Georgia Institute of Technology.

———. "Miss Newman's Unwritten Books." *Atlanta Journal* 18 Nov. 1928: 3, 24.

———. "Peachtree's Fame in Fiction: It Started with Frances Newman, Georgia's First Modern Novelist." Atlanta History Center, Library/Archives, Frances Newman Personality File.

Davidson, Donald. "The Artist as Southerner." *Saturday Review* 2 (15 May 1926): 781–83.

———. "Frances Newman." *Critics Almanac* 13 May 1928. Rpt. *The Spyglass: Views and Reviews, 1924–1930*. Selected and ed. John Tyree Fain. Nashville: Vanderbilt UP, 1963. 26–29.

———. "A Mirror for Artists." *Twelve Southerners* 28–60.

———. *Southern Writers in the Modern World*. Athens: U Georgia P, 1958.

———. "The Trend of Literature: A Partisan View." *Culture in the South*. Ed. W. T. Couch. Chapel Hill: U North Carolina P, 1934: 183–210.

Dollard, John. *Caste and Class in a Southern Town*. 2nd ed. New York: Harper and Brothers, 1949.

Dounce, H. E. "A Style, a Sultana and a Peri: Evidently Brainy Georgian and Benighted Virginian Femininity Are Sisters Under Their Skins" (Rev. of *Dead Lovers Are Faithful Lovers*). *Evening Post* 5 May 1928. Scrapbook, Frances Newman Papers, Archives, Library and Information Center, Georgia Institute of Technology.

Dowling, Linda C. *Language and Decadence in the Victorian Fin de Siècle*. Princeton: Princeton UP, 1986.

Drake, Robert Y., Jr. "Frances Newman: Fabulist of Decadence." *Georgia Review* 14 (1960): 389–98.

"Drug Killed Noble Writer." Folder 16, Frances Newman Papers, Archives, Library and Information Center, Georgia Institute of Technology.

Duggan, Margaret Manning. Preface: The Apprenticeship of Frances Newman. *"The Gold-Fish Bowl": Miss Newman's Five-Finger Exercise*. Diss. U South Carolina, 1985. Ann Arbor: ULMI, 1985. 8518022. x–lxxi.

DuPlessis, Rachel Blau. *Writing Beyond the Ending: Narrative Strategies of Twentieth-Century Women Writers*. Bloomington: Indiana UP, 1985.

Ehrenreich, Barbara, and Deirdre English. *Complaints and Disorders: The Sexual Politics of Illness*. Old Westbury, NY: Feminist Press, 1973.

Essig, Carolyn. "Atlanta Women Become Famous." *Atlanta Journal* 9 Sept. 1928: 6.

Evans, Elizabeth. "Frances Newman." *American Women Writers: A Critical*

Works Cited

Reference Guide from Colonial Times to the Present. Ed. Lina Mainero. Vol. 3. New York: Frederick Ungar, 1981. 253–55. 4 vols.

Evans, Hiram Wesley. "The Klan's Fight for Americanism." *North American Review* (Mar. 1926). Rpt. in Mowry 137–45.

Evans, Sara M. "Women." *The Encyclopedia of Southern History.* Ed. David C. Roller and Robert W. Twyman. Baton Rouge: Louisiana State UP, 1979. 1353–55.

Faust, Drew Gilpin. *Mothers of Invention: Women of the Slaveholding South in the American Civil War.* Chapel Hill: U North Carolina P, 1996.

Feinberg, Leonard. *Introduction to Satire.* Ames: Iowa State UP, 1967.

Fiedler, Leslie A. *Love and Death in the American Novel.* Rev. ed. New York: Stein and Day, 1966.

"Finds Veronal in Body of Frances Newman." Folder 16, Frances Newman Papers, Archives, Library and Information Center, Georgia Institute of Technology.

Flora, Joseph M. "Fiction in the 1920's: Some New Voices." *The History of Southern Literature.* Ed. Louis D. Rubin, Jr., et al. Baton Rouge: Louisiana State UP, 1985. 279–90.

Foster, Virginia. "The Emancipation of Pure, White Southern Womanhood." *New South* 26.1 (1971): 46–54.

Fox-Genovese, Elizabeth. *Within the Plantation Household.* Chapel Hill: U North Carolina P, 1988.

"Frances Newman." *Twentieth-Century Authors: A Biographical Dictionary of Modern Literature.* Ed. Stanley Kunitz and Howard Haycraft. New York: H. W. Wilson, 1942. 1018–19.

"Frances Newman Paid Last Honor; West View Burial." *Atlanta Journal* [24 Oct. 1928]. Folder 16, Frances Newman Papers, Archives, Library and Information Center, Georgia Institute of Technology.

"Frances Newman Shocked the Neighbors, She Admits." Scrapbook, Frances Newman Papers, Archives, Library and Information Center, Georgia Institute of Technology.

"Frances Newman's End Like a Page From Her Book." [*Post-Dispatch Sunday Magazine*]. Folder 16, Frances Newman Papers, Archives, Library and Information Center, Georgia Institute of Technology.

Frank, Joseph. "Spatial Form in Modern Literature." *Sewanee Review* 5 (1945): 221–40, 433–56, 643–53.

Gallo, Louis. "Frances Newman." *Dictionary of Literary Biography Yearbook 1980.* Ed. Karen L. Rood, Jean W. Ross, and Richard Ziegfeld. Detroit: Gale Research, 1981. 276–79.

———. "Notes on Some Recently Found Lost American Fiction." *Missouri Review* 4.3 (1981): 91–98.

Gilbert, Sandra, and Susan Gubar. "Introduction: The Female Imagina-

Works Cited

tion and the Modernist Aesthetic." *Women's Studies* 13 (Dec. 1986): 1–10.

———. *The Madwoman in the Attic: The Woman Writer and the Nineteenth-Century Literary Imagination.* New Haven: Yale UP, 1979.

———. *The War of the Words.* New Haven: Yale UP, 1988. Vol. 1 of *No Man's Land: The Place of the Woman Writer in the Twentieth Century.* 3 vols. 1988–1994.

Glasgow, Ellen. *A Certain Measure: An Interpretation of Prose Fiction.* New York: Harcourt, Brace, 1938, 1943.

———. *Life and Gabriella.* New York: Doubleday, Page, 1916.

———. *The Romantic Comedians.* 1926. Virginia ed. New York: Charles Scribner, 1938.

———. *They Stooped to Folly.* 1929. Dolphin Books ed. Garden City, NY: Doubleday, 1961.

———. *Virginia.* New York: Doubleday, Page, 1913.

Glenn, Isa. *Southern Charm.* New York: Alfred A. Knopf, 1928.

Green, Paul. "A Plain Statement About Southern Literature." *Reviewer* 5 (Jan. 1925): 71–76.

Haardt, Sarah. "The Southern Lady Says Grace." *Reviewer* 5 (Oct. 1925): 57–63.

Hall, Jacquelyn Dowd. *Revolt Against Chivalry: Jessie Daniel Ames and the Women's Campaign Against Lynching.* New York: Columbia UP, 1979.

Hanna, Evelyn. "Dead Rebels Are Faithful Rebels." Folder 24, Frances Newman Papers, Archives, Library and Information Center, Georgia Institute of Technology.

Hansen, Harry. " 'The Hard-Boiled Virgin' Arrives; Study of a Budding Amazon." *World* 28 Nov. 1926: 10m. Scrapbook, Frances Newman Papers, Archives, Library and Information Center, Georgia Institute of Technology.

Hardwick, Elizabeth. Introduction. *Dead Lovers Are Faithful Lovers.* 1926. Rpt. New York: Arno Press, 1977.

Hargrett, Lester. "First Novel by Clever Atlanta Woman Original In Form and Bold In Content." *Enquirer Sun* 26 Dec. 1926. Frances Newman Collection, Special Collections Department, Robert W. Woodruff Library, Emory University.

Harris, Barbara J. *Beyond Her Sphere: Women and the Professions in American History.* Westport, CT: Greenwood Press, 1978.

Harris, Corra. "Is Modern Woman Happy?" *Atlanta Constitution* 18 Nov. 1923: 7, 21.

Harris, Julia Collier. "Interview With Miss Frances Newman, Southerner Who Won Fame Overnight." [*Columbus Enquirer-Sun* 25 Jan. 1925?]. Frances Newman Collection, Special Collections Department, Robert W. Woodruff Library, Emory University.

Works Cited

Hart, Frances Noyes. "The Feminine Nuisance Replies." *Bookman* 54 (Sept. 1921): 31–34.

Heilbrun, Carolyn G. *Reinventing Womanhood*. New York: WW Norton, 1979.

———. *Writing a Woman's Life*. New York: WW Norton, 1988.

Hergesheimer, Joseph. "The Feminine Nuisance in American Literature." *Yale Review* 10 (July 1921): 716–25.

Herrick, Robert. "A Feline World." *Bookman* 69 (Mar. 1929): 1–6.

Hibbard, Addison. "Literature South—1924." *Reviewer* 5 (Jan. 1925): 52–58.

Hooks, Bell. *"Ain't I a Woman": Black Women and Feminism*. Boston: South End Press, 1981.

Hoyt, Clement. "Hardboiled Virgin Is Not Hardboiled But Good Reading." *Houston Post-Dispatch* 23 Jan. 1927. Scrapbook, Frances Newman Papers, Archives, Library and Information Center, Georgia Institute of Technology.

Hubbell, Jay B. "Southern Magazines." *Culture in the South*. Ed. W. T. Couch. Chapel Hill: U North Carolina P, 1934. 159–82.

Huf, Linda. *A Portrait of the Artist as a Young Woman: The Writer as Heroine in American Literature*. New York: Frederick Ungar, 1983.

Johnson, Gerald W. "The South Takes the Offensive." *American Mercury* 2 (May 1924): 70–78.

Johnston, Mary. *Hagar*. Boston: Houghton Mifflin, 1913.

———. "The Woman's War." *Atlantic Monthly* 105 (Apr. 1910): 559–70.

Jones, Anne Goodwyn. *Tomorrow Is Another Day: The Woman Writer in the South, 1859–1936*. Baton Rouge: Louisiana State UP, 1981.

———. Foreword. *Dead Lovers Are Faithful Lovers*. By Frances Newman. Athens: U Georgia P, 1994. vii–xxxvi.

"Judge William T. Newman." *Book of Georgia*. Ed. Clark Howell. Atlanta: Georgia Biographical Association, 1920. 521, 554.

Kaplan, Sydney Janet. *Feminine Consciousness in the Modern British Novel*. Urbana: U Illinois P, 1975.

Katz-Stoker, Fraya. "The Other Criticism: Feminism vs. Formalism." *Images of Women in Fiction: Feminist Perspectives*. Ed. Susan Koppelman Cornillon. Bowling Green, OH: Bowling Green U Popular Press, 1972. 313–25.

Kaufman, Gloria. Introduction. *Pulling Our Own Strings: Feminist Humor and Satire*. Ed. Kaufman and Mary Kay Blakeley. Bloomington: Indiana UP, 1980.

Kennard, Jean E. *Victims of Convention*. Hamden, CT: Archon Books, 1978.

King, Richard. *A Southern Renaissance: The Cultural Awakening of the American South, 1930–1955*. New York: Oxford UP, 1980.

Works Cited

Kirchwey, Freda. *Our Changing Morality.* New York: Albert and Charles Bond, 1924. Rpt. ed. New York: Arno Press and The New York Times, 1972.

Kolodny, Annette. "Some Notes on Defining a 'Feminist Literary Criticism.' " *Critical Inquiry* 2 (Autumn 1975): 75–92. Rpt. *Feminist Criticism: Essays on Theory, Poetry and Prose.* Ed. Cheryl L. Brown and Karen Olson. Metuchen, NJ: Scarecrow Press, 1978. 37–58.

"The Lady from Georgia" (Rev. of *Frances Newman's Letters*). *American Mercury* [Mar. 1930]. Folder 23, Frances Newman Papers, Archives, Library and Information Center, Georgia Institute of Technology.

LaFollette, Susan. "Women and Marriage." *Concerning Women.* New York: Albert and Charles Boni, 1926. Rpt. Rossi 553–63.

Langfield, William R. "Fiction Without Shock-Absorber" (Rev. of *The Hard-Boiled Virgin*). Scrapbook, Frances Newman Papers, Archives, Library and Information Center, Georgia Institute of Technology.

"Latest Fashions of Paris Daring to the Extreme." *Atlanta Constitution* 18 Jan. 1920: A11.

Lauter, Paul. "Race and Gender in the Shaping of the American Literary Canon: A Case Study from the Twenties." *Feminist Criticism and Social Change: Sex, Class and Race in Literature and Culture.* Ed. Judith Newton and Deborah Rosenfelt. New York: Methuen, 1985. 19–43.

Lieberman, Marcia R. "Sexism and the Double Standard in Literature." *Images of Women in Fiction: Feminist Perspectives.* Comp. Susan Koppelman Cornillon. Bowling Green, OH: Bowling Green U Popular Press, 1973. 326–38.

Little, Judy. *Comedy and the Woman Writer: Woolf, Spark, and Feminism.* Lincoln: U Nebraska P, 1983.

Lubbock, Percy. *The Craft of Fiction.* New York: Charles Scribner, 1921.

MacDonald, Edgar E. "The Ambivalent Heart: Literary Revival in Richmond." *The History of Southern Literature.* Ed. Louis D. Rubin, et al. Baton Rouge: Louisiana State UP, 1985. 264–78.

Macy, John. "Women Are Witches." *Bookman* 67 (1928): 429–32.

Makowsky, Veronica. *Caroline Gordon: A Biography.* New York: Oxford UP, 1989.

Manning, Carol S., ed. *The Female Tradition in Southern Literature.* Urbana: U Illinois P, 1993.

Mansfield, Katherine. *Selected Stories.* London: Oxford UP, 1953.

May, Henry F. "Shifting Perspectives on the 1920's." *Mississippi Valley Historical Review* 43 (1956): 405–27.

McGovern, James R. "The American Woman's Pre–World War I Freedom in Manners and Morals." *Journal of American History* 55 (Sept. 1968): 315–33.

Works Cited

Mencken, H. L. "Sahara of the Bozart." 1917. *Prejudices.* 2nd ser. New York: Alfred A. Knopf, 1920. 136–54.

Merrill, Lisa. "Feminist Humor: Rebellious and Self-Affirming." *Women's Studies* 15 (1988): 271–80.

Milford, Nancy. *Zelda.* New York: Avon, 1971.

Mims, Edwin. "The Revolt Against Chivalry." *The Advancing South.* Garden City, NY: Doubleday Page, 1926. 224–56.

Mitchell, Mary. Letter. [*New York Herald Tribune Books.*] 17 June 1928. Scrapbook, Frances Newman Papers, Archives, Library and Information Center, Georgia Institute of Technology.

Morgan, Ellen. "Humanbecoming: Form and Focus in the Neo-Feminist Novel." *Images of Women in Fiction: Feminist Perspectives.* Ed. Susan Koppelman Cornillon. Bowling Green, OH: Bowling Green U Popular Press, 1972. 183–205.

Mowry, George E., ed. *The Twenties: Fords, Flappers, and Fanatics.* Englewood Cliffs, NJ: Prentice Hall, 1963.

"Newman Parody Portended Death." *Evening Post* 27 Oct. 1928. Adrienne Battey Collection. Hargrett Rare Book and Manuscript Library, University of Georgia Libraries.

O'Brien, Michael. *The Idea of the American South, 1920–1941.* Baltimore: Johns Hopkins UP, 1979.

O'Conner, William Van. "The Genteel Tradition." *The Age of Criticism 1900–1950.* Chicago: Henry Regnery, 1952.

Olsen, Tillie. "Silences: When Writers Don't Write." *Images of Women in Fiction: Feminist Perspectives.* Ed. Susan Koppelman Cornillon. Bowling Green, OH: Bowling Green U Popular Press, 1972. 97–112.

Overton, Grant Martin. *The Women Who Make Our Novels.* New and completely rev. ed. New York: Dodd, Mead, 1928.

Page, Thomas Nelson. "The Great American Question: The Special Plea of a Southerner." *McClures* 28 (Mar. 1907): 565. Quoted in Ruoff 130.

Painter, Nell Irvin. " 'Social Equality,' Miscegenation, Labor, and Power." *The Evolution of Southern Culture.* Ed. Numan V. Bartley. Athens: U Georgia P, 1988. 47–67.

"Parody Newman Review Coincides With Her Death." Adrienne Battey Collection. Hargrett Rare Book and Manuscript Library, University of Georgia Libraries.

"Parody on Novelist Paralleled Her Death." Adrienne Battey Collection. Hargrett Rare Book and Manuscript Library, University of Georgia Libraries.

Paterson, Isabel. "Phantom Lover" (Rev. of *Dead Lovers Are Faithful Lovers*). *New York Herald Tribune Books* 6 May 1928, sec. xii: 3–4.

Pratt, Annis. *Archetypal Patterns in Women's Fiction.* Bloomington: Indiana UP, 1981.

Works Cited

"Probers Seek Source of Drug Fatal to Writer." *Evening Journal* Friday, 26? Oct. [1928]: 1, 18. Adrienne Battey Collection. Hargrett Rare Book and Manuscript Library, University of Georgia Libraries.

[Ransom, John Crowe]. Introduction: A Statement of Principles. Twelve Southerners ix–xx.

Ransom, John Crowe. "Modern with the Southern Accent." *Virginia Quarterly Review* 11 (Apr. 1935): 184–98.

——. *The New Criticism.* Norfolk, CT: New Directions, 1941.

——. "Reconstructed but Unregenerate." Twelve Southerners 1–27.

Riddell, John [Corey Ford]. "Meaning No Offense: Parody Interviews in the Respective Manners of Frances Newman and Carl Van Vechten." *Vanity Fair* 31.3 (Nov. 1928): 89, 102.

Roberts, Diane. *The Myth of Aunt Jemima: Representations of Race and Region.* London: Routledge, 1994.

Rosowski, Susan J. "The Novel of Awakening." *The Voyage In: Fictions of Female Development.* Ed. Elizabeth Abel, Marianne Hirsch, and Elizabeth Langland. Hanover, NH: UP of New England, 1983. 49–68.

Rossi, Alice S., ed. *The Feminist Papers: From Adams to de Beauvoir.* New York: Columbia UP, 1973.

Rothermel, Winifred. "Aristocratic Writer, Daughter of South, Taken By Death in Gotham: Her Ideas on Death, Dress, and Literature Were Unusual, Interviews Reveal." [*Birmingham News-Age Herald* c. 22 Oct. 1928]. Atlanta History Center, Library/Archives, Frances Newman Personality File.

Rubin, Louis D., Jr. "Southern Literature and Southern Society." Rubin and Holman 3–20.

Rubin, Louis D., Jr., and C. Hugh Holman. *Southern Literary Study: Problems and Possibilities.* Chapel Hill: U North Carolina P, 1975.

Ruoff, John Carl. "Southern Womanhood, 1865–1920: An Intellectual and Cultural Study." Diss. U Illinois, 1976.

Ryan, Mary P. *Womanhood in America: From Colonial Times to the Present.* 3rd ed. New York: Franklin Watts, 1983.

Sam, Conway Whittie. *Shall Women Vote? A Book for Men.* New York: Neale, 1913. 309–10. Quoted in Ruoff 180–81.

"Says Miss Newman Took Her Own Life." 25 Oct. 1928. Folder 16, Frances Newman Papers, Archives, Library and Information Center, Georgia Institute of Technology.

Scott, Anne Firor. Foreword. *The Hard-Boiled Virgin.* By Frances Newman. 1926. Rpt. Athens: U Georgia Press, 1980. v–xix.

——. "The 'New Woman' in the New South." *South Atlantic Quarterly* 61 (1962): 473–83.

——. *The Southern Lady: From Pedestal to Politics, 1830–1930.* Chicago: U Chicago P, 1970.

Works Cited

Scott, Bonnie Kime, ed. *The Gender of Modernism: A Critical Anthology.* Bloomington: Indiana UP, 1990.

Seabury, Florence. "Stereotypes." Kirchwey 219–31.

Seidel, Kathryn Lee. "The Comic Male: Satire in Ellen Glasgow's Queenborough Trilogy." *Southern Quarterly* 23.4 (Summer 1985): 15–26.

———. *The Southern Belle in the American Novel.* Tampa: U South Florida P, 1985.

Showalter, Elaine. "Toward a Feminist Poetics." *Women Writing and Writing About Women.* Ed. Mary Jacobus. London: Croom Helm, 1979. 22–41.

Singal, Daniel Joseph. *The War Within: From Victorian to Modernist Thought in the South, 1919-1945.* Chapel Hill: U North Carolina P, 1982.

Smelstor, Marjorie S. C. "Frances Newman: A Rediscovered Novelist." *Southern Quarterly* 18.2 (Winter 1980): 5–17.

Smith, Lillian. *Killers of the Dream.* New York: WW Norton, 1949.

Soskin, William. "Books on Our Table: A Communication on the Death of Miss Frances Newman." [*New York Evening Post* 16 Jan. 1930]. Folder 23, Frances Newman Papers, Archives, Library and Information Center, Georgia Institute of Technology.

Spacks, Patricia Meyer. *The Female Imagination.* New York: Knopf, 1975.

Stevenson, Frederick Boyd. "Brooklyn Has No Censorship of 'Bad' Books." Scrapbook, Frances Newman Papers, Archives, Library and Information Center, Georgia Institute of Technology.

Stubbs, Patricia. *Women and Fiction: Feminism and the Novel 1880-1920.* Sussex: Harvester Press; New York: Barnes and Noble, 1979.

Suckow, Ruth. "Frances Newman a Thin and Brittle Novelist" (Rev. of *Dead Lovers Are Faithful Lovers*). *World* 20 May 1928: 9m. Scrapbook, Frances Newman Papers, Archives, Library and Information Center, Georgia Institute of Technology.

Sultan, Stanley. *Eliot, Joyce and Company.* New York: Oxford UP, 1987.

Symons, Julian. "About Frances Newman." *London Magazine* 6.3 (1966): 36–48.

———. *Makers of the New.* New York: Random House, 1987.

Talmadge, John. "Frances Newman." *Notable American Women 1607-1950.* Vol. 2. Ed. Edward T. Jones. Cambridge, MA: Belknap P Harvard U, 1971. 622–23. 4 vols.

Tannenbaum, Frank. *Darker Phases of the South.* New York: GP Putnam, Knickerbocker Press, 1924.

Tate, Allen. *Collected Essays.* Denver: Alan Swallow, 1959.

Trotti, Lamar. "Tragic Love Is Theme of Miss Newman" (Rev. of *Dead Lovers Are Faithful Lovers*). Scrapbook, Frances Newman Papers, Archives, Library and Information Center, Georgia Institute of Technology.

Works Cited

——. "Work of Frances Newman Praised." Scrapbook, Frances Newman Papers, Archives, Library and Information Center, Georgia Institute of Technology.

Twelve Southerners. *I'll Take My Stand: The South and the Agrarian Tradition*. New York: Harper and Brothers, 1930.

Untermeyer, Jean Starr. Reply to Elizabeth Brewer's "Flappers" ("In the Bookman's Mail"). *Bookman* 57 (June 1923): 480–81.

Wagenknecht, Edward, ed. *The Letters of James Branch Cabell*. Norman: U Oklahoma P, 1975.

Welter, Barbara. "The Cult of True Womanhood: 1820–1860." *American Quarterly* 18 (1966): 151–74.

West, Rebecca. "Battlefield and Sky." *Strange Necessity: Essays*. Garden City, NY: Doubleday, Doran, 1928. 321–33.

Westling, Louise. *Sacred Groves and Ravaged Gardens*. Athens: U Georgia P, 1985.

Wheeler, Marjorie Spruill. *New Women of the New South*. New York: Oxford UP, 1993.

White, Barbara. *Growing Up Female: Adolescent Girlhood in American Fiction*. Westport, CT: Greenwood Press, 1985.

Wolock, Nancy. "Cross-Currents: The 1920s." *Women and the American Experience*. New York: Knopf, 1984. 381–418.

"Woman's Mind Known to All Equally as Well as to Writer." Scrapbook, Frances Newman Papers, Archives, Library and Information Center, Georgia Institute of Technology.

Woolf, Virginia. "Modern Fiction." *The Common Reader*. 1925. Introd. and ed. Andrew McNeillie. 1st ser. Annotated ed. New York: Harcourt Brace Jovanovich, 1984. 146–54.

——. *Mrs. Dalloway*. 1925. Middlesex, England, and Victoria, Australia: Penguin, 1966.

——. "Professions for Women." 1931. *Women and Writing*. Introd. and ed. Michèle Barrett. New York: Harcourt Brace Jovanovich, 1979. 57–63.

——. *A Room of One's Own*. New York: Harcourt, Brace, 1929.

——. *To the Lighthouse*. New York: Harcourt, Brace and World, 1927.

——. "Women and Fiction." 1929. *Women and Writing*. Introd. and ed. Michèle Barrett. New York: Harcourt Brace Jovanovich, 1979. 43–52.

Yellis, Kenneth A. "Prosperity's Child: Some Thoughts on the Flapper." *American Quarterly* 21 (Apr. 1969): 44–64.

Zeman, Anthea. *Presumptuous Girls: Women and Their World in the Serious Woman's Novel*. London: Weidenfeld and Nicolson, 1977.

INDEX

Index

Index

Index

74; marriage in, 68–69; women's employment in, 81, 84–85
Hall, Jacquelyn, 32–33
Hamilton, Edward (*The Gold-Fish Bowl*), 99–100
Hanna, Evelyn, 35
Hansen, Harry, 143–44
Hard-Boiled Virgin, The, 61, 126, 127; aristocracy in, 44; autobiographical elements in, 2, 3, 105–6; as *bildungsroman*, 97, 106–11; complex sentence structure in, 159–60; courtship in, 36–39; dual perspective in, 144–47; education in, 72–73, 107; episodic structure of, 128–30; free association in, 150–51; Katharine Faraday as narrator of, 143–44; male misreading of, 111–13; marriage in, 65, 108–11, 175 (n. 2); negatives in, 153, 161–62; psycho-narration in, 148–50; racism in, 41; reactions to, 16, 19–20, 21, 24; religion in, 41, 45, 171 (n. 13); repetition in, 130–33; sexuality in, 155–60, 162–63; Southern Agrarian view of, 92; story/drama motif in, 133–37; women's employment in, 81, 110–11, 136–37; writing of, 11, 13, 15–16, 18
Harris, Barbara, 64
Harris, Corra, 78
Harris, Julia, 23
Hart, Frances Noyes, 172 (n. 17)
Hawthorne, Nathaniel, 10
Heilbrun, Carolyn G., 21, 106, 124
Hemingway, Ernest, 16
Henry, O., 8
Hergesheimer, Joseph, 57
Herrick, Robert, 57
Hibbard, Addison, 33, 87
Hofmann, David (*The Hard-Boiled Virgin*), 135, 136
Holman, C. Hugh, 94
Honeywell, Edmonia (*The Romantic Comedians*), 55
Honeywell, Gamaliel (*The Romantic Comedians*), 55
House of Seven Gables, The (Hawthorne), 10
Howe, Doctor (*The Hard-Boiled Virgin*), 130–31, 135
Hoyt, Clement, 62
Hubbel, Jay, 94

Huebsch, Benjamin, 14
Huf, Linda, 111
Hurston, Zora Neal, 167 (n. 2)

I'll Take My Stand (Ransom), 89
"I'm a Fool" (Anderson), 14–15
Importance of Being Earnest, The (Wilde), 2
Industrialization, 88–89

James, Henry, 9, 10, 156
Jenkins, Herbert George, 102
Johnson, Gerald, 170 (n. 7)
Johnston, Delia, 14
Johnston, Mary, 6, 35, 36, 68–69, 166; education in novels of, 73–74; southern lady as portrayed by, 47–51; women's employment in novels of, 81, 84–85
Jones, Anne Goodwyn, 50, 68, 126, 171 (n. 9), 175 (n. 6); on *The Hard-Boiled Virgin*, 109, 128, 137, 145, 151; on superficial social change, 60
Joyce, James, 8, 126, 143, 165

Kaplan, Sydney Janet, 127
Katz-Stoker, Fraya, 93–94
Kaufman, Gloria, 172 (n. 18)
Kennard, Jean, 97, 98, 101, 103, 104
Killers of the Dream (Smith), 31
King, Samuel (*The Hard-Boiled Virgin*), 135
"Klan's Fight for Americanism, The" (Evans), 47
Kolodny, Annette, 113, 121–23

LaFollette, Susan, 64–65
Laforgue, Jules, 18, 19
Langfield, William, 156–57
Lardner, Ring, 14
Laura (*Southern Charm*), 81, 86–87
Lawrence, D. H., 7, 8, 165
LeGrand, Mrs. (*Hagar*), 73–74, 84
Lesbianism, 160
Lewis, Sinclair, 16, 36
"Library Literary Notes," 6
"Library Notes": on other southern women writers, 48; on suffrage, 174 (n. 8)
Lieberman, Marcia, 105
Life and Gabriella (Glasgow), 47, 54, 113;

Index

education in, 75; marriage in, 69–70;
women's employment in, 81, 85–86
Lightfoot, Amanda (*The Romantic Comedians*), 55, 63
"Literary Complexes," 7
"Literary Independence," 9
Little, Judy, 57
Littlepage, Agatha (*They Stooped to Folly*), 64
Littlepage, Mr. (*They Stooped to Folly*), 56
Liveright, Horace, 127, 168 (n. 12)
Long, Susan, 3, 11, 12, 20
Love and Death in the American Novel (Fiedler), 170 (n. 5)
Lubbock, Percy, 141
Lumpkin, Neal (*The Hard-Boiled Virgin*), 38
Lynching, 31–33, 43–44

McBride, Robert M., 8, 98
McCullers, Carson, 167 (n. 2)
MacDonald, Edgar, 53
Macy, John, 156
Madwoman in the Attic (Gilbert and Gubar), 113
Main Street (Lewis), 36
Mallard, Louise ("The Dream of an Hour"), 123
Manning, Carol S., 35
Mansfield, Katherine, 126, 127, 138, 155, 166; narrative voice in writings of, 147–48, 150; Newman's praise of, 8, 9
Marriage, 175 (n. 2); and angel in the house, 114–19; in Glasgow's novels, 69–71; in Glenn's novels, 65, 67–68; in Johnston's writings, 68–69; Katharine Faraday's rejection of, 65, 108–13; as prostitution, 65–68; self-sacrificial, 70–71; and superficial social change, 64–65
Marriage plot convention, 97, 98–105; in *Northanger Abbey* and *The Gold-Fish Bowl* compared, 101–4. See also Courtship
Mary Victoria (*They Stooped to Folly*), 64, 70–71
May, Henry F., 93
Mencken, H. L., 7, 10, 15, 23, 167 (n. 5); on southern sterility, 34
Menstruation, 157–58, 160

Mims, Edwin, 71, 76
Mind of the South, The (Cash), 28
Modernism, 126, 143; feminist, 166
Moreland, Catherine (*Northanger Abbey*), 102–4
Morgan, Ellen, 110
Mrs. Dalloway (Woolf), 138, 150
Munford, Beverly, 71
Myth of Aunt Jemima, The: Representations of Race and Region (Roberts), 28–29

Narcissism, 67–68; defined, 175 (n. 6)
Narrated monologue, 147–48
Narrow House (Scott), 7
Negatives, Newman's use of, 153–54, 161–62
New Criticism, 93–95
New Criticism, The (Ransom), 93
Newman, Fanny Percy Alexander, 3
Newman, Frances: childhood of, 3–5; contradictory traits of, 1–3; death of, 19–24; education of, 5–6; funeral of, 24–25; illnesses of, 17–19, 168 (n. 9); influences on, 9, 102, 126–27, 156, 163, 166; insecurity of, 10–11, 12, 15, 17–18; as librarian, 5–6, 11–13; love affairs of, 19–20; nonfiction writing of, 6–7, 8–11, 13–15; notoriety of, 16, 156–57, 164–65; on racism, 41–44; satiric voice of, 34–36, 57–58, 87, 145, 146, 149; on sexuality in her writings, 157; and Southern Agrarianism, 87–88, 90–92; and southern literary canon, 93–95; writing process of, 9–10, 15–16. See also *Dead Lovers Are Faithful Lovers*; *Gold-Fish Bowl, The*; *Hard-Boiled Virgin, The*
Newman, Henry, 24, 25
Newman, William T., 3
"Newman Parody Portended Death," 21–22
Nightmare Abbey (Peacock), 11
No Man's Land: The Place of the Woman Writer in the Twentieth Century (Gilbert and Gubar), 166
Norris, Charles, 23
Northanger Abbey (Austen), 101–4

O. Henry award, 8, 168 (n. 6)
O'Connor, Flannery, 167 (n. 2)

197

Index

O'Hara, John (*Life and Gabreiella*), 69–70
Olsen, Tillie, 111
"On the State of Literature in the Late Confederacy," 168 (n. 8)
Overton, Grant, 140
Overton, Sally ("Rachel and Her Children"), 123–24, 175 (n. 2)

Page, Thomas Nelson, 32, 57
Paterson, Isabel, 4, 36, 66, 67, 118–19; on structure of *Dead Lovers Are Faithful Lovers,* 114, 139
Patricia Brent, Spinster (Jenkins), 102
Patterson, John, 25
Patterson, Margaret, 10, 13, 23, 25, 168 (n. 13)
"Peachtree's Fame in Fiction: It Started with Frances Newman, Georgia's First Modern Novelist" (Daniel), 24
Peacock, Thomas Love, 11
Pelops (*The Gold-Fish Bowl*), 82, 99, 103
Pendleton, Gabriel (*Virginia*), 56
Pendleton, Mrs. (*Virginia*), 55–56, 85
Pendleton, Virginia (*Virginia*), 53–54, 62–63, 70, 118
Penhally (Gordon), 174 (n. 11)
Penis envy, 39
Perryman, Mrs. (*Dead Lovers Are Faithful Lovers*), 66, 122
Peterkin, Julia, 177 (n. 8)
Petronius, 123
Peyton, John (*Life and Gabriella*), 69
Pirandello, Luigi, 136
Porter, Katherine Anne, 167 (n. 2)
Portrait of the Artist as a Young Woman, A (Huf), 111
Pratt, Annis, 106, 112
"Prelude" (Mansfield), 138, 147–48, 155
Prince, Gerald, 145
Priscilla, Miss (*Virginia*), 74–75
"Profession of Letters in the South, The" (Tate), 90
"Professions for Women" (Woolf), 114–15, 165
Proust, Marcel, 129
Psycho-narration, 147, 148–51; in *Dead Lovers Are Faithful Lovers,* 151–55
Pulling Our Own Strings: Feminist Humor and Satire (Kaufman), 172 (n. 18)

Quoted monologue, 147–48

"Rachel and Her Children," 11, 97, 123–24, 168 (n. 6), 175 (n. 2)
Rachel (*Hagar*), 68–69
Racism, 28–33, 41–44, 55–56, 88
Ramsay, Isabel (*Dead Lovers Are Faithful Lovers*), 40, 62; employment of, 81, 83; negatives regarding, 162; as other woman, 119–21; psycho-narrative viewpoint toward, 153–55; and racism, 42, 43–44; and religion, 46–47; sexual imagery regarding, 164; and time, 138; viewpoint of, 114, 121, 139–41
Ramsay, Mr. (*To the Lighthouse*), 148–49
Randolph (*The Gold-Fish Bowl*), 99, 103
Ransom, John Crowe, 88–89, 93, 94
"Real Beginnings of the Southern Renaissance, The" (Manning), 35
"Real Womanhood," 169 (n. 2)
Reinventing Womanhood (Heilbrun), 124
Religion, 41, 45–47, 171 (n. 13)
Richardson, Dorothy, 8, 143
Riddell, John, 21
"Rising Age of Heroines, The," 2
Roberts, Diane, 28–29
Romantic Comedians, The (Glasgow), 16, 47, 53, 55, 63–64; women's employment in, 86
Room of One's Own, A (Woolf), 111
Rosowski, Susan, 106–7, 108–9
Rossetti, Christina, 108
Rossetti, William Michael, 108
Rossi, Alice, 169 (n. 1)
Rothermel, Winifred, 1, 2–3, 12
Rubin, Louis D., Jr., 94, 174 (n. 10)
Rucker, Louis, 11, 20–21, 25
Ruoff, John, 77, 173 (n. 5)
Rutledge, Sarah (*The Hard-Boiled Virgin*), 44, 157, 158, 175 (n. 2)
Ryan, Mary P., 80

Sacco, Nicola, 168 (n. 12)
"Sahara of the Bozart" (Mencken), 34
Salome (Wilde), 167 (n. 2)
Sam, Conway Whittie, 77
Satire, 34–36, 87; as critique of social order, 57–58; didactic, 47–48; and narrative viewpoint, 145, 146, 149

198

Index

Index